The Flame Within

The Flame Within

Memoir of a Firefighter

WAYNE MUTZA

McFarland & Company, Inc., Publishers
Jefferson, North Carolina, and London

LIBRARY OF CONGRESS CATALOGUING-IN-PUBLICATION DATA

Mutza, Wayne, 1951–
    The flame within : memoir of a firefighter / Wayne Mutza.
       p.   cm.
    Includes index.

    ISBN 978-0-7864-7276-5
    softcover : acid free paper ∞

    1. Mutza, Wayne, 1951–   2. Fire fighters — Wisconsin —
Milwaukee — Biography.   I. Title.
TH9118.M88A3 2013
363.37092—dc23
[B]   2013010277

BRITISH LIBRARY CATALOGUING DATA ARE AVAILABLE

On the cover: In what is traditionally called "organized confusion,"
firefighters scurry about to get the upper hand of this blaze that has
full possession of the upper floors of this residence (courtesy MFD
Historical Society); flames (Stockbyte/Thinkstock)

Manufactured in the United States of America

McFarland & Company, Inc., Publishers
  Box 611, Jefferson, North Carolina 28640
  www.mcfarlandpub.com

Table of Contents

Preface   1

Introduction   7

1. The Road to the Glass House   19
2. The Glass House   31
3. Interlude   55
4. Back to School   63
5. Engine 5   81
6. Scary Stuff   119
7. Truck Man   128
8. An Officer and a Gentleman   155
9. Brady Street   166
10. More Characters on Brady Street   190
11. The Beginning of the End   215
12. Later Lessons   219

Epilogue   232
Index   239

Preface

Damn, it's hot! Unbearably, ear-blistering hot. Cinnamon-colored smoke swirls around me. Through the brown haze a yellow glow beckons, daring me like a deadly siren's call. "C'mon with that line!" one of my two mentors scolds, his voice muffled by the bulky face-piece of his breathing apparatus. Crawling on the attic floor, soaked with sweat, panting, my heart racing, I strain to pull the hose. Stiff with water pumped at 150 pounds per square inch, it's like dragging a tree limb. *Isn't anyone below us helping pull this damn thing?* Sweet, intoxicating wood smoke leaks into my face-piece, stinging my eyes and piercing my nostrils. Slick with sweat, the rubber one-size-fits-all mask doesn't seal well.

"Keep moving, keep moving," a voice coaxes. *Crawl, pull. The smoke darkens to black. Blindness. Spooky. Scary shit, this firefighting. Control the fear. Stay in control.* Our lowly trio inches forward on hands and knees, never rising above a crouch because a few feet above our heads searing heat waits to inflict unspeakable pain on exposed flesh. We bulldoze through unrecognizable objects, stumbling, cursing. Bill Kaminski is behind me, Ken Grabske, my other mentor and our senior "first pipeman," is next to me, guiding, protecting. Darth Vader–like, each labored breath is amplified by the clicking mechanical valves of our masks. The eerie sound competes with the fire's mocking crackle. Separating the dark side from the tiny world inside my mask is a clear plastic shield, through which I stare wide-eyed at ... at what? *How much heat can this thin plastic withstand?* Venturing into this eerie, deadly world makes me feel small and isolated. It throws my senses off kilter, magnifying tiny elements, such as the nagging pain of a face-piece buckle digging into my forehead, and the weight of the air tank on my back — but God bless every cubic inch of pressurized air in that steel cylinder. *Who would dare tramp into Satan's lair, and do it again, and again?* Admittedly, the excitement is unrivaled. The challenge is obsessive.

Suddenly, another engine company's heavy stream hammers loudly against the ceiling below us. Its power vibrates the floorboards on which we

1

crawl. They're pushing the fire; they've cornered the beast, it's pissed off and it's coming after us. The glow becomes panoramic, threatening to envelop and consume us. We push on. It suddenly gets hotter; white molten metal hot. "Hit it!" a voice commands. I quickly lean back on my heels and cradle the nozzle. I turn its steel barrel fully to one side, making sure it is set on *straight stream*, not *spray*, which would create a steam cloud that would horribly scald us. Fresh from training, I remember to open it slowly, away from the fire, so the air trapped in the line doesn't give the demon the oxygen it craves. A long, strong hiss, then water. *Tip the nozzle up, open it fully, lean slightly into the back pressure, work it in large arcs.* I can't see the white, solid stream, but I smile as I hear it whistling through the nozzle, punching the devil's friend in the gut. A gloved hand rests heavily on my shoulder, reassuring, teaching. "That's it. Good. Whip it around. Overhead, overhead — huge figure-eights. Don't let it get behind you." The glow disappears, and it has cooled down to a couple of hundred degrees. A slap on the shoulder. "Okay, shut it down."

Crawl forward. The glow reappears, lower this time. *It must be reflecting off of water on the floor.* Crash! *What th...* Nothing but air under me, and a lightning bolt cracks through my groin. *Ah, Christ!* My legs dangle, but held by a floor joist planted firmly in my crotch, I'm prevented from falling through to the burning floor below. *Oh, what fucking agony!* Even worse, I drop the nozzle and my air hose has been sliced. The poison cloud attacks my throat, narrowing it to a pinpoint. Can't breathe. *What the hell am I doing here?*

"Gimme the line!" one of my partners yells. *Screw the line. I'm dangling up to my jewels in a blast furnace and I'm gettin' outta here!* I hear the stream thundering against the walls, feeling its cooling effect as I'm pulled backwards and out. Bells are ringing; alarm bells on breathing apparatus announce: *You're damn near out of air and you have just a few minutes to save yourself.* Muffled shouts behind us. The cavalry has arrived.

I discovered later that those flames weren't reflecting off of water on the floor; we were looking at fire on the floor below through glass windows laid across openings in the attic floor. A fiendish booby trap, or unbelievably poor maintenance? I had my first "worker" under my belt. *What an interesting career this could be.*

I got the strange feeling that I was again in a war, facing a ruthless enemy, and operating under ill-defined rules of engagement. This enemy wasn't shooting bullets; nevertheless, it wanted to kill me, and it demanded respect. Bill understood, perfectly. We had mutual respect, having discovered that we served in Vietnam in the same areas, during the same time frame, performing equally dangerous missions. Ours was a bond that none could penetrate and few could understand.

On the way to the fire, standing by the pumper's jump seats, hanging on tightly, we had strained to spot the telltale smoke. The first-arriving engine company's anxious radio call came first: "We have a working fire!" As I squinted into the wind blasting over the cab, a gloved hand reached across the engine cover and tugged at my heavy coat. It was Bill, looking at me with a big grin on his weathered face. It was easy to read his dark, liquid eyes. We were back aboard a Huey helicopter, thundering into the unknown, skimming the treetops, fire ahead, and there was no turning back. When we rolled into the brown, pungent fog, Bill shouted over the engine's roar and the siren's wail, "Like goin' in on a combat assault, ain't it?" "Amen, Bro," I yelled back. *Amen.* He flashed the grin again. The bond was forming. Although brimming with anticipation, I was confident and determined. My senses were piqued.

When we pulled up to the huge flat that belched flames and smoke, our company officer jumped out of the cab and disappeared. He wasn't my regular boss, thankfully. By the time I had grabbed my breathing apparatus and yanked the heavy water-filled hand-pump extinguisher from its rack, he was nowhere to be seen. *Too bad. I'd like to jam this hand pump's hose up his ass to prove I would stay dutifully behind him.* I didn't see him till the fire was out. The look he gave when he found me with my pants down in the cab of the pumper checking my injuries was priceless. Despite his reputation as a scatterbrain, he would become a "white shirt," our slang for chief.

I limped during the remainder of my shift, but didn't dare tell anyone about the huge welt and cut on my inner thigh. And no one asked. That was the mindset then.

Driving home the following morning, tired, reeking of smoke and my head throbbing behind my eyes, I thought about the job offered me by New York Life Insurance Company after I came out on top in the interview process. I would have worn a suit to work, flown periodically to the Big Apple, and had my own office and secretary. That didn't sit well with Pat, my wife at that time, but she wasn't crazy about my becoming a firefighter either. It was a wash. Besides, living on the edge was a suit I would be more comfortable wearing. And I was no stranger to the road less traveled.

After leaving the army, which was followed by six months of raising hell, I decided to find my place in society. Dream offers from the CIA for work in Southeast Asia and the lure of smoke-jumper school in Montana slowly dissipated in the wake of foundry and road construction jobs, along with a relationship that promised fulfillment. I even considered medical school, but I had screwed around too much in high school, certain that I lacked the intelligence for such lofty aspirations. Besides, I was a restless sort with an adventuresome spirit that couldn't be stilled. The next best thing, it seemed, that might fulfill my desire to help others while satisfying my appetite for adventure was the fire service, and its new dimension, called Emergency Medical Services, or EMS. Jobs with two ambulance companies and enrollment in fire technology courses marked the pathway toward my newfound goal.

The appeal of the fire service loomed bigger than life. And there were episodes that tantalized, fanning the embers of obsession. While bartending, I met Werner Weissenborn, a tough, grizzled Milwaukee Fire Department battalion chief. Beneath his weathered exterior and gruff tone, I detected in his eyes and in his voice not only passion for the job, but gentleness, a profound sense of humanity. I connected with that. Then, through a mutual interest in photography, I met King Monaghan, a Milwaukee firefighter. King had been told he'd never walk again after his legs were crushed by a car that smashed into his fire truck. After 13 months in the hospital and agonizing therapy, King was back on the job. Such determination inspired me. He invited my brother, Dale, and me, along with a couple of friends, to his firehouse, Engine Company 18 and Ladder Company 10 at Third and Auer streets. What I saw fanned the flames.

The station was dubbed "The Butcher Shop," and the men called themselves "The Gas House Gang." I was allowed to peek into the fraternity of firefighters and firehouse life. Raucous and bawdy, they seldom revealed the serious side of what they did. I did, however, see their tears one hot Memorial Day, when they pulled from the Milwaukee River the bodies of two teenagers who had tested the rain-swollen waters with a homemade raft. With the ghetto around them teeming with life on a hot summer night, the Gas House Gang gabbed with the neighbors and played pranks on each other. Motown tunes pushed through the screen door of Trotter's tavern next door, and black kids thrilled at being included in the endless water fights. Beer was kept cold hidden in toilet tanks, the summer punch had more "punch" than the rules allowed, and Pearl was always willing to flash her ample breasts from the window across the gangway.

Life was good. These boys worked hard and played hard. I was hooked. I wanted in. I knew where I belonged.

Following Engine 18 and Ladder 10 to fires, it was the old-timers, seasoned and wise, I noticed most. Their actions were marked by purpose and confidence. Again, gentleness crept through. I longed to be one of the young pups; awkward but eager students whose respect for the old scouts was obvious. Without seeing their faces in smoke and darkness, the distinction between them was clear. The cubs' black helmets shined like waxed Volkswagens, while helmets worn by veterans were discolored, cracked, and even warped by countless confrontations with the devil's only friend. The colored helmet front-pieces that identified the companies to which they were assigned were barely discernable, having been baked and blackened. It didn't dawn on me then what the smoke and heat that signed their helmets was doing to their lungs and blood vessels. Both of my mentors, my friends, Bill and Ken, would be dead from heart attacks before they reached the age of 52.

After Vietnam, I felt that I had seen the extremes that life had to offer; the fire service could show me nothing new. This book illustrates how wrong I was. My old man, gone three decades now, was quite a character. The ultimate provider, he was as gentle and caring as anyone could be, yet tough as nails. I wish that he had jotted down his experiences for me to read when I want to remember him. With that in mind, I have centered these pages on my years with the fire service, purely my choice, even though others encouraged me to write about my youth, or my experiences as a soldier during the Vietnam War. I may never be ready or willing to do that. The fire service, on the other hand, became an identity, and therein is a story to tell. But more than a story about Wayne Mutza, this is a story about humanity — a story that peers into the hearts and minds, the very souls, of those who slipped the boundaries of human soundness and uttered the words most difficult to say: "Help me." It then too becomes the story of those who, humbled in their own human frailty, came to help.

Someone I'll always remember once wrote, "Mechanics fix cars, doctors fix people, teachers teach kids. Most professions start with something and end with something. But writers start with nothing, often just an idea, and end up with something that lasts forever. It's god-like because what writers do is at a higher, more abstract level. They master the process of creation." While seemingly high praise for the spawning of a simple idea, these words exemplify my love of life and my desire to share my experiences, with the hope that someone can learn from them, and that my kids and grandkids will gain a better idea of who I am. Like the love that I have for my family and friends, my fire for the profession will always burn, until the angels close my eyes.

Despite being urged by many to write this book, I found it difficult to write about myself. I craftily managed to put off building the manuscript for a number of years. I even side-stepped the project by deciding it was easier to write about others in the profession. The result, my book *Life Lines: Stories from the Firehouse*, is a success. But I was only kidding myself. My cerebral gremlins teased and prodded, not allowing the project to remain merely spools of thought on the dream weaver's loom, never letting me rest until I picked up the pen to feed my passion — to fan the flame within.

Introduction

The city of Milwaukee is 100 square miles of residential and commercial real estate, teeming with a population of 600,000. Its eastern edge is the Lake Michigan shoreline. Tall buildings steadily sprout, filling Milwaukee's skyline. Once known as a brewing and manufacturing powerhouse, Milwaukee evolved into a moderately progressive metropolis that has a widely diverse population and embraces strong cultural influences. "A great place by a great lake," goes the city's motto. Milwaukee's cityscape, still rife with ethnic strongholds, reflects the large influx of European immigrants during the middle and late 19th century, along with the migration of blacks from the South. Hispanic families moved from the West and Southwest, while the arrival of Asians and Russians spawned other ethnic neighborhoods.

Like most major cities, Milwaukee fell victim to the times, struggling with the turbulent 1960s, a decline in manufacturing, and "white flight," the latter the result of the expansion of the predominantly black inner city. But the city endured and even grew, architecturally and culturally if not in populace. The winds of change swept clean pockets of the cityscape that begged for revitalization, giving rise to new leadership to confront new problems. And through it all, the Milwaukee Fire Department struggled to keep pace with the changing face of the city.

The Milwaukee Fire Department (MFD) has long enjoyed a reputation as one of the best in the nation, its members having forged a proud history of serving with distinction and professionalism. The department's training and strategies proved superior to those of many other cities. We called ourselves an "inside fire department," meaning we went into a building to find the fire, and to attack and kill it. The main body of the department, the firefighting division, is 1,000 strong. To provide optimal response times throughout the city, 36 fire stations are dispersed among five geographical battalions. Each station, or firehouse, houses the basic unit, an engine company, or pumper, with a crew of four or five. Sixteen firehouses are assigned a ladder company, now referred to as a truck company in a return to

Milwaukee's historic Metropolitan Block building succumbed to fire in 1975, becoming an artful study in line as aerial ladders and master streams angled upward toward it. The massive, five-story landmark burned out of control for 11 hours. A firefighter became trapped on an upper floor during the five-alarm blaze and was rescued (courtesy Dale Mutza).

the traditional designation. Truck companies are staffed by four or five firefighters.

When Emergency Medical Services (EMS) came into its own during the 1970s, it meant sweeping changes for the MFD. The EMS training program was born of the public's awareness of a higher class of EMS available to them. Milwaukee police ambulances shouldered the load, but since police rigs no longer met federal standards, and police officials declined budgeting of the emergency medical technician (EMT) training mandated by 1977 state law, the fire department in January 1978 assumed EMS responsibility. The EMS concept was valuable but fell short of the true life-saving capability then catching on. In the trend-setting cities of Los Angeles and Seattle, a new word — "paramedic" — was heard, from which Milwaukee took its cue. Milwaukee suburbs West Allis and Wauwatosa established the first two units, in 1973 and 1974, respectively, and Milwaukee's Med 3 began service in November 1977. The Milwaukee Fire Department paramedic program was established amid a political maelstrom that marked the arrival of women in the fire service. As of this writing, the department operates 12 paramedic units.

At the forefront of the department's modernization efforts was the establishment of a hazardous materials team, a heavy urban rescue team, and the Bureau of Technical Services. A dive rescue team has been in existence since the 1950s. Administration, training, and construction and maintenance bureaus complete the organizational chart.

A call to 911 for a structure fire brings a response of three engine companies, one or two truck companies, a battalion chief, and, if people are reported trapped, a rescue squad or paramedic unit. A fire exceeding the capabilities of that much equipment and manpower calls for additional units and a variety of special equipment, usually in the form of "greater alarms," which are ranked from a second to a fifth alarm. In typical firehouse jargon, they are called a "two-bagger," a "three-bagger," and so on. They are initiated, usually by on-scene chiefs, who are said to "pull the hook," a throwback to when alarm boxes with pull handles for summoning help stood as sentinels on street corners. The term "leaning on it" describes a chief leaning on the handle, or hook, as he considers calling for additional resources. Expert fireground tacticians know that the actions taken during the first few minutes of a fire determine the course, and the outcome, of the event; that can be hours, or even days, later.

Engines carry a few thousand feet of hose and are equipped with a 500-gallon water tank for a "quick attack." For unlimited water supply, pumpers connect to hydrants that are fed from the great lake through pumping stations. Simply, engine crews must get water on the flames, preferably as close to the "seat" of the fire as possible. Deep inside a building is where this gets tricky. Using a combination of aerial ladder and ground ladders, truck crews must ventilate the building, usually by making a large opening in the roof over the fire, a most dangerous place. The timing and coordination of attacking and ventilating the fire is critical because working powerful hose streams in an unventilated building not only pushes fire throughout the structure, it also can turn the building into a painfully scalding steam chamber.

Paramount among operations at a structure fire is rescue. It is everyone's job and is often performed in conjunction with advancing hose lines and ventilating the building. Second in the prioritized order of "sizing up" a fire is protecting the exposures. Sometimes a building is allowed to burn, with first-laid hose lines instead trained on buildings threatened by the blaze, a tactic most confusing to the uninitiated — "covering the exposures," we called it. The fire is then confined, extinguished, and overhauled, the latter entailing the process of removing and wetting down anything that has burned. Often, this includes methodical demolition to find hidden pockets of fire, lest firefighters be called back to the scene hours later for a most embarrassing "rekindle." Buildings that become so heavily involved with fire that interior attacks are ruled out become write-offs, in a procedure better known as "surround and drown." Fire companies, after losing a building, are ribbed by their merciless peers as having "saved the basement" or "created a new parking lot." No one is immune.

Since firefighters respond to more medical than fire alarms, nearly everyone in the firefighting division is trained as an emergency medical technician (EMT). In what is termed a tiered response, the closest engine company arrives first. After making an assessment, the EMT-trained crew assesses the patient and then calls for a private ambulance, or, if advanced life support is necessary, a paramedic unit. In order of frequency, EMS calls are in response to cardiac, respiratory, and trauma episodes. The remainder, ranging from kids with runny noses to elderly persons in need of assistance, bring total annual EMS alarms to more than 40,000, accounting for more than 70 percent of the department's total number of about 67,000 alarms. Alarms other than structure fires or EMS run the gamut, from gas leaks to recovering bodies from water. Regardless of their differences, all are representative of human imperfection and frailty, requiring intervention by those who make the fire service their calling.

In a recruiting video, former Milwaukee fire chief Doug Holton extols the department's motto: "Courage, Honor, and Integrity." Such virtues are a tall order for any of us, and rather than goals to be achieved, they are hallmarks of a person's journey through their career.

There are a number of reasons why people join the fire service. Some fulfill childhood dreams, while others hunger for challenges not found in more conventional jobs. Others satisfy curiosity or find job security. Many are drawn to the excitement, and even danger. But what makes people seek danger, either consciously or subconsciously? It may be the need to confront fears, and the fire service easily embodies everything that we fear. Confronting fear constitutes courage. Ralph Waldo Emerson, in my opinion, said it best: "Heroism feels and never reasons and is therefore always right."

Heroes. I've been called a hero more times than I care to remember, and I've always been uncomfortable with the term. I believe that the bravest thing I've done in terms of the fire service was to raise my hand when I was sworn in, and anything that happened after that was just part of my job. My personal creed is best summarized by a poster I had taped to my locker; it showed a firefighter giving mouth-to-mouth resuscitation to a child outside of a burning home. Below the image were the words, "I shall pass through this world but once. If therefore, there be any kindness I can show, or any good thing I can do, let me do it now — for I shall not pass this way again."

Society has categorized heroes. The distinctions vary from someone who is dedicated to a humanitarian effort to the soldier who saves comrades under withering fire in the heat of battle. I believe that heroes are defined by the choices they make, particularly while doing things they are afraid to do. Especially baffling is that true heroes, whether acting instinctively, or kinetically responding to their core values, find their actions unremarkable, despite the danger involved. I never saw my actions that were deemed heroic as anything more than the outcomes of choices I had made.

We need heroes. Children need heroes. But since 9–11 the term has been overused. I'm convinced, after seeing banners strung from rural firehouses beckoning, "Be a hero, join the fire department," and having witnessed major city firefighters signing autographs and encouraging people to take their picture, that the label has lost its special significance. Its meaning has become blurred. True, the members of the fire service who walk among us are a special breed, and their work is admirable, but it has made some of them believe they can do no wrong. This heroic self image clouds their perception of purpose. The time had come for rescue workers to simply do their job and remember that they raised their hands vowing to serve and protect.

I want to tell you about my heroes. They are unassuming, ordinary people who rallied against all odds to find deep in their souls the importance and meaning of placing others above themselves. Theirs is a special love of life. While stationed downtown, my first pipeman, Ken Grabske, possessed endless wit and quick humor, and dispensed expert tutelage, which made him a joy to be around. We became friends to the extent that we could reveal to each other personal things that otherwise would have become fodder for the merciless rumor mill. I never saw beneath his raucousness until the day we were called to an accident down the street from the firehouse. A truck had literally driven over a car, whose young woman driver was crawling from the wreck. Ken jumped off of the engine and ran to her. Kneeling in fresh fallen snow, with the injured woman's head cradled in his lap, Ken comforted the shaking, sobbing woman while brushing snowflakes from her face. Someone brought a blanket, which Ken tucked gingerly around her shoulders to seal out winter's wind. He kissed her gently on her forehead and didn't let go of her hand until she was lifted into an ambulance. I feel blessed to have that image etched into my memory. I wonder if the woman remembers.

Equally memorable is an encounter with a man whose courage I will always remember. He never humped a hose line into a burning building, or breathed life into an unconscious victim. I don't remember his name. He is, nonetheless, my hero.

I met him in an east side apartment building to which my Engine Company 6 had been summoned to assist an invalid. We found the elderly man sitting on the floor. He flushed with humility, forcing a smile through an obvious flood of pain as we approached. Kneeling respectfully to face him, I saw on his face how the pain consumed him. Hooded eyes, seasoned with life, darted upward to meet mine.

"Hi, looks like you have a problem," I started.

"Yes," he hissed through clenched teeth. "I believe I do."

"What's your name, sir? How can we help you?"

He didn't appear injured, but pain gripped him. I offered my hand, which he grasped weakly to steady himself. He went on to explain how he was simply trying to get to his chair, but fell. Questions about his medical problems revealed that he was in the advanced stages of bone cancer. The pain that racked his body was unimaginable.

We were humbled by his apologies for having to call us, bothering us, not having anyone else on whom to rely. Usually, in the small, spartan surroundings of the elderly who live alone are photographs of kids or grandkids, the emotional tether to which they cling. I looked around. There were none. Moved by his determination to remain self sufficient, despite intolerable pain, I could only offer to do whatever made him comfortable. In his condition, the only comfort he could know would be a merciful passage into the hereafter. He asked only to be helped into his chair. He gritted his teeth and winced as we ever so carefully eased him up into his well-worn, cushion-y domain.

"Can we get you something? Water? A pillow?"

His moist eyes twinkled. "No, thank you. You know, I've always admired firemen. My dad was a Chicago fireman."

"Is that right?" I perked.

He started by saying how he remembered his dad's stories about the horses. He stopped short, flushed with embarrassment, the light in his eyes quickly dimming. "I'm keeping you. I'm sorry."

Quickly, I brushed off his apology and said that we'd like to hear about his dad. My crew nodded. Keying my radio button, I informed the dispatcher that we were in service, but would remain on the scene.

Staring into the past, disconnecting from his fragile frame, he told us how his dad took care of the fire horses; how he fought blazes in the frigid winter. Our attention was more precious than any medication we could give him, more meaningful than any service we were conditioned to provide. That we provided a diversion from his pain for 15 minutes of his life was a lesson in humility. We left him in his pain, his loneliness, and when we said goodbye, we knew that we would not see him again. After we crowded into the elevator, staring through the door, I muttered, "God help me if I ever complain about trivial crap again." Silence. You could have heard a pin drop in that elevator. I turned to look at my crew. There wasn't a dry eye among those weathered faces. Staring through the windshield during the quiet ride back to the firehouse, I thought about, and agreed with, the old man's decision to end his battle outside of a care facility. And I thought about heroes I have known. True heroes.

There are others of the same grain with whom I've had the good fortune to brush shoulders. Others like 36-year veteran Dick Kovatch, who, because of his brash selflessness, asked that I not spread the story of how, during a church service, he leaped from his pew to perform CPR on his pastor, who had collapsed from a heart attack at the pulpit. He saved the padre's life. Kovatch possesses drive that permeates his being, reaching to the depths of his soul. I marveled when he told me, in confidence, the details of how he pulled a man from the bowels of a burning building. As a chief, he arrived first and went in alone. He didn't have to; he was a white shirt; he could have waited for the cavalry, but he was a firefighter to the core. Crawling through the hot, smoky maze, he found the man and brought him out. With wonderment in his voice and his eyes energized with sincerity, Kovatch confided, "I made all the right moves. I knew every turn, as though the power up above was guiding me." And no one knew.

Many believe that such actions are spiritually governed. I've often believed that powers beyond this earth allowed me to accomplish things I should not have survived; powers that, at once, made me feel invincible and small; powers that allowed me to look the reaper in the eye and brazenly taunt, "Fuck you. I'm not finished here," while fully understanding that death was one of the cards I might be dealt.

Oh, there were glory hounds; there were braggers and boasters who, when it came time to stare into the face of death, cowered and even wet themselves. And there were others who did not seek, or receive, recognition for their daring deeds. For example: once, while working as a motor pump operator at a fire where an occupant reportedly was trapped, I saw Clarence Kuehmichel single-handedly raise a ladder to a second-floor window at the rear of the building. He then crawled into the brown smoke pushing through the opening, and disappeared. Eventually, the arms and head of a limp body plopped through the smoke, followed by Kuehmichel, who struggled to carry the man down the ladder. After I hollered for the rescue squad crew to get over there to grab the victim, Clarence flopped at the base of a tree, retching, head down, arms draped over his raised knees, exhausted. Tears flowed down his blackened, smoke-stained face and his eyes were constricted and bloodshot, making a grotesque mask of his angular features. Later, when I told him that I had seen his life-saving exploit, and that he could get an award, his brush-off with a flip of his hand was what I expected. "Besides," he croaked, "I found the guy in bed. When he woke up he fought with me, so I decked him. Made it easier to get 'im out." And no one knew.

Then there was the unassuming duo of Dick Kaiser and Roger Semenske, who literally pulled my ass from the fire, a story that I've recounted elsewhere in this book.

In terms of the fire service, the world is indeed a stage, upon which a host of characters play out their careers. We would like to think that emergency service workers fit a certain profile; that they come from strong family backgrounds; that they are answering a calling, but that isn't always the case. There is no denying that people who have crossed that career threshold undergo an unplanned metamorphosis. And through the transformation, most become competent and dedicated, regardless of the different classes with which they are identified. In rare cases, miscreants are attracted to the job, bringing with them their unshakable, insidious attributes. Deceptively hidden among our ranks were an armed robber, a serial rapist, a child molester, and even an arsonist or two. I knew and worked with them all, and never had a clue.

There is a unique psychological dimension associated with firefighters and rescue workers that may account for their particular behavioral patterns, as well as varying degrees of intensities in their personas. It makes them complex. The intensity with which a soldier engages in a firefight is not unlike that enveloping a firefighter crawling into a burning building, or a paramedic tending to a gunshot victim in a hostile setting. Such intensity presents itself as bonding. Men bond in physical activity. They bond in sharing grief. They tell their families and friends about the exciting and the funny happenings, but little about the losses. In grief, they can look at each other and know what the other is thinking. "We lost someone today." *We.* Grief results from situations in which they no longer have control. Control is important to rescuers; they need to have control of a situation. And they bond in foolishness, which is evidenced by the pranks they play on each other, and their often crude firehouse banter. Despite the public's perception that the life of a firefighter is a drama, it is really a comedy; a comedy interspersed with chaos, fear, intense emotion, and professionalism. The humor ranges from uproarious to rude and utterly tasteless. It is merciless, to the delight of most of them. Arguably, this dimension makes the fire service a trying environment for women.

I joined the ranks when firehouses were strongholds of masculinity. The Milwaukee Fire Department, like others across the nation, was slow to accept females and minorities. Even after women cracked the profession's hard shell, firefighters clung to the term "brotherhood" and the media continued to call them "firemen." Their rituals, their sense of fraternity, and their traditions link them to firefighters of past centuries. Many would agree that tradition is the cornerstone of the fire service. So steeped is the profession in tradition that often it has been called "200 years of tradition unimpeded by progress." When the FDNY confronted the unimaginable on 9–11, not only did the public and the media raise firefighters to unparalleled status, it reinforced the term brotherhood. Firefighters typically share the combat soldier's and police officer's view of outsiders. We stay within our own circles and trust few others. And given the new admiration for firefighters and subsequent cultural shifts, those same outsiders seemingly grant the fire service a pass on its struggles with diversity. Flirting with, and even embracing, racism and sexism, yet risking it all for complete strangers, underscores firefighters' complexity. My overall take is that there's a little Archie Bunker in all of us. In one aspect of the way in which the fire service mirrors society, the male-female issue, the black-white issue, and the gay-straight issue will never go away. Ego often gets in the way of young firefighters, whereas older, experienced firefighters, who better understand the stresses and danger of the job, find it easier to put ego aside.

Saving life not only fortifies ego, it generates an extreme adrenaline rush. Firefighters and paramedics will tell you that it also has a spiritual element. Intervening in death's summons explains the God complex. Smashing the proverbial clock said to be set for all of us — performing life-saving miracles that ordinarily are reserved for gods and poets — gives a sense of control. It always seemed strange altering someone's destiny with CPR, but I had made it a point to spit in the reaper's eye, so why not do it through someone else? The combination of such godlike ability and the rush of risking one's own life to save lives gives rescuers a sense of accomplishment. Their bonding and zest for life likely is derived from having seen death in all its horrible forms. They find merit in the saying, "What doesn't kill you makes you stronger." The worse the emergency, the stronger their resolve. It has to be that way; 9–11 proved that.

The discipline necessary to do the job is one of the reasons why the fire service is called a quasi-military organization. The fire department's very structure, right down to its uniforms and rank system, revolves around discipline, both imposed and inherent. Such disciplines, combined with a sense of purpose and distinction, fuel rescue workers' motivation. How else would it be possible for them to operate in such dangerous environments, and do it again and again? Discipline on the fireground is a world apart from discipline in the firehouse. The latter has its place, but discipline where "the hot bricks fly" is really about doing what's right, and damn the circumstances. It means staying alert, thinking on your feet, and not giving in to complacency, exhaustion, and panic. Giving in to them invites carelessness and overconfidence. Giving in to them invites injury and death. It's bad enough that emotional stresses at the brink of death are in high gear, and often are coupled with the reason-bending effects of toxic smoke and gasses.

I accepted that fear was my companion when things got hot. So I reasoned that it was important to not only control fear but make it work for me, since it prompts sharp decisions and heightens the senses. In the heat of fighting fire, my senses were at fever pitch. My intuition came alive. Some call it a sixth sense. And I recall vividly experiencing euphoria during and immediately after a tough fire. You become light-headed. An animal instinct possesses you. You feel elated and almost inebriated from the thrill of the event; punch-drunk, if you will. Your comrades feel the same so you are a slap-happy, loud band of brothers who love each other.

Helping keep it all in check are leaders. Leaders run the gamut. There are leaders who can make their people do something simply by suggesting it, while others couldn't get someone to follow them to the john. Good leaders lead by example. Their actions — their very characters — are contagious. They are comfortable with who they are. Good leaders remember where they came from — "We all rode the tailboard" was the phrase we used. Good leaders know that respect is a two-way street. And good leaders are passionate about leading; they care about their people, and it shows. The grunts in the ranks are seldom fooled by "plastic" leaders. Once leaders lose the confidence of their people, they lose the ability to lead. It doesn't matter why they lost confidence. We are judgmental that way.

While I was assigned to a ladder company, the boss of the engine company in the same firehouse consistently experienced "mask trouble." The term was twofold. It meant that you had a problem donning the face-piece of your breathing apparatus, or that you consistently diddled with your mask at fires, while the rest of your crew passed you on their way into hell. The man climbed the promotional ladder, and when I worked with him, everything he said to me seemed empty and meaningless. The system had flaws.

The system harbored other peculiarities. Often, a battalion chief hand-picked favorites for assignment to his battalion, a practice within the realm of his rank's privileges. The move was prudent if he selected firefighters known for their firefighting abilities. But sometimes the firefighter was selected for no other reason than that he was a good cook, or the chief's golfing buddy.

Like any testosterone-fueled work environment, the fire department protected its own. What today's human resources call conflict resolution, department officials usually handled by transferring the problem. When a female claimed sexual harassment, the male was transferred. When racial tension flared, someone was "getting a ride" to another firehouse, likely to become someone else's problem. Even when a firefighter I worked with confided in me that another guy on the departing shift was having a tryst with his wife, the department transferred his hormonal friend. Those at the management level were not exempt from the practice. Battalion chiefs who rubbed against the bureaucratic grain were transferred to outlying battalions, effectively ending their climb up the promotional ladder.

The dramatic photograph of Milwaukee firefighter Tom Klatt was nominated for a Pulitzer Prize and was used as the cover for a congressional report titled "America Burning." The photographer says, "The Milwaukee firefighters, that day, changed my life forever! The passion of the men at the scene to save children's lives is an image that has forever humbled me and made me respectful. Thank you all!" (courtesy Ronald M. Overdahl).

I've often felt that the character of a firefighter would be one of the most challenging, yet interesting, studies a psychologist could undertake. I categorized firefighters as the best and the worst people I've met; nothing in between. This very black-and-white assessment was based on my expectations of an individual to meet the demands of the profession. As an indelible part of the city's fabric, firefighters know that all that is expected of them is that they do their job. It is a matter of course to the public that if they call for help, someone will come. My destiny was to be one of those who came to help.

1

The Road to the
Glass House

I remember instructors saying that responses to emergency situations begin long before the alarm is received. It goes back to preparation and training, they said, but I believe it goes much farther back. It goes back to the development of the firefighters themselves, long before they make the decision to become dedicated to helping others, even if it means facing danger. It goes back to their upbringing and their character development. It goes back to family. It goes back to the choices they make while traveling the road to their future.

The road I traveled took me to the Glass House, the nickname given the firehouse to which I was first assigned. Although the road to the Glass House was winding and rocky, and in spots strewn with boulders, I was fortunate to have navigated its rugged length. I never forget that I shouldn't have survived the trip.

As a young boy, I was a curious blend of rebel — yearning for adventure and finding school a waste of time — and dreamer, savoring every moment of my youth. My interests were of my choosing, and they were wide-ranging. I hung with the toughest street kids, all of us too young to carry the folding knives we hid in our pockets. We dared each other to jump from the highest roof, or climb the highest tree — the angels began to hover. Yet, I had no aversion to writing a poem, planting flowers, or learning how to cook and sew. I loved animals. My curiosity abounded, ranging from fascination with outer space to being thrilled by the discovery of how a machine worked by taking it apart. I indulged my creative side, taking great pride in making things; it didn't matter whether my medium was a hammer, an artist's brush, or a pen. I loved music but hated going to Saturday morning choir lessons. Having become fascinated by the martial arts during my teens, I became a student of karate and judo, embracing their disciplines. Those lessons would pay dividends in the years ahead. I was adaptable — I could be a city kid or a country kid. And there were girls; always girls. By the time I had reached my late teens, my loving and hard-working parents had come to realize there was no harnessing their rough-and-tumble son; the sleep they must have lost, the stress they must have endured. Their marriage had begun to unravel and without family bond and structure, I felt that I was left on my own to chart my future. Individually, they remained loving and supporting, but I missed the family unit.

Despite the rocky situation at home, I was excited about the future, which could only mean being a soldier. From early on, it was the only thing I wanted to do with my life. Preparation started early; Boy Scouts and the Civil Air Patrol's cadet program. There was hope for Phil and Lenore's boy.

That my dad had waded ashore at Normandy on D-Day and marched across Europe in World War Two had nothing to do with my aspirations. More memorable was his candor: "We got our asses kicked on the beaches. I was scared to death." Even more impressionable, and probably influential, was his work ethic, which was fueled by his sense of responsibility. After all, I was one of five kids, having two older sisters, Marcy and Carol, a younger sister, Nancy, and a brother, Dale. Plus, my grandmother lived with us. His refrain, "I have eight mouths to feed," was never lost on me. Unbridled humor and affection countered his junkyard-dog tenacity. Such simplicity and balance would crumble in the wake of stresses those tumblers of Old Granddad could not calm. I would forgive him for his whiskey-induced violent behavior, and make peace with him before he died in 1980. I knew that he was proud of my choice to become a firefighter.

That choice had foundation. My army service significantly influenced my career considerations. Amidst the gray moral parameters of the war in Vietnam, I not only strived to keep intact my sense of humanity, I jealously guarded it. The violence I had witnessed committed by both sides made me question my decision about a career wearing army green. Helping people simply had more appeal. Saving lives, not taking them, was something I could get my arms around. Too often I agonized over the helplessness of being ill-equipped, under-trained, or under the charge of inept supervisors when people were wounded or needed help. I vowed never to feel so helpless again, promising commitment — a self-imposed atonement, perhaps — to helping others.

After my "freedom bird" touched down in Oakland, California, in 1972, I stepped onto rough surface of my road to the future. Vietnam had left a bad taste in my mouth and I decided to leave the army. My first act after embracing my surprised mother was to unceremoniously strip off my dress greens and dump them on the floor. I didn't realize then that it broke my proud mother's heart. She soon figured out that her soldier son's dream had been shattered. My old man's cooler-than-expected reception stemmed from his violently abusive drinking in my absence. Now he expected retaliation, or at the very least, that he would have to toe the line.

I was without a sense of direction and purpose. I felt as though I had climbed into a little raft and gone adrift. I drank too much, spent endless days watching the waves of Lake Michigan lap onto shore, and had meaningless romps with people whose names I sometimes didn't know. I didn't carry a gun like some combat veterans who felt naked without one — I carried two. The only way it seemed I could differentiate between day and night was knowing that the enemy attacked during darkness. More than once my poor, worried mother told me that I walked at night and warned her to get to a bunker. I kept friends at a distance and trusted only the few combat vets I knew. A dose of survivor's guilt brought me even closer to the train wreck I was becoming. Fortunately, the counselor I was ordered to see when I nearly lost my driver license was a Vietnam combat vet, First Cavalry Division. He said, "Wayne, I know where you've been and I know where you are." I wasn't alone. Seeing that he had saved himself, and that he trusted me to straighten up, helped turn me around. Within a few months, I reasoned that I had survived to serve a purpose; I just didn't know what that was. I remained a wild card but I knew I had to begin a new life. I had to change.

Remembering the natural high of being in top shape during my paratrooper days, I began biking, running and weight lifting. The work ethic of my youth, fueled by a lust for independence and the child's self-imposed endurance of task I possessed, became energized. Possibly because I was a survivor, and could still taste the satisfaction of saving lives in Vietnam, I felt an overwhelming desire to help others. My compulsion to become a police officer ended abruptly one early foggy morning on my way to the cinder running track on the lake drive. An older, burly cop emerged out of the fog to give me a speeding ticket, unfairly, I thought, because I couldn't see the posted sign and the area was a ghost town that time of morning. He wouldn't relent during my explanation, so my impulsive side had had enough of the prick. I told him I had been going through the police exam process but I would pull out because I didn't want to end up like him. I rolled the ticket into a ball, tossed it against the dashboard and drove off into the fog, mumbling a wish that I never get that ugly if I didn't get laid. I did quit the police candidate process and eyed the fire department, wondering why I hadn't started with that in the first place. I started planning my new course, and I felt great about having goals.

Aware that trying for civil service positions was a long and arduous process, I began preparing by finding books and enrolling in fire technology courses at the local college. I knew I was becoming hooked when I began watching the new TV series *Emergency!*, which showcased the exploits of Los

Angeles firefighter-paramedics Roy and Johnny. Another upside was that I got to know my younger brother, Dale, better than I ever had. We shared common interests, including photography. We took lots of photos on the streets, including of fires, which Dale processed in his own darkroom. It was

The author combined his interest in photography and the fire service and took this shot of hose laid at a five alarm blaze in Milwaukee in 1973. For obvious reasons, in fire service jargon, this was called "spaghetti." The photograph appeared in various publications and was used as an advertisement by a company that manufactured fire hose.

a fun learning and bonding experience. Dale made a career of his expertise and talent that I admire so much. Finding work with two local ambulance companies was easy since they liked my military training and combat experience that dealt with trauma. And I didn't require any type of license. I found it odd that the people who cut my hair or served me a drink had to be licensed, but the people who might hold my life in their hands did not. But that soon changed, thanks, in part, to the show *Emergency!*.

One ambulance company folded and the other was part time, so I needed a full time job. I found work in a foundry, which I equated to a surreal, primeval cave in hell, complete with thunderous din, smoke and fire. I was certain that at times I had seen Satan cavorting among, and sabotaging, our monolithic, groaning, smoke-breathing machines. Being badly burned twice by molten metal, and hearing the screams of a coworker set afire by a shower of molten zinc, steeled my determination to spend the next 30 years or so of my life elsewhere. With the foundry temperature edging past 120 degrees, at noon most of my coworkers raced to the tavern to refuel and cope, while I ate lunch outside, where I had a view of a firehouse. Periodically, the fire truck emerged from its cave, beaming radiantly as the sun ignited its red metal, its riders pushing arms into black coats, and strapping on helmets. *I wonder where they're going and what purpose they'll serve.* The boy still could dream.

I was no stranger to hard work, which kept the wolf from the door. I laid some of Milwaukee's streets with a road crew, and delivered beer and booze to Clark Beer Depot's thirsty customers. I worked as a maintenance man at St. Joseph's Hospital, where I often sneaked to the roof for the glorious view, and got giddy as a schoolboy when nurses flirted. All the while I kept my ear to the ground for fire departments that were hiring. I took the exams for suburban departments and kept close tabs on hiring in Milwaukee and Chicago. The big cities were where it was happening, and finding a position in one became my goal.

I was elated when the City of Milwaukee Fire and Police Commission in 1974 began accepting applications for the position of firefighter. Pat and I had tied the knot the year before, and as we foundered through the uncertainty of oneness, we moved from rent to rent. I passed the written exam, sweated through the physical agility, and sweated again as I explained during the interview why I had spent a night in jail after a drunken spree following my army discharge. Amazingly, they understood and gave me a pass to the medical exam.

Having a hearing loss from the war, I nervously bullshitted my way through the hearing test, which consisted of a ragamuffin physician, with cigarette dangling from his lips, quietly muttering selections from an eye chart.

After complying with "Bend over and spread your cheeks" during the dubious rectal exam, I did hear him say, "Very nice." Bolting upright, I snapped, "Physical's over and I pass. Right?"

I placed number 79 on the eligibility list of 800. Being in the top ten percent meant that I stood a good chance of becoming a firefighter. It was important to me that I be established in my career occupation by the time I was 25 years of age. It appeared I would reach that goal, but during the months of waiting on the eligibility list, the road again turned rocky when ratio minority hiring became a much publicized issue. I paid close attention to the controversial process, which Fire Chief William Stamm explained, tended to "eliminate past racial prejudices." I didn't care what color a firefighter was, as long as he was hired under the same standards to which I was held. And I surely didn't want the selection process slowed for unfair hiring practices.

Our first son, Jeffrey, was born during April 1976, and three months later, on the same day, I received letters of acceptance from the Milwaukee and South Milwaukee fire departments. I tossed South Milwaukee's in the trash. It was an easy decision, especially after discovering that South Milwaukee had bumped me from number one to number three, handing the first two appointments to the sons of city officials.

> Dear Sir:
>
> Your name has been certified for appointment as Firefighter in the Milwaukee Fire Department, and you are herewith ordered to report to the Office of the Fire Department, 711 West Wells Street, 3rd Floor, on Tuesday, September 7, 1976 at 8:00 A.M. for the purpose of taking the oath of office and to be assigned to duty.

Hot damn! Only having watched Jeff come into the world eclipsed my excitement.

Twenty-three of us milled about to be sworn in on the third floor of the main station. The scene reminded me of my induction into the army; a pack of apprehensive young men about to embark on a new career, who, days later, would appear to have come from the same mold. Well, almost; nine of our group were black and one was Hispanic. Two were sons of Milwaukee firefighters and three of us were Vietnam veterans. Early the next morning, our motley group gathered at the Bureau of Instruction and Training on the city's far north side, the next leg of my journey down the road to the Glass House. Clean shaven, with fresh haircuts and clad in red jumpsuits, we got right down to business. Our instructors wasted no time finding out how serious we were about becoming firefighters. Their aim, in fact, was to make *us* question how serious we were. Physical training began immediately and by the third day we were in the smoke tower for their first attempt at thinning out the group.

Huddled into a room of the imposing, cold concrete building, metal shutters and doors were closed with a loud, sobering clang. Eyes darted nervously about the damp, blackened enclosure as though they expected to see dried blood stains from previous recruit classes. Eventually all eyes focused on a discolored metal 55-gallon drum in the middle of the room. Holes had been punched along its bottom edge and straw-like packing material and lumber scraps overflowed its rim. Nearby was a large brass, water-filled hand pump. I found the prospect of what we were about to endure more interesting than frightful. After all, this was part of what I had signed up for, and I was sure this had great importance in performing the job. I had faith in the experience of the instructors. In my mind flashed an image of my instructors in Army Airborne school — tough no-nonsense gorillas who wore black baseball caps. Their white T-shirts hugged massive muscle as they ran backwards, taunting us on five-mile runs wearing combat boots in 95-degree Georgia heat. But they were human like me, and if they could do it, I could do it. Quitting was not an option. These fire guys were no different. True, they looked softer than jump school's Black Hats, but I knew not to underestimate them. They had seen and done things that I hadn't, and they were compelled to teach matters of life and death, and I respected that.

The slight pop of the match striking flint startled the still group. The lieutenant touched the tiny flame to the straw. As the flame grew and danced atop the barrel, the lieutenant talked. Like an Indian council chief imparting wisdom before the fire, its yellow flames flickering in his eyes, he spoke of the importance of learning how to function in smoke, how to breathe through your nose to slow breathing. And he stressed the importance of self control, keeping your cool, because we'd be working in smoke all the time, so we had to get used to it. He explained that we wouldn't always have the luxury of breathing apparatus, and in some instances we wouldn't take the time to put it on, or it might fail. We could run out of air if we were trapped, so we had to be able to fall back on this training and say, "I know how to operate in smoke, I've done this before." The firelight in his eyes brightened and glowed on his face, throwing sinister shadows. He advised watching the smoke's movement, foretelling its behavior. We were told how it stratifies, meaning it will form layers as it rises with the heat. When it hits the ceiling, it will spread laterally and bank down the walls, called "mushrooming." It fills upper levels and the ceiling it forms lowers. When the eerie gray-brown mass was near head level, causing the tall guys to duck, he admonished us to stand upright and try to breathe normally. The flames dove down into the barrel to meet the air the fire sucked in through the bottom vents. The fire, though contained, had become a living thing. Smoke now poured from the barrel, and when flames erupted, the lieutenant had a recruit pump the water can as he wet down the burning material to generate more smoke. Down the smoke ceiling came, enveloping our heads. And with that came coughing and clipped curses.

Visibility was erased as it reached my eyes; it had the familiar sting of tear gas. And when I inhaled it through my nose, my instant thought was that no human could possibly breathe in this stuff for long. It attacked our mucous membranes on the way down to our lungs. It was miserable, it felt tortuous, but it was possible. We stayed in it until we wheezed only short breaths. *Sweet Jesus, this ain't normal!* In the blinding smoke came a reassuring voice: "Stay calm, breathe normal." Just when I wondered how everyone else was doing, I heard a shout and panicked movement. I sensed the air pattern shift as a door to the clean outside world slammed open. Someone had bailed. The door slammed shut. "All right," the voice commanded, "get down on one knee." That brought us just under the smoke ceiling and a wonderful reprieve from the torture just two feet above our heads. I could see through teary, blurred eyes that everyone looked like hell. Tears and sinuses ran freely, streaking our smoke-stained faces. Coughing and wheezing were rampant. It sounded like an emphysema ward. "Stand up!" *Holy shit!* As we disappeared back into the layer, the smoke and gases renewed their attack on our bodies. "Breathe easy. Do it!" There were no slackers because there was no escaping the smoke. I thought of how we were in this together and that the instructors were human, like me. *But how did they endure so much of this nasty crap?*

"Lie on the floor." Twenty-two bodies instantly plopped on the deck, not caring if we got a boot in the face or an elbow in the ribs. Down at that level was left only a slight amount of heavenly breathable air. We learned to put our noses to the cool concrete and lie sideways so our hearts didn't beat as hard. It was psychological, really. "Now kneel!" *My God, the smoke ceiling is now thick at this level!* There was nowhere left to go. Our throats were down to a pinhole and we were feeling the effects of the toxic gasses. *Stay calm.* I heard someone losing it, and there went that infernal pumping again. *Christ, how much smoke can that barrel put out?* I heard shuffling and pounding on the metal door. He's signaling someone outside. "Out! Out!" He didn't have to say that twice. We felt a rush of cool air and I was carried with the crush of bodies stumbling out into brightness and fresh air. We coughed, gagged, and some guys leaned over the railing, puking like seasick sailors. The lieutenant reminded us that this was "clean" smoke and what we'd encounter in the field will be nastier and more deadly. *Amazing.*

We repeated the process until we learned that we could live in the nasty stuff, but the guy that panicked bolted two more times, and he was washed out. The next test of will was climbing a 100-foot, unsupported aerial ladder mounted to an impressive truck. Although we'd heard that this was another common elimination event, everyone made the climb. More difficult than the climb, as the aerial swayed and bounced, was buckling in a waist belt at the narrow tip and leaning backwards with arms outspread to stare at the heavens. I was grateful for having converted my fear of heights to respect for heights at an early age.

During 12 weeks of training, we became intimately familiar with that tower, the gym and the classroom. We donned masks, raised and lowered ladders, laid and operated hose lines, swung axes and ran in our sleep. Working in smoke became second nature. Nothing on this earth, we were convinced, could have made us more appreciative of breathing equipment than those days in the smoke filled tower. When we were finally introduced to breathing equipment weeks later, it quickly became apparent that this was the most vital aspect of our training. Called SCBA, for Self-Contained Breathing Apparatus, or, simply "mask," the unit consisted of a compressed air tank, regulator, harness, and face-piece with hose. The total weight was 30 pounds and, although it was rated at 20 minutes of air, the realistic figure was 15 minutes, figuring that the firefighter was breathing hard, thereby increasing the demand for air and depleting the supply. A warning bell signaled a few minutes of air remaining. During donning drills, we had only 24 seconds to get the mask from the floor to fully donned and operational mode. Often, we were sent to another area while instructors sabotaged the masks so we had to quickly correct malfunctions. We learned how to remove the mask while negotiating tight spaces during blindfolded victim searches, and while following, by feel, a hose line out of the building. And we learned how to buddy-breathe in smoke made ink black by burning tires. I was sure the death of a firefighter due to smoke inhalation a few years earlier had much to do with the emphasis the old scouts placed on mask training and the buddy system. "Two go in — two come out" was heard repeatedly.

Physical fitness was stressed throughout training. It made sense because being fit not only prevented injuries, it paid dividends in performance. At the end of every week, the instructors graded us on the number of push-ups and sit-ups we could do. I was never good at sit-ups but I could pump out over 100 push-ups. I held the class record until Tommy Heine, a true Adonis, easily surpassed my total, and he held perfect form, not like my own version the instructors called "Mutz-ups." The instructors eventually nicknamed me Tank to characterize my short, thick stature and the way I bulldozed through evolutions, not to mention locked doors. My classmates ribbed me in a heavy European accent that I was "strong like bull."

We sweated weekly written exams. We could tie knots blindfolded, we learned water systems, hydraulics and electrical systems, we gained insight to the arsonist's trade, and we could recite the flash points of flammable liquids.

We learned building construction and how to methodically take a building apart to find hidden fire. We learned how to use every tool in the inventory. Ground ladders ranged from 14 feet to 50 feet, the latter weighing in at a hefty 360 pounds. It took a five-man raise to get the thing vertically unsupported, and then we teased our self confidence and trust in our classmates by climbing it that way, going over the top and climbing down the other side. We became so used to climbing the vertical cat ladder hugging the five-story tower that some guys were skipping up the rungs. Our confidence was showing. Practice fires were lit in various parts of the tower building so we could apply the combinations of things we had learned to put them out. As I neared the final curve of my road to the Glass House, our class rotated through engine and ladder teams to attack fires set in vacant houses. There we especially learned the critically important coordination and timing of hose lays, laddering the building, ventilating and the all-important search and rescue. We came to realize that fire, with its awesome ability to turn day into night, wreak carnage, and summon demons, could be beaten.

Since I had been testing myself since I grew out of diapers, I was compelled to challenge myself once again. Here, it seemed important. We were led down into a smoke-filled basement of a vacant house to become familiar with navigating in blinding smoke. When an instructor ushered us out, I hung back and disappeared, knowing that an instructor was still down there somewhere. Larry Ceretto's reputation as a smoke-eater was unmatched but I wondered if he was trying to find his way out, or simply testing himself. This was another case of, "if he can do it, I can do it." Being alone down there, groping in blindness, hearing only the sound of my own breathing in my face-piece was frightfully eerie, but knife-edge exciting as I felt my way along walls, remembering directions and counting turns. Eventually, Ceretto appeared in front of me, inches away, his serious eyes staring through his face-piece into mine. "Let's go out," he said calmly. He didn't lead me; he simply disappeared as though knowing I could stay with him. Once outside, we peeled off our face-pieces, but the ass-chewing I expected never came. He just smiled.

As our load lightened, we received first-aid training, toured the alarm bureau, donated blood, and received a heavy dose of reality witnessing burn management at St. Mary's Burn Center. A cruise in the choppy harbor aboard the fireboat *Deluge* one cold day under a gray woolen sky made the landlubbers among us glad to return to dock, but it only reaffirmed my fondness for work boats.

As we neared the end of training, we anxiously awaited field assignments to an engine or ladder company. Being full of piss and vinegar, most of us desired the busiest companies. Traditionally, tall recruits went to ladder com-

Wearing self-contained breathing apparatus, the author scales a ladder to enter a burning building during his recruit training in 1976. Fires were set in vacant houses during latter weeks of training so recruits could apply their learned skills. Rubber turnout gear would soon be replaced by Nomex fire resistant coats and bunker pants (courtesy Dale Mutza).

panies, while the remainder were assigned to engine companies. The rationale was that bigger guys could better handle ladders, while smaller guys could better negotiate the confines of building interiors. As expected, such distinction fueled boasts by truck men about being bigger and stronger. When talk turned to a graduation party, we were reminded of a party the cops had thrown recently that had made front page news, and not in a good way. It was customary to try to outdo previous classes, regardless the amount of alcohol and the number of women we wouldn't take home to meet Mom that took. I found it humorous that one of our instructors who warned us had entertained a crowd of reveling firefighters by wearing a nude dancer as a party hat. He was one of the best firefighters I've ever met, so how he played mattered little to me.

Lieutenant Richard "Kogee" Kovatch while assigned to the Fire Academy as a training officer. The author would share assignments with Kogee four times throughout his tenure with the Milwaukee Fire Department: as a recruit, instructor, firefighter and officer. Attached to Kogee's coat buckle is a medal of Saint Florian, the patron saint of firefighters.

When the list of company assignments was read, I was somewhat disappointed to hear, "Mutza — Engine 20." I would be a "downtowner," a "looper," a label no doubt borrowed from Chicago. I quickly shifted my attitude about working in a ghetto firehouse, realizing that downtown would offer a tremendous variety of alarms and serve as a good learning ground. I was going to the largest firehouse in the city; the only "triple house," meaning it housed two engine companies and a ladder company, in addition to a variety of equipment. Being headquarters, and more modern than other 19th-century brick firehouses, earned it the name "the Glass House."

2

The Glass House

Above the expansive apparatus floor of the Glass House were living quarters for the 23 men assigned per shift, and above that, on the third floor, was the hub of the department, which incorporated the Bureau of Administration and the office of the chief engineer, his assistant, and the firefighting deputy chiefs. The term *third floor*, I would discover, identified headquarters and its hierarchy. Classmate Glen Allen also was assigned to the Glass House, on the same shift, but on the ladder company. We were the tallest and the shortest in our class, and we often joked that we had flubbed a ladder raise so thoroughly that our punishment would be to become loopers. Then we could show everyone our clown act.

We worked a three-platoon, 24-hour shift, and had 48 hours off. It was a terrific system, but often you stayed awake for 24 hours, working, and spent the first off day resting. You were refreshed the next day off, but returned to work the next morning. That drew no sympathy from envious neighbors and relatives who spurned "tax-robbing" city workers, and saw only the firefighter relaxing when they returned home from their sweaty eight hours. A colorful firefighter who showed disdain for such critics would say, "Screw those eight-hour-a-day, time-clock-punching, brown-bag-carrying sons of bitches!" I was fortunate; like most of my relatives, I was hard-working factory stock, and we held mutual respect for our jobs. I was "their fireman," and they saw honor in my chosen career. It was important to make them proud.

Four or five firehouses comprised a battalion, of which there were seven in Milwaukee. Stations having one engine company were called single houses, while those with an engine and a ladder were called double houses. My Engine 20, along with our partner Engine 2, ran with a crew of five, which consisted of an officer (a lieutenant or a captain), a motor pump operator (MPO), who drove the rig and operated the pumps, and three firefighters, the most senior of which was the first pipeman. The position holds awesome responsibility; whether a fire is beaten often depends solely upon the skill and aggression of the person controlling the nozzle, or pipe. My boss was Lieutenant Dick

This fire occurred in the Manhattan Apartments on State Street in 1978, during the author's days as a "looper" in the downtown district. Ladder Company 2's crew prepares to put its "Big Stick" into operation as a water tower (courtesy MFD Historical Society).

Rajchel, a soft-spoken, gray-haired man not easily given to humor. Maybe it was because I was there and he now had to mind his Ps and Qs to set a good example. His quiet, rapid speech was difficult for me to hear, and my refrain, "What was that again?" seemed to irritate him. Most of the men assigned there, I noticed, talked in fast, clipped sentences in a language tailored to the demands of sudden urgency. Rajchel had served much of his career, having come up through a time when, as the old timers put it, "You lived off the pipe." It described how, before SCBA appeared, leather-lung firemen put their noses close to the nozzle to breathe air being expelled with the pressured water. Lieutenant Rajchel also wasn't quick to grab a mask when he had a cub under his wing. *The more you operate in smoke now, the more you'll appreciate your mask later.*

My MPO, Herb Zautke, was in the twilight of his career. He was a pleasant man, serious and expert in his work, and I expected to learn much from him. On stage, the blue-helmeted MPO was a detached observer, watching from his position at the rig the white-helmeted director and his black-helmeted and red-helmeted actors. At fires, our MPOs had the best seat in the house, giving them unmitigated license to critique the incident, though seldom were they so inclined. But since they saw things we did not, they sometimes offered their perspectives.

Although standard operating procedures were in place, tactics and company policies differed according to location and officer preference. How we operated at alarms often was dictated by the nature of the emergency. Flexibility was vital; we switched roles and split crews often. Ladder 2, like all ladder companies, ran with a crew of five: an officer, driver, and three firefighters, one of whom doubled as tillerman if the truck was a tractor-trailer type. Typically, the boss and the rookie, or "cub," worked as a team, while the remaining three handled the roof operation. If opening up the roof to vent the fire was ruled out, the entire crew might perform search and rescue, ventilate the building, or be assigned forcible entry. Ladder assignments were favored by some since their crews operated more independently than those assigned to engines. Adding to the appeal of ladder companies was the fact that engines went on EMS calls, which were scorned by many who claimed their job was strictly to "fight the red devil" and not play nurse. At fires, and major alarms, battalion chiefs ran the show, doling out assignments as companies arrived. Often, hand signals sufficed. Sometimes when we pulled into greater alarms, the chief merely pointed at the pair in the cab and raised two fingers, meaning we were to drop two big lines and get a water supply. Now, *that* I thought was professionalism!

Until our one-year anniversary date, we were probationary firefighters undergoing on-the-job-training. We would be tested by the school monthly and we would be evaluated and monitored closely in the field, lest we kill someone, or ourselves. There would be no down time except for sleep at night. There was never a reason to be idle. I knew every inch of my rig, a massive diesel-powered 1973 Pirsch-Hendrickson that could pump 1,500 gallons per minute. I could easily name, describe, and demonstrate the equipment in any compartment when someone pointed to it. There were always manuals to be read, something to be cleaned, or helping hands needed somewhere. Often that was in the kitchen, where tradition also reigned. Cooks were exempt from doing dishes, and the senior firefighter washed, while the next in line was the "dipper," who rinsed. Next lowest in the pecking order was the "wiper," who dried the dishes and put them away. Dare he pass back to the washer a dish still dirty, he was chastised with, "A good wiper could clean that." The cub mopped the floor, while the MPO took out the garbage and cleaned the stove. And God help anyone who disrupted the order. Firehouse maintenance routines too were governed by tradition, with specific chores done on designated days. For example: Monday was "mask day," Tuesday was "ladder day," Wednesday was "windows day," Thursday was "kerosene day" (the most dreaded since it meant cleaning the underside of the rigs), Saturday was "brass day," and Sunday was welcomed as "holiday routine." After the evening meal, we cubs studied for monthly exams and logged every box alarm that punched in on the teletype register, called the joker stand. We became expert at identifying, by the number of punches, where a box was being pulled and what companies responded. And there were always drills and lessons to be learned in between alarms. Young guys were glad to see us so they could relinquish their "cub" status. Newcomers seldom were warmly welcomed and often were called "cub bitch." And with that came a regular dose of hazing, a true test of the thickness of one's skin.

Firefighters, it seemed, had mastered the dark art, of which there were few limits. Anything to do with a cub's characteristics, physical and otherwise, was game, as was his personal life. Admittedly, sometimes lines were crossed and tempers flared. So I learned to walk a fine line, to take whatever good-natured ribbing that came my way in stride, and become the best firefighter I could be. One of the age-old unofficial requirements of cubs was that they make popcorn at night for the brothers. Regardless how much flak I took for not making popcorn, I simply would not do it. The subservient nature of that rankled me, as did the expectation that the cub make the deputy chief's bed. Not once during my fire service career did I make popcorn or make any-one's bed other than my own. I needed to maintain some sense of self control so I drew the line at these two cub chores. Prior to my arrival, a firefighter's refusal to make the chief's bed had made front page news. Looking deeper into why firefighters "worked on" cubs, and each other, it seems that it is, however Neanderthal in nature, a test of stress limits, perseverance, and their own level of self assurance. And, in a way, it is bonding. Being worked on had little effect on me. Much of it, I knew, was positive attention. I would earn my reputation by doing my job. *Make your own damn popcorn.*

I was anxious to do just that — to get out into the streets to face whatever an emergency could throw at me. There were big hurdles to jump: my first "worker," my first "crispy critter," my first "floater"; the list of firsts was long. All firefighters endure indescribable anticipation of their first fire, that first opportunity to prove to others — and especially to themselves — that they're up to the task of performing the job they've been trained to do, the job they chose. "It'll come, kid," the old timers croon: "it'll come soon enough."

My very first run was for a Christmas tree that burned outside of Gimbel's Department Store on downtown's busy Wisconsin Avenue. *Bring the hand pump and an axe, stay glued to the boss, and do exactly as told.* But I wasn't used to crowds of onlookers. It was an easy fire, even novel. My next one was not so novel.

With siren screaming and the air horn parting traffic, our massive Hendrickson pumper roared west on Wisconsin Avenue to a tall apartment building. A fire had been reported on an upper floor of the building, in an occupied apartment. *This could be bad.* And it showed on the faces of my two pipemen, Ken Grabske and Bill Kaminski. Lieutenant Rajchel and I headed straight for the building. Looking up, we spotted light smoke drifting about the upper floors. We knew that inside was a less passive scene. We skipped taking the time to don masks, the procedure being that the old heads would put theirs on and bring ours up with them. Time was critical and we needed to be as light as possible to make the climb. Elevators are seldom used as they tend to be busy at a time like this, can malfunction, and heat sensitive call buttons can take you straight to where the real heat is; bad news any way you look at it. We have more latitude on the stairs. I had all I could do to keep up with my boss, who carried a small pry bar, a hand lantern, and a walkie-talkie. I lugged the clumsy hand pump extinguisher and a 16-pound fire axe.

We pushed past people streaming down the stairs, some hollering, "Top floor." *Of course.* I was in shape but this was punishing. We ran 13 floors — 26 flights of stairs — I was exhausted when we hit the top landing and we hadn't even begun work. The smoke was heavy but livable, for us, at least. *Thank you, training lieutenants.* An elderly woman wasn't finding it so livable and Rajchel told me to get her to the stairs. I stumbled into Bill and he took her by the arm. I crawled back to find Rajchel, but he was gone. *Shit. You never, never lose your boss.* In a running crouch, dragging the hand pump, I heard in the smoke, "Goddammit, Mutza, get that can in here!" I made out his form, kneeling in the doorway of the burning apartment. We crawled in to see flames roaring up the kitchen walls and beginning to spread across the ceiling. *We'll just be able to nail this nasty bitch.* I handed him the snake-like small rubber hose and pumped like there was no tomorrow. We knocked down the fire and quickly crawled into the apartment to search for victims, at the same time fiddling with stuck windows to open them. *No breaking out the glass this high up.* The shards can sail like daggers into crowds far below. Finding no one, we backed out into the hall where Bill and Ken had our masks and a hose line.

While they went in to finish off the fire, Rajchel and I shamelessly blew the black phlegm hanging from our mouths and noses and hurriedly donned the masks to savor their clean air. Back in we went to help overhaul and ventilate. When everything was clear, Bill and Ken commented on the obviously gay trappings in the apartment, which included sketchings of nude men. When the obviously gay occupant showed up and complained about the damage, Bill faced him, shrugged, and quipped, "We don't start 'em, we put 'em out." Then he lazily rolled his eyes, dropped his shoulders and his tone, adding, "Love what you did with the place, though," leaving the man speechless. I was reminded that dealing with distraught people was one of the things we weren't taught in the academy.

This was a one-room fire, and despite the effort to reach it, it doesn't qualify as my first bonafide worker. That came shortly thereafter and is the fire I describe in the preface.

I didn't have to wait long to encounter my first dead person. The call came in at night, reported as a car fire below a stretch of the maze of downtown freeway overpasses. My engine and our Ladder 2 responded. There, fully aflame on a hillside, was the hulk of some sort of vehicle. We quickly went to work with a quick-attack line, and when the smoke cleared, we were looking at the charred, twisted carcass of a semi truck cab. Using pry-bars, the ladder crew partially lifted the hulk, while we knelt to peer underneath. *We can smell you, but we can't see you.* Lights revealed a charred body. *Aha, the driver.* But we had to lift the entire thing to check for other occupants and make it easier for investigators who would have to sift through the mess. Even though the body was charred, it was obvious the driver was a big man. Kneeling down with a sheriff to peel away the remains of a wallet seared to the torso's crisp hip, I tried to ignore the stench of roasted flesh. We were, however, somewhat fascinated by the torso's erection, not an unusual occurrence in fire deaths, as intense heat contorts muscle and tissue. More disturbing were the occupants of cars that had pulled over on a nearby ramp and peered through the chain link fence to gawk at the carnage. We had covered the body, but when I saw those faces pressed against the fence, it incensed me enough to throw back the tarp and snap, "Here, is this what you ghouls want to see?" They quickly

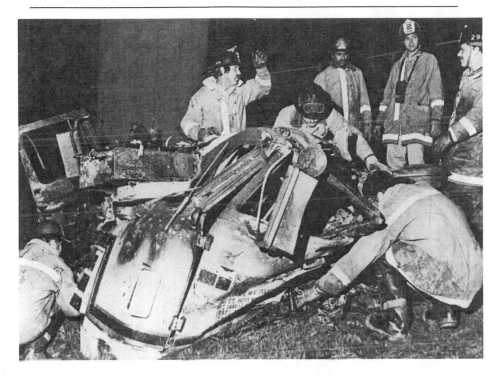

The first fatality the author encountered as a firefighter was underneath this truck cab, which plunged 100 feet from a freeway overpass. Mutza (at far right) converses with Ken Grabske (with hand raised), while Ladder 2's Lieutenant Dick Fehr and Firefighter Glen Allen look on (courtesy *Milwaukee Sentinel* © Journal Sentinel, Inc., reproduced with permission).

turned away. Being a cub, that was a bold move, but the others understood and never brought it up.

Among the ashes, we found opened beer cans. The driver, it turned out, had begun his long trip in Ohio. A sheriff pointed upward to an elevated curve of road. "The rest of his rig," he said, "is up there." When he lost control, his cab separated from his trailer and he plunged 100 feet down, the end of his trip. A photo in the next day's paper showed me smiling over the charred wreck as I talked with Ken. Obviously, I was already somewhat immune to tragedy. Having seen tragedy since I was 18 years old —first with the Eighty-Second Airborne Division — taught me self-control, and I was still learning. Was I desensitized or did I simply accept death as part of life? Horrifying experiences can have positive effects. I knew that traumatic emotional events could change my perception and how I acted, but they didn't have to be debilitating. Glen, too, was getting his share on the "big stick" (our nickname for Ladder Co. 2). I saw his eyes well up after working at a blaze in a home for the developmentally disabled, where two young patients burned to death. I saw the look again after an early morning run to a bad accident one December morning in the downtown Marquette Interchange. A taxi cab had been pummeled and cut in half by trucks skidding on fresh snow. It took some time to shake the image of the cab driver's shoes burning from a fire that burned so hot we couldn't get near until we got water. Glen's ladder truck got there in time for him to hear the trapped driver's screaming pleas.

I stayed in touch with some of my recruit classmates. Word quickly spread about Mike Warzala's first encounter with fire death, which was worse than we could imagine. One bitterly cold January day, Mike's Engine Company 30 pulled up to a house fire at 29th and Center streets in the inner city. Although the fire had full possession of the house, Mike and his crew fought valiantly to enter to save kids they were told were still inside. The anguish still shows on Mike's face when he describes how they knocked down the fire in the stairwell but couldn't get past the massive fire. They punched through an adjacent wall with axes in a desperate attempt to get to the victims. When their axes broke through the wall, tiny burned legs tumbled through the openings. Six children died in that inferno. We did not envy the anguish that crew, and those families, suffered. Gung ho as Mike was, he was ready to quit, but he went on, put it all in perspective, and retired as an officer. Mike walked proudly in the footsteps of his father, Don Warzala, who had also felt the sting of flame and had seen the face of death.

Being a looper did, indeed, provide the widest variety of alarms. All the potential was there: every kind of building and occupancy, including residential, apartment complexes, high-rise, industrial, mercantile and everything in between. Besides fires and vehicle accidents, we responded to drownings in the Milwaukee River, suicides (successful and not) — those from heights we called "jumpers" — chemical leaks, cave-ins, people stuck in elevators, industrial accidents, explosions, water leaks, alarms sounding, and the rapidly increasing medical emergencies. I learned to work in a world where I regularly bumped up against towering structures, massive machinery, overpowering sounds, and flurries of emotions, and keep it all in perspective. I learned to work in weather extremes: temperatures so hot that guys were tipping over and relief came only from sticking my head under an open hydrant; and so cold that we had to use tools to chip ice from our coats to remove them. Sometimes we saw our rigs cocooned in ice, frozen to the street in winter's grip. "We'll come back for it in April," we joked. There is nothing like being roused from half-sleep and 90 seconds later feeling sub-zero wind blasting your face. And then a few minutes after that, to open a nozzle and feel icy water run down your sleeve, past your underwear and into your boots. It was unnatural. We joked that the mind-numbing, teeth-rattling cold made our manhood "turn turtle," not to emerge until spring. I learned to work for long durations under combinations of extremes. The longest I recall spending at an alarm was about 13 hours at a stubborn auto scrapyard blaze in the industrial valley. Some of those hours were spent in an elevated turret of our fireboat *Deluge*, manning a giant turret nozzle downwind of the vessel's exhaust stacks.

After a few months, Glen and I switched places so I could gain truck experience and he some time "on the pipe." Working overtime and relief shifts meant working in other houses, which broadened our experience. Being downtown, we didn't get the steady regimen of dwelling fires familiar to inner city companies, but we discovered that variety was, indeed, the spice of life, and death. One windy morning we were atop a high-rise building wrestling a huge sign with ropes, and that afternoon Glen and I were ordered to climb the 100-foot aerial ladder to stop a ranting, belligerent man from jumping out of a window on an upper floor of the Wisconsin Hotel. Glen and I gave each other that classic *you gotta be shittin' me* look when, thankfully, the police broke through the inside door and captured the maniac.

The old hotels — the Wisconsin, the Antlers, and the Belmont — in particular, gave us plenty of work. Unlike our contemporaries working the ghettos, we often worked above two floors and had more people in a building to worry about. Often, just reaching the fire was an all-out effort. We relied heavily upon our aides, the battalion chiefs' drivers, who usually arrived first and carried only a walkie-talkie. They were experienced, hand-picked firefighters who dashed into buildings to serve as the eyes and ears of chiefs running the show from street level. Being first in and carrying no equipment whatsoever, aides accounted for more saves than anyone. Most were experts at "reading" fire and showed great courage. And, of course, they had "leather lungs." I admired our aide, Dan Shea, who drove First Battalion Chief Bob McCann. Being of slight frame, fair skinned and with a bushy shock of blonde hair topping his youthful face, Dan didn't look the part. But perform he could. Crawling down the smoky hall of a nasty fire on an upper floor of one of the old hotels, he scooted past us and disappeared in the smoke. When he came back, he had a victim. It wasn't unusual to crawl deep into a rooming house or hotel, bump into Dan, and have him tell us where the seat of the fire was, or what direction to go. Once, we met him crouched at the doorway of an apartment fully involved with fire. As flames roared over his head, he pointed just inside the doorway and shouted, "Can't do anything for that one!" Barely visible in the flames was a black body sitting in a chair tilted backward against the wall. The form looked weirdly relaxed, although fully aflame. *Win some. Lose some.*

I was earning my keep as well as a good reputation for putting out 100 percent and keeping my nose clean. I loved the work and the challenges, and it showed. I could think on my feet and stay calm regardless the stress of an incident. As I gained experience, I took risks, though carefully thought through. "Everything in moderation," they say, but I was never sure what moderation was. Nor was I sure what constituted calculated risk, but I convinced my family I was being careful. And I was becoming accepted. It didn't take long to figure out who I could trust with my life, and who were the slackers and posers. One fire, in particular, spotlighted the various types.

The four-story flophouse on 12th and State Streets was called the Journal Arms, which we debased to "the Urinal Arms." All of the fire companies in that part of the city knew it well. It housed the worst of society, and we went there often for fires and other problems. No sooner would we pick up our hoses and gear from a fire there than the drywall truck was pulling up so the dump could be patched up to squeak pass code for habitation.

One cold winter day I came in to work and discovered that my regular boss was off and that we would spend the shift under the charge of a newly promoted lieutenant. I knew the guy and it made me uneasy because I thought he spouted off too much and was very much a weasel. In the middle of the night the warbler jolted us from our beds. It is a most tense, heart-pounding moment between the fifth ring and hearing the dispatcher call off the companies responding, where, why, and any other critical data. After calling off a host of companies, the dispatcher chimed, "You have a fire—12th and State—people trapped." For him to say confidently "You have a fire" meant multiple calls were received, making it a sure thing. He didn't give us the building address—he didn't have to—he knew we'd see it. Because it was so cold, I sat in the roomy cab between the MPO and the boss.

The dump was only six blocks away so we spotted smoke haze almost immediately after leaving the barn. Herb got us there in zip time and as we pulled up, ugly gray smoke pushed from every window of the top floor; licks of flame darted through the billowy mass. Glancing upward through the windshield, I saw there, kneeling on a narrow, sloped third floor ledge, a young man, clad only in underwear. His knees were drawn tightly up to his chin and I could see the terror in his eyes. Smoke cartwheeled out of the window behind him. I was surprised at how he managed to cling to a ledge that extended no more than a few inches. Even in the closed cab, I could hear someone screaming. This was a real "Oh, shitter." We were first in and we had to act, fast. That's where the boss takes center stage. But this first-day-as-a-lieutenant, chock-full-of-advice expert froze. I looked at his face, his small eyes set deep above high cheekbones staring straight ahead. I couldn't believe it. He blanked. Before I could say something to snap him out of it, Herb reached across my chest and grabbed his coat, shaking him, hollering, "Do something!" It was an order more than a plea. "You got people trapped, man!"

Herb quickly zeroed in on a nearby hydrant, and when he jumped out of the cab I spilled out after him. Ken, Bill and I masked up and laid a large line as far into the main doorway as we could. The Big Stick was right behind us and they got the guy on the ledge down. People were stumbling down the stairs, hollering. One guy, obviously out of it, badgered us to get upstairs to save people. We finally shoved him out the door. It sounded like Bill decked him to keep him out, and alive. Ken and I began working our way up the stairs to the top floor, working the line as we neared the landing. The smoke was hot and black. Rivulets of bubbling paint ran down the stairwell walls. Flames, at times, were near the floor. My time had come. Ken shoved the pipe into my hands, and I was fine with that. I felt his shoulder against my arched back, expertly taking up the back pressure of the hose. Farther back, someone fed us line, struggling with the rock-hard hose, pushing its huge rigid loops along walls. Intermittently opening the pipe to knock down flames produced scalding steam that stung our ears, pushing us face-down into warm, filthy water. The pain of kneeling on hot embers made us constantly shift stance. Ken stayed glued to me, shouting encouragement as we fought the beast room by room, down the hall, never giving in, and finally ended up at the rear of the building. Some of the floor had burned through and a rear porch and stairway had collapsed. I was wasted. I couldn't stand. I was dizzy, but I had crawled the length of the building and knocked down the bulk of the fire. There was just enough light to see Ken's broad grin under his Yosemite Sam moustache.

We staggered outside and found Bill on a hillside behind the building, straddling a large hose line. He had laid the line by himself to set up a water curtain to protect nearby Mt. Sinai Hospital from the blaze. He had all he could to do keep from sliding on his butt down the slush covered hill as back pressure from the hose worked against him. To help control the nozzle, he used the trick of forming a huge loop and placing the nozzle under the heavy loop, and then straddling the point where hose intersected. I was proud of my crew and our efforts. There is intense pride in "making the fire" and not giving in to it. Everyone did what had to be done, expertly. Oh, the new lieutenant? We didn't see him until the overhaul stage, when he gave some sort of order about picking up equipment. We didn't pay close attention. We knew what we had to do.

Later, when we unwound and relived our part in the action, I was humbled yet pleased to hear Ken brag about how I moved aggressively through the fire and beat it down. Tom of Ladder 2 told how he had climbed an extension ladder he had placed below a window to rescue a man trapped on an upper floor. When he neared the top, the man swore at him, calling him everything but a white man, and pushed the ladder away, with Tom teetering on the top rungs. Tom tried again, only to be met with the same pushing and the crazed man's vows that no "honkey mothafucka" was gonna save his ass! "Ain't ya'll got no niggas to come save this nigga?" he yelled. *Well, actually, sir, we do employ African-Americans, but they're busy right now.* That was enough for Tom. On his third climb, he bellowed at the belligerent would-be victim that he'd punch his lights out if he touched that ladder again. The man knew Tom meant it and got out onto the ladder, mumbling and cursing. I would see over and over, firsthand, examples that not everyone we were sent to help saw us as lifesaving angels.

Equally memorable were the unusual calls. One day we were summoned to retrieve a jumper who bailed out of an upper-floor window. We searched a lower roof of an abutting building but were stymied when we couldn't find a body. We were about to dismiss it as a malicious call when someone heard moaning coming from a two-foot square air shaft. Peering in, we were amazed to see a woman stuffed neatly inside. After carefully freeing her from her sheet metal trap, we unfolded her compacted body. We knew that, at the very least, she should have had parts severed by the sharp edges of the shaft when she fell into it. We were astounded to find that she suffered only bruises; her mental state we labeled as inebriated. She explained that she was sitting backwards in her hotel window many floors above, and remembered then feeling a flying sensation. Fortune smiled on the woman that day. In your best efforts, you could not duplicate her dive into that narrow shaft and emerge unscathed.

Another jumper we had two weeks earlier had not been so fortunate. His intended plunge was successful. As we walked along quiet Wisconsin Avenue early one Sunday morning, blood running off of a marquee onto the sidewalk made it easy to find that victim. I was grateful that no one had to see that. Less considerate was a young man who one day waited for a bus to come along on busy Water Street. When the bus pulled up, he stepped purposely in front of it. Since he was obviously dead, our first priorities were covering his remains and tending to bystanders who had seen and heard the sickening impact. I felt for the distraught bus driver and those who witnessed his selfish act, and I was angry at the dead guy for subjecting so many to his thoughtlessness. When the police had cleared the scene, we scooped up brain matter from the pavement. Our gallows humor kicked in to deal with it. Out of public earshot, among us could be heard, "There's third grade," and "I've got the piano lessons." We then laid a line and flushed away the remnants of the man's life. Just when we thought the runs couldn't get any weirder, something new would come up. It was one of the great aspects of the job; no two days — no two runs — were alike. I'll leave you to guess the comments made after a call to Ambrosia Chocolate for an industrial accident. It required that we search a vat of chocolate the size of an upturned Volkswagen to find a black worker's finger severed by mixing blades.

Not all of fire service life was death and destruction. There had to be balance. Often, especially in slower houses, there were long periods between calls that made the troops bored and restless. It dulled the edge and gave them more time to play games. Although the Glass House was more spit-and-polish than most, the boys found ways to stir up trouble. It made you believe that when they were kids, they said to their parents, "When I grow up I want to be a fireman," and that the parents replied, "You can't do both." Working on each other was incessant. It was a way of firehouse life. You were always on the defensive. It even showed in our speech. And there were pranks, some of which were time-honored, such as setting water traps in kitchen cabinets, and limited only by the prankster's imagination. The cubs, of course, were the usual targets. A common shocker was hiding nude in a cub's locker and jumping out when he opened it. Another tease had two guys pointing out to the cub which bed was his, and noting that the two beds pushed tightly against

Deputy Chief's Aide Frank Rozek and a company officer place the body of a person killed in a fire onto a police department stretcher for transport to the morgue. Firefighters' acceptance of losses in fires didn't make the grim task any easier (courtesy MFD Historical Society).

it were theirs. Once, I awoke in the dorm to what sounded like a chicken clucking. Sure enough, when I scanned the huge dorm, there, tethered to Frank Rozek's bed, was the head-bobbing bird. A guy known for his frugalness took it home, where it became dinner. Frank was a wise old-timer and the deputy chief's driver, a position of honor. I learned much from him. Frank was also a cut-up, always quick with a line or a story. I heard he was quite the firefighter in his day and had distinguished himself by talking a woman out of jumping off a bridge on his way home from work. I guessed that Frank told her jokes, but he never shared the details. We had fun working on Frank, but he asked for it, especially when he paraded through the place at night, wearing an oversized pith helmet down over his eyes, lugging a flashlight, and yelling, "Lights out!" It was common, especially on windy days, for the guys to line up in front of the firehouse and watch the "skirts" go by, on their way to downtown offices. Most of them seemed to enjoy the attention, and when one of us struck up a conversation with a pretty lass, Frank would say, "Ah, geez, there goes the wife, the kids, and the 200 dollars in the credit union." When Frank retired, on his last day, he got up quietly before dawn and ran a hose from the apparatus floor up a pole hole into the dorm. He then secured it to a railing, aiming the nozzle so it covered the entire dorm full of sleeping bodies. And just before he walked out of the firehouse for the last time, Frank turned the water on.

And there were water fights, even in the Glass House. Some days, especially hot ones, we spent hours mopping up water. Only the bosses were exempt — sometimes. The shenanigans all but stopped when someone waited for unsuspecting quarry to appear at the bottom of a hole for a sliding pole. The next person to walk by took the full brunt of a bucket of ice cold water. With his hair plastered to his forehead, stern, no-nonsense Deputy Chief Gus "Casey" Koleas looked up and saw the shocked face of Lenny of Engine 2. We scattered to escape the wrath of the chief we called "the Greek fire god." Guys even hid in lockers. We could hear the squishing noises made by Casey's shoes as he plodded upstairs where Lenny waited to take his punishment. Chief Koleas shot Lenny his fiery look, pointed at him, and said quietly, "Young man, you'll be out of here soon." And within weeks Lenny was getting a ride to Rescue Squad 4, known to be the busiest "puker" in the city. He hated it.

Lenny seemed to have a stream of bad luck. We almost lost him once, in a bad attic fire. Engine 20 had taken its turn guarding the Summerfest grounds at the lakefront, where the long, hot, 12-hour shift was spent watching the girls and hoisting kids up onto the rig. The union guys manning the nearby "Fill the Boot" fund-raising table were off duty so they imbibed steadily, bringing trays filled with foam-topped cold ones from a beer tent.

On the sly, Lenny sampled his share and by the time Summerfest closed, he was well on his way to being three sheets to the wind. Just after midnight, as we were backing into quarters, the radio came alive, dispatching us to a fire in the projects to the north. Already mobile, it was a cinch we would arrive first. That we did, and hurriedly got a line up the stairs to the attic. The attic was "rolling" and just as we got past the landing, the fire flashed over, meaning everything was superheated and simultaneously and violently ignited. It would have been more prudent to have waited for a ladder company to get onto the roof and open up. Instead, the oxygen-seeking fire went for the stairwell we were on. Not realizing how loaded Lenny was, we had allowed him to take his honored position on the pipe. The fire bowled him over, blowing his helmet off. He plowed backward into us and the three of us rolled down the stairs, the blaze roaring over our heads. Lenny got his ears burned; maybe it served him right, I thought. He's lucky he didn't lose them. He toughed it out because if he went to the hospital and they took a blood test, he would have been out of a job, or, at the very least, suspended, along with the acting boss.

Much time was spent in the kitchen, the very heart, the forum, of the firehouse. There, problems are solved, training conducted, gossip exchanged, and views aired. As a cub, I learned to become an assistant cook, called the bull cook. Not only did I enjoy it, I learned culinary skills from experts. Despite my activity level, it was difficult to keep off extra weight. In what other workplace does one eat fresh bakery goods in the morning, a full-blown meat-and-potatoes meal at noon, another cooked meal at 5 P.M., and have a kitchen to rummage through during an entire work shift? Even if, in the middle of the night, we transferred to another house to cover for a company tied up at a blaze, we raided their refrigerator. Of course, beer-batter fish fry required at least a six-pack, and, with permission from the chief, a glass of red wine was allowed with an Italian dinner. Food was, and remains, very important to firefighters. Everyone was a critic. If supper was late, the cook heard, "The whole world eats at five." If the boys found a meal under par, they demonstratively looked under their plate for change. Digging through what he called a "honeymoon salad" (lettuce alone), Frank Rozek would say, "Gee, I'd have given you another quarter if you needed a tomato." No mercy. Once, while cooking with Pepie Du De Voire, we pulled from the massive industrial oven a monstrous pan loaded with many pounds of cooked roasts, potatoes and vegetables. We struggled and lost our grip on the steaming, heavy load and it tilted, splaying a meal for 23 hungry fire guys across the floor, gravy and all. We looked at each other, and then looked around. No one had seen the fiasco. Without saying a word, we closed the kitchen door, rolled down the huge shutters to the dining room, and grabbed dust pans from the broom closet. On hands and knees, we skimmed the dust pans around the floor like boys playing with toy cars. Squinting at the scraping noises that might attract attention, we managed to scoop everything back into the huge pan, muscle it onto the stovetop, and mop the floor. Then we called the hogs to dinner. Only a couple of suspicious eyes were cast our way when we begged off the meal with, "Ya know, when ya spend the day in a hot kitchen, you just lose your appetite." When someone complimented the meal, Pepie and I tried not to look at each other, knowing we'd lose it. And no one knew. I hope the statute of limitations on kitchen mishaps is up.

One of my favorite among our cast of characters was Paul Collova, who had cut his teeth in the busy Second Battalion. Assigned to Engine 2, Paul was a burly guy who I never tired of listening to. His deep brow furrowed over dark brown eyes, emphasizing the clear enunciation of his words. Paul's back had never been right ever since he had fallen through a floor of a burning building, landing on a kitchen table, his back jolted by his breathing apparatus. He held my respect because not only was he honest about his fears and his opinions, he once dashed in his engine to the hospital with a badly injured young boy, rather than wait for the paramedics, who were delayed. He took heat for making that call, but many of us admired his quick thinking that saved the boy's life. Sometimes, on a sub-zero cold night, when the howling wind pushed against the windows and rattled the big apparatus bay doors, Paul would drill through us with those big browns, his brow would crease and he'd say, "Tonight could be the night we pull up and they'll be tap dancin' on the window sills." And sometimes he was right.

I liked working with Paul. He was reliable and sensible. He could think on his feet and he was funny. He and I once volunteered to go deep into a smoke-filled brewery warehouse to bring out a large acetylene tank that blow-torched bright orange flame from where its valve had been knocked off. Then-booming Pabst Brewery was a regular source of work for us loopers. Periodically, grain in storage silos ignited, or we were called for an ammonia leak, which had us ventilating and dissipating the noxious irritant with hose spray. Often, we were invited by grateful brewery workers to their lunchroom, where they enjoyed sharing their occupational perk — access to "shorties" kept in a large cooler. More than once I heard clinking noises coming from a stash of shorties in the hand-pumps as the fire boys returned to their rigs.

During a shift when Paul and I worked on Ladder 2, we ended up dragging a large, heavy attack line into the Hack's Furniture warehouse in the Third Ward factory district. In the blinding smoke, we had stopped short of high-stacked furniture storage platforms to reposition the line when the massive racks, with a thunderous roar, collapsed in front of us, knocking us over. We lay on the cold floor in dust and smoke, forehead to forehead, staring at each other, frozen, silent, knowing that had we advanced just a few feet farther, we both would have been crushed like bugs.

I never got used to working in blinding conditions. It was spooky. You never knew what danger awaited feet, sometimes mere inches, away. It made you move slowly, and it humbled you. During a shift when I was assigned to Ladder 2, we were sent at night with a full assignment to an explosion on the west end of State Street in an industrial area. True to my cubly status, I stuck with the boss. Through the smoke we noticed that the top front portion of the building's wall protruded outward over the sidewalk, buckled as the result of an explosion. My lieutenant sent a warning over his walkie-talkie. Slowly feeling our way through the smoky interior, we stayed in voice contact, commenting about the odd curvature of the floor on which we stood. As the smoke lightened, we realized we had been standing in the bottom, curved portion of a huge cylindrical tank. The rest of the tank was gone. The next morning, we were humbled to see that the metal buckles of our turnout coats, any metal we wore, and even the coins in our pockets, had turned a corrosive green color. Instantly, we thought of what it had done to our lungs after we removed our masks during overhaul.

Our work gave us an inside, close-up look at all parts of society. Some calls, however, were more close-up than we preferred. One such alarm came in on June 30, 1978. We responded to a report of a fire in an underground parking garage at fashionable Juneau Village, just over a mile away. Such fires are particularly nasty because the heat and smoke are confined. This turned out to be even nastier. We made a long hose stretch and made our way through the blinding smoke, which had a sickening, familiar odor. We discovered that a car had exploded. Despite what you see in movies, this is a rare occurrence, even if the vehicle is on fire. Among the shredded, pulpy and charred remains of the driver, under the front seat of the wreckage was the lower leg, the fetlock portion, of a large animal, such as a horse or a deer.

It didn't take long for us to figure out that this was a car bombing and that the fetlock held some mob symbolism. Amid such carnage some of the old heads with strong stomachs still managed the expected wisecracks about wise guys. And who could resist recalling images from the film *The Godfather?*

We later discovered that Milwaukee mafioso and reputed informer August "Augie" Palmisano was the victim of the car bomb, a weapon frequently used by the mob for settling scores. I was reminded of another mob killing three years earlier when an informer had been gunned down in front of his home. I would rather have been at that scene.

One of the nicknames by which Milwaukee mob boss Frank Balistreri was known was Mad Bomber, derived from his preference for car bombs. A few days after the remains of Balistreri's former acquaintance were scooped into evidence bags, Mr. Big was quoted as saying, "He called me a name — to my face — and now they can't find his skin." What a guy! A decade later, I would be involved in the cleanup of another bloody mess left by Milwaukee's mob.

The dark humor we often exhibited, also called gallows humor, seems insensitive, but it was a way of coping with stress. Even our dispatchers retained the odd brand of humor from their past as firefighters. But sometimes our coarseness backfired. For example: one day while Paul Collova and I were giving a tour at the Glass House to two large groups of children with female chaperones, the warbler sounded for the rescue squad. The groups stilled as we heard the dispatcher over the loudspeaker announce the unit to respond. "Squad 1," the old-timer chimed. Whoever picked up the phone confirmed the assignment by repeating, "Squad 1." Captivated by the alarm coming in, the now quiet tour group heard the dispatcher follow with, "Squad 1, ya got a lady bleeding from the snapper." Audible gasps filled the huge apparatus bay before the dispatcher finished giving the address. The red-faced squad men scurried past the crowd into their ambulance as Paul and I exchanged blank looks, his mouth agape. The dispatcher, "Huge Nuge," received a good ass-chewing for that one.

Nuge himself told the story of a distraught black woman who called because her parakeet got loose in her house, and she couldn't coax the bird back into its cage. Nuge's initial response to her was, "You got a gun, lady?" When she wailed back, "You ain't funny, motherfucker," Nuge retorted, "Ah, its wings'll get tired and it'll set down." Nuge's dispatching career ended shortly thereafter.

Few jobs, I knew, offered the variety of situations we faced day after day. And where else do you not only share danger with coworkers, but live with them? I didn't embrace the "brotherhood" and the "second family" nature of the job that many preached. I loved the job and was fiercely proud, yet it was important that I maintained balance and remained objective, clung to values, if you will. Job was job and family was family, so I kept the two separate. Happily, the job was a constant learning experience. In short order I was exposed to the variety of cultures in this great city. Despite any image I may have evoked of being hardened and old school, those close to me knew that the color of someone's skin, their beliefs, or their sexual orientation didn't matter to me. Hell, I didn't care if they had blue skin and barked at the moon. I didn't care if they were male or female and with whom they got it on — as long as they didn't do it on my front lawn, I always said. *Just don't try to sell me your beliefs like insurance.* I grew tired of guys who made a show of over-defending their masculinity, who allowed it to be threatened. I valued the trust of coworkers who confided in me, a couple of whom were gay. I guarded their secret lest they be persecuted. I worked with a woman who did not flaunt her lesbianism, but neither did she suppress it. I found that courageous. She was a hard worker and a friend, and I admired her. The contagious smile she always wore went a long way with me.

The gay element was prevalent in the downtown area. In fact, opposite the parking lot of the Glass House was a gay establishment we called the Brown Door. In deference to the sobriquet, the door was painted brown. I found it humorous that every time Police Chief Breier's troops came to raid the after-hours bathhouse, the joint had been tipped off, and little came of the raids. It was no wonder, for we regularly saw big names, including politicians, frequent the place, not to mention a firefighter's car or two.

Christmas Eve our chief gave permission for us to invite family to the evening meal. Nearly 40 people crowded the kitchen when the warbler squealed five rings, indicating a fire response. The crowd stilled and we heard the address of the fire building — it was the Brown Door. We had only to look out the windows since our kitchen faced the place. Sure enough, into the parking lot spilled guys clad only in towels, or less, scurrying for cover, and, I'm sure, concealment. Light smoke followed them out the door. My acting boss and I slid down the pole to the apparatus floor, where we suited up and grabbed the tools we would need. After making the short dash across the parking lot, we crouched and quickly pushed past coughing bodies stumbling through the brown door. Making our way down a hall, we knew we were close, as the brown smoke got thicker. Finally, we heard the familiar crackle and felt heat. Finding a cubicle wrapped in flames, we knocked the fire down and backed out so a crew with a hose line could go to work.

During overhaul, amongst scantily clad guys scurrying about to gather belongings, one of our guys, who could never qualify as a PR specialist, came up with a can of Crisco and asked loudly if it was for making popcorn. The chief, whom I greatly respected, snapped, "Knock it off!" But it got worse. He kept it up, blurting out for the benefit of the already pissed off manager other rude innuendos about gays. The chief had had enough. He leaned into the guy, glaring, jerking his thumb over his shoulder toward the door: "Out! I'll talk with you later." I felt the chief was right; the guy was one of us but he was unprofessional and embarrassing. *And we of the glass house shouldn't throw stones.*

It turned out that a couple had gotten so immersed in wishing each other merry Christmas that they hadn't noticed a candle igniting the wall trappings. Later, back in the firehouse kitchen, I found it interesting that our female guests, in particular, bubbled with curiosity about the bathhouse. The fire at the Brown Door remained a popular topic, and the boss and I took a lot of ribbing about how we found the fire so fast, as though we were familiar with the layout. I rolled with it, answering, "Are you kidding? Of course we knew exactly where that cubicle was." *Can't get to me 'cause I've been worked on by experts.*

Another aspect of the job to which I became accustomed was injuries. Singed ears and nail punctures, despite steel boot soles, were a dime a dozen. Smoke inhalation, cuts, and debris in the eyes were common. Regardless how careful we were, some injuries couldn't be avoided. They came with the territory. Stitches, sprains and open burn wounds meant off-duty time. More thought provoking were events where a miss was as good as a mile. One experience on my list of "shouldn't have survived" episodes occurred at a large mercantile building called Sydney Hih. Filled with trendy shops reminiscent of the sixties hippie era, the four-story, multi-colored complex had had more than its share of fires, which usually grew into "greaters." During overhaul at one of the blazes, I was leaning out of the lower broken-out portion of one of the upper floor's massive plate glass windows. My sixth sense told me to quickly duck back inside. No sooner had I jerked my head back when the upper portion of the huge glass plate gave way. I saw the awful blur and felt my helmet move as it slid past. Had my head been where it was a second earlier, I would have been decapitated. A chill braced me when I heard the heavy glass slab impact the sidewalk below. I didn't want to look.

The angels would close the distance many times over the years. They once froze my foot in mid-step on a roof shrouded in smoke. My next step would have been to the pavement three stories below. My angels had friends. I was in awe when Ken Grabske told how he was spared during his days at busy Truck 7. He and his partner had gone to the roof to open up over a nasty attic fire. After hooking his roof ladder on the peak, he began pulling his axe from his equipment belt to begin a vertical cut. His partner, invisible in the thick smoke, straddled the peak near Ken to begin a horizontal cut with his axe. When the head of Ken's axe blade was flat in front of his face, his partner's first swing hit it dead center. Long after the pain ceased, Ken still heard the mind-numbing clunk as metal hit metal. But he was spared from being cleaved in a most horrible way, suffering instead a smashed nose.

I was finding the job to be a real hard-knock lesson at developing people skills. And we usually dealt with people at their worst, whether they were victims, perpetrators, or in some way related to either. Sometimes, it was difficult not to pass judgment. *Just do your job and move on. Don't take it home with you.* But that was easier said than done. For example: at a bad freeway crash, we tended to a 26-year-old woman who was trapped in her mangled car after she had been hit head-on by a drunk driver who, somehow, had gotten onto the freeway going the wrong way. She was in horrible shape but able to talk to us while we worked to free her. We encouraged her, even joked with her to distract her from her pain, but she would die of her massive injuries before the sun set that day. The drunk driver was staggering about complaining of his banged-up knees. Before the sheriffs cuffed him, I wanted a piece of him. We all did. But none of us acted on it. That was great restraint. Dealing with people, with their emotions, was something they should have at least touched on at the academy.

We dealt with the wide range of emotions of individuals, and with the collective, contagious emotions that gripped panicked crowds. We faced the latter at an apartment building blaze on 18th and Clybourn streets one night. When we pulled up, bedsheets tied together hung from windows belching gray-black smoke. Broken bodies littered the ground around the building. Survivors joined neighbors pleading with us to save those still inside. *We can't deal with you now. We have work to do.* A woman with long, dark hair appeared at a third floor window, the moonlight illuminating her white nightgown, her pale face. Dark smoke framed her squatting form filling the opening. We shouted, pleaded: "Stay put! Hang on. We're coming." She was eerily silent, reposed. She knew. She looked down at us, as in forgiveness, and tipped backward, swallowed by the black maw. Seeing that, having been so close, but losing her, screwed me up so bad that I felt awkward trying to deal with the survivors. That wasn't me. Yes, dealing with people and their emotions should have been covered at the academy. Down the road, I would have the opportunity to change that. Periodically, Deb and I venture into that area to a popular restaurant. Despite having put my past in perspective, when I look at that plain building, I still see in the pale moonlight those bedsheets hanging from the windows, and I look at *that* window to see if anyone's there.

It never ceased to amaze me the situations that people could get into. Maybe it was the gods laughing at the humans. Given the number of tall buildings in our area, elevator emergencies were commonplace. Usually, occupants were trapped in them and we would override their mechanical systems, or use force, to free the hapless riders. One day, what sounded like a routine call surprised us. A call for a man stuck in an elevator turned out to be a man stuck *outside* an elevator. It was gruesome. Somehow, the elevator mechanic had gotten himself wedged between the outside of the car and the wall of the shaft. The car had shifted, twisting and pinning him, with his head and shoulders above the door opening at floor level. He remained conscious and was able to talk to us. As with the young woman in the car wreck, we tried to divert his attention from his predicament, no easy task. It gives you an idea of the calmness and tact a rescuer must have. The first paramedic unit to enter service with our department was with us, monitoring him and starting an IV. I was surprised that he seemed to have little pain. But when we finally sprang the man's trap with power tools, his eyes shut, his head dipped and he died, before we even got him out of the shaft and onto the floor. *What th ... but we were just talking to you. How could you die on us so suddenly?* I was stunned since he had never given the appearance of hanging on by a thread. The paramedics later explained that such an occurrence is common with massive compression injuries where the compression is the only thing literally holding the insides together, allowing them to still function. Upon release, they instantaneously fail. Doing CPR was pointless. I felt for his family the awful news they would receive, and, in a selfish way, I wished that I, we, had said something more appropriately fitting his final moments, although I couldn't imagine what that would be. We worked hard, we did our best, but he died. We were upset not only at the loss, but that we didn't have total control over the outcome. We usually bawdy bunch of firefighters were silent as we gathered our tools and made our way back to our rigs. Back at quarters, members of other companies read on our faces that this was one of those rare occasions when wisecracks were a bad idea. But we would snap back and store this one in the gray matter — along with all the others. Later, it dawned on me that only a couple among us seemed to know everything we needed to know about elevators. That too I would have the opportunity to change.

When EMS began to play a larger part in our operations in 1977 as a result of federal mandates, I volunteered for EMT training, which was being given at hospitals. Deputy Chief Koleas admired my ambition, but he explained that I did not have enough time on the job to qualify. I was giving my all and I was determined to continue pouring myself into my work, not missing any opportunity to learn. It must have showed. One night the guys were crowded into the dayroom and when I walked in, they leveled their best shots at this cub. As usual, either I ignored them, grinned, or gave short neutral answers. Captain Dick Butz, whom I greatly admired, was the ranking "house captain" and stood among them. When I walked by, he stopped me and asked, "Say, Mutz, how's everything going?"

"Great, Cap."

"And how do you like the job?" he pressed.

"I love it, Cap." *Now what are these jokers up to? They're too quiet and showing no emotion. And gentlemanly Butz usually doesn't go in for the foolishness.* Butz swept his arm across the group, turned back to bore his steel eyes into mine, and asked, "And what do you think of these guys?"

I hesitated as though deep in thought, scanned the group waiting anxiously for my reply, put my hands on my hips and went for it: "Ya know, Cap, I've had about enough of these cocksuckers!" The place went nuts. They broke into a roar, doubled over with laughter. I had to duck the barrage of magazines and debris that sailed at me. There were handshakes all around and slaps on

This memorial of helmet, boots, and coat stands at Milwaukee's Fire Headquarters and is dedicated to Milwaukee firefighters who answered "The Last Alarm." The tradition of posting on a firehouse apron the personal gear of a firefighter killed in the line of duty is as old as the department itself. To date, this has taken place 106 times.

the back. Ken stuck his tongue in my ear. I had earned my stripes. I proved myself by doing my job and they showed their respect with acceptance. I was especially honored because I was still weeks away from my coveted "year on," which, traditionally, was cause for great celebration. When the animals settled down, Captain Butz extended his hand, beamed, and said, "Great job." *Great job, indeed.*

For all the great things the job offered, there were lows that tempered the highs. On November 17, 1977, Firefighter Walter J. Nell, Jr. died. Young Wally died after being thrown from Ladder 6 when it was struck by a car while responding to a call for an alarm sounding at an industrial complex. I had met Wally at his south side firehouse when my company transferred there to cover while they were tied up at a fire. The day he died, his new twin babies were 13 days old. Knowing that there are no empty pews at firefighters' funerals, many of us stood outside. Down the street was the firehouse from which Wally made his last run. In a tradition as old as the fire department itself, on the apron in front of the gleaming red trucks and saluting firefighters was his boots, coat and helmet. His flag-draped casket was borne on one of our pumpers. Attending Nell's celebration of life stripped away some of my invincibility.

Before two quick years had passed at the Glass House, my name was on a "shift list," transferring me to Engine Company 31, a much slower, single house on the south side. I was disappointed but I had to play the hand I was dealt. The old heads said, "Your first transfer is the toughest, kid." Tradition showed me favor on the morning after my last 24 hours of duty at the Glass House. Shift change was marked by roll call at 8 A.M. with both the on-coming and off-going shifts standing in front of their rigs. It was impressive, actually, rows of khaki contrasted proudly against their massive red and chrome mounts. After rounds of handshakes, "Good lucks," and the expected smart-ass remarks, most of the guys quickly broke off, climbing into the cabs of the many rigs filling the apparatus floor. I had no idea what was going on. An ear-splitting cacophony of sirens and air horns shattered the air, filling the building, vibrating the walls. I was frozen with chill. The astonishing din was accompanied by a mesmerizing display of emergency beacons and flashers that splashed dazzling light patterns across the cavernous bays. The doors were open, and out on the street, people stopped, gaping. Traffic stopped. I stood there, overwhelmed. This fantastic sound and light show was for me. I had been given the most honorable salute firefighters could render a parting comrade. The drive home was difficult, trying to see through misty eyes.

3

Interlude

The south side. What a reality check that was. Thankfully, it turned out to be only a way-stop on my journey.

Every firehouse seemed to have a personality all its own, based on the ethnic flavor of the neighborhood it protected. Engine 31's area was a bastion of Polish immigrants where small one-and-a-half and two-story homes stood shoulder to shoulder. The tidy lots on which old ladies raked leaves against the wind were becoming shabby parcels chafed free of grass. Like many Milwaukee neighborhoods, the near south side was undergoing transition as legions of hard-core Polish shared sidewalks with poor whites and minorities. Drugs were making inroads to the area, which could only mean despair and more work for us.

Engine Company 31 was typical of the fire companies established around the turn of the century to keep pace with the growth of Milwaukee's residential areas. The old firehouse was a rectangular, two-story brick, occupying a corner lot for easy street access. I expected to see the ghosts of old firefighters wearing suspenders and huge moustaches plodding up the creaky, curved wooden stairs, and remnants of hay in the corners of back rooms where fire horses once waited anxiously in their stalls. Some of the terms that hark back to the days of the horses, such as "getting a hitch" and "chief's buggy," survived and remained in use. Even our engine was a throwback to the old days: a 1949 Mack with open cab and a pumping capability only half that of the monster rigs I was used to. And it was one of the last pumpers in city service without a water tank. That meant if we couldn't put the fire out with the few gallons in my hand pump, we had to do a hose layout and find a hydrant. "Waiting for water" took on a whole new meaning. We three firefighters rode the tailboard. Our MPO, Don Wolf, gave me plenty of time behind the wheel. I enjoyed driving manual transmission trucks, but buffs and old car collectors drooling over our antique classic only confirmed that the old girl had served her time.

We often joked that each part of town was a separate fire department as a result of demographics and frequency of alarms. I found that to be true. Older guys commonly were assigned to slower firehouses. The closer to the fringes of the city, the slower the house. Since Engine 31 logged only sporadic runs, it was considered a "slow house." There were days we didn't turn a wheel. I felt I was too young, too new to the job to be stuck on the south side, living and working with old timers. *This doesn't make sense. What am I doing here?* I tried not to take it personally, but that was difficult when people asked who I pissed off to end up there.

My boss was Lieutenant Bob Jendrzejek, a wise, gentlemanly old-timer of Polish stock. He noticed how I lit up while listening to radio chatter of a fire developing across town. And he understood. It took a long time for me to understand his oft repeated advice: "Don't wish your life away, kid."

I missed the excitement and challenge, the camaraderie, and the spirited bluster of busier houses. The fundamentals of the job remained the same, but I had to learn about the new people I worked with, from the guys next to me on the tailboard, to our chief. *How do they do things here? What are my limits? Who can I trust?* If we went north with busy Engine 12, I knew their crew was younger and more aggressive; if we went south, we could expect the opposite. It only enhanced my adaptability.

Engine 31 offered barely enough work to keep me from going stir crazy. Much of my learning would come from reading, but that accounts for only ten percent of what we retain, compared to 90 percent retained from hands-on experience. A couple of the old-timers seemed obligated to remind me that I was the youngest member, the most wet behind the ears. I volunteered to cook, but that spot was tied up by the guy with the shakes who saw grocery shopping as an opportunity to stop and hoist one, or a few. Thankfully, I was finally accepted for the 80-hour EMT training course held at the training academy. It got me out of the place, and I was learning useful and interesting skills far beyond the first aid taught during recruit training.

Admittedly, I didn't expect the number of crime-related runs to be so high in our quiet corner of the south side. Many were drug- and alcohol-related, and gang influence was becoming more apparent. Young people injured in fights were a dime a dozen. A violent run that stands out in my mind was a 15-year-old girl strung out on drugs and being sexually abused by her father. Then there was the call for a "man down," who we found lying face down on someone's lawn. As we approached him, we smelled gasoline. I started to kneel down to check him out and the next thing, my helmet was flying through the air. Luckily, his wild swing was a glancing blow. I recovered quickly, and he was on his feet, ready to go to war with us. *Great.* There was no talking down this crazed, foaming-at-the-mouth, glassy-eyed maniac. The boss called for police assistance and we circled him, but kept our distance.

Our MPO that day, Russ, was a big man, so of course, our friend zeroed in on Russ and they traded a few blows, with Russ letting him know he was in a scrap. He was in a rage, ranting about his brother, so we all got on the rig and slowly pulled away, certain that the boys and girls in blue would arrive soon. He attacked us three on the tailboard so we kept him busy swinging our heavy metal spanner belts at him. We drove around the block and when we returned, our friend was engaged in Wrestlemania with a group of coppers. They finally subdued and cuffed him. Later a cop told us the guy had a long rap sheet and was pissed off about his brother being convicted of caving in someone's skull with a hammer. He was trying to kill himself by drinking gasoline. Dryly, I said, "I should have offered him a cigarette." Another lesson learned: approach with caution even if you *can* see their hands.

Then there was the shooting of a young man during a holdup. This one stands out because the sad outcome may have been the result of bungling by our own people. It happened at a gas station only a few blocks away. In fact, we were so close that the police had yet to arrive. We found the guy lying on the floor in the back room. The room was tiny but I squeezed in by the victim's head to check him out. My partners obligingly stepped aside, knowing I would step in. I found a small bullet hole in his shoulder, but he complained more about back pain. That reminded me how bullets can fragment or deflect off of bone and travel in any direction inside the body. That, and his back pain, told me not to move him, as the bullet could be near his spine. When the paramedics arrived, I was still jammed in the tiny room, and told the senior med what I found, including the young man's vital signs, such as blood pressure and pulse. He didn't seem overly concerned since the victim had good "vitals" and the entry wound was small. I warned him not to be fooled by that small hole and that the bullet could be anywhere. But his priority was to get the guy out of that cramped area. I stood my ground with the med, saying that this guy had to be "boarded," meaning completely immobilized on a back-board, lest we move that bullet. The med, known for his cockiness, wasn't going to let a young firefighter tell him what to do. With that, he grabbed the guy's hands and pulled him to a sitting position. The guy screamed and I got in the med's face, shot looks at his two partners challenging them to intervene, and said, "You're making a big mistake." He ignored me and pulled the sitting victim through the doorway. Once on the stretcher, the victim was quiet. I asked him about his back pain, and he murmured that he didn't feel it any more. I found out later that that small-caliber bullet had deflected off of his curved shoulder bone and had indeed lodged against the young man's spine, paralyzing him. All we had to do was slide the "long-board" under the victim, but the haughty med, for some reason, was in a rush and didn't bother to send someone to fetch the board. As much as I respected and admired the training and experience of our paramedics, I vowed never to allow this prick's ego to get in the way of being responsible and open-minded. The complaint I registered about the incident, expectedly, dead-ended. The life of a 20-something-year-old may have changed dramatically because he was not only the victim of the ills of society, but a victim of our system.

An inordinate number of alarms for kids hit by cars was a signpost of declining family values in the area. We logged an amazing nine "child struck by auto" runs within a two-week summer period. One of them was my first fatality at Engine 31. A boy only two or three years old had been brought to the sidewalk. When the boss and I leaned over him, he looked ashen and life-less. He had no pulses. He was a beautiful boy with blonde hair. When I leaned into him to begin CPR, I hesitated. I saw my son, Jeff, who was the same age. Grabbing my shoulder, Jendrzejek bent over to look me in the eye and snapped, "Can you do it?"

"Yeah, yeah, I can, Loot," I answered.

I knew our efforts were futile by the gurgling noises and fluids coming from his ears every time I blew into his mouth. Man, that was tough. Any emergency professional will tell you that losing kids is the toughest. The next day at home, I couldn't stop looking at Jeff and thinking, *God, I could never handle losing one of my kids.* Just when I thought they couldn't be any more precious, they became even more so.

The runs weren't any weirder than what I had seen as a looper, but they were interesting, nonetheless. There were more vehicle accidents and just as many suicides. Fires were infrequent and usually the result of maliciousness. Late one night, we were sent with an "emergency response assignment" to one of the many taverns along 6th Street. The dispatcher added, "Ya got people in the water." Behind the tavern was one of the stretches of open aque-ducts that carried rainwater to the lake. The past few days had seen heavy rains and flooding, so the aqueduct was topped off and had the current of a respectable river rapids. The Fourth Battalion chief had gotten there first. I jumped off the rig and went for the rope we carried. Center stage in the pierc-ing light of our hand lanterns were a man and a woman chest-deep in the dark water, desperately trying to hang on to a concrete wall at the mouth of a tunnel. Their faces were contorted in fear. Their mouths moved, but we could only guess what they were yelling over the rush of the water. Our MPO immediately brought our engine around so it faced the water, which brought its headlights into use, not to mention two bumper-mounted tow hooks. *Nice work, Don.* No contenders stepped up to arm wrestle me for the plunge into the churning rapids. *Okay, then the kid is going to show you what he learned in school.* My choice was the bowline knot, which I tied around myself. The others wrapped the rope around the tow hooks as I hustled over to the retaining wall. I came alive teetering on that wall, about to be lowered into the violent torrent. I glanced backwards to get my bearings. The woman was still there in the spotlight. The man was gone.

Down I went, into the shocking cold. The noise and power of the pounding water were awesome, a stark reminder that I couldn't swim a lick. As I descended, the guys on top seemed a mile away, but I knew they had a better grip than the current. Trying to keep my footing as I made my way to the woman, I thought, *How can you still be upright and able to hang on in this current?* Many things are possible if you're scared witless.

When I reached her, she was shaking uncontrollably and babbling incoherently. Despite the water's smell, the booze on her breath came through. Now I could see into the dark tunnel and there, clinging to its wall, wide-eyed, was the man we thought the current had carried downstream. My look told him to hang on. *This can only go one at a time, so I'll have to come back for you.* He seemed to understand, closing his eyes. I tied the tail of my rope to the woman, raised my right arm to signal I was ready, locked her in my arms and let them do the work of pulling us in. When we got to the wall, I yelled to them that I had spotted the man and would go back. I had really hoped I was done and could get out. I was relieved to see he was still there, and repeated the process. After they pulled me up, I was so exhausted I couldn't stand.

The story later unfolded that two men and a woman had sat at the bar into the wee hours. By closing time, they had put away enough liquid courage to decide that a romp in the water would be fun. One went in on a dare and the others tried to save their drinking partner. I never saw the third of their trio. Unable to hang on, he had taken the long water ride out to the lake before we arrived. His body was found in the harbor a couple of days later. The only emotion I recall about the event was being glad that I handled the live victims and didn't have to deal with the bloated one. How sad, I thought, that drinking to excess and then being stupid was at the top of their list of "things to do today." Sad too was that I could relate.

The only other out-of-the-ordinary run that I recall during my tenure at Engine 31 was being part of a large response to the ship docks at Jones Island. The call came in as an "explosion aboard a ship." Any sailor or firefighter will tell you that fire of any magnitude aboard a ship warrants special tactics and precautions. And it greatly increases one's "pucker factor." I envisioned crawling into the ship's bowels, through blinding, poisonous smoke among a maze of compartments whose steel walls glowed cherry red.

There was not a wisp of smoke. Good sign. We trailed behind the first-arriving companies, climbing steep, narrow walkways that had cables for rails.

The excessive clanging and swaying of the old walkway made me wish there weren't so many of us weighing it down. No one seemed sure what had happened, so we had to go aboard. Once on deck, the scene that hit us reminded me of the aftermath of a gunfight. Bodies were scattered about, some surrounded by widening pools of blood. The rescue squad crew went straight for one who was eviscerated, meaning his torso was split open and his intestines, grayish-yellow and glistening in the sun, lay beside him on the steel deck. My crew spotted a guy whose left arm was nearly amputated. We went to work immediately trying to pack the gaping hole that was his upper arm. He was conscious and able to tell us that a hawser winch had exploded as they worked on it. I didn't understand what a hawser winch was, much less its mechanics that could wreak this much havoc. A short distance away I noticed that the squad crew had piled their victim's intestines atop his torso and had covered them with a sterile dressing, which they kept wet. He too was conscious, and I hoped that he knew how fortunate he was to be in the care of these two seasoned squad men. Five crewmen had been hurt, three critically.

I got our guy involved with explaining the hawser system, and he stayed relatively calm throughout his ordeal. The decision was made to carry these guys down the steep, shaky catwalk to the dock. I didn't relish the plan but there was no other way; we didn't have time to set up a crane or wait for a helicopter. Besides, I had had enough of smelling blood warmed by the sun on the metal deck. Since the walkway was wide enough only for one, Chief Koleas directed that the strongest men take the head and tail of the wire stokes baskets loaded with victims. He looked at me with that glint in his piercing eyes and asked if I was ready to take the front. *How do you answer that? God, that man knows how to motivate.* "Got it chief," I snapped, as though this was a daily occurrence.

I hoisted the litter to my shoulder to keep our guy level, grabbed the cable and started down. *God, please stop this awful swaying.* I doubt that I, or my partner, could have done the carry under normal conditions, but we were operating on adrenaline, focusing on getting our guy down safely. It helped that a brief kinship had sparked between victim and rescuers, not an unusual occurrence, and now we were helping our friend.

Someone had taken my helmet so it wouldn't slip down over my sweaty forehead on the rigorous descent. The next day, my father-in-law, Leroy, beamed proudly as he told everyone how he watched me on TV come down that walkway holding the litter high with one hand. I was, after all, "their fireman."

A bothersome run I was glad to have missed occurred on one of my scheduled off-days. A young boy was trapped in a house fire. Not only did

In which is traditionally called "organized confusion," firefighters scurry about to get the upper hand on a blaze that has full possession of the upper floors of this residence (courtesy MFD Historical Society).

the operation go badly, the chief, I was told, froze, so the first-arriving companies took independent action. The fire was put out but the boy perished. The chief's behavior may not have made a difference in saving the boy, but I couldn't help feel that had this occurred in the ghetto where younger, more aggressive firefighters worked, the boy might have been pulled out sooner. I didn't know the chief well, but he had a lot of years under his belt. I knew not to pass judgment or venture into this psychological dimension, remembering what it was like to have a superior freeze during combat in Vietnam. Everyone has their limits and everyone handles things differently. Regardless, the incident steeled my determination to get out of the south side at the first opportunity. And that came sooner than I had expected.

Someone must have remembered. My boss handed me the department phone one day, his brow creased in curiosity: "It's for you. It's Chief Seelen," he almost whispered. Deputy Chief Seelen stood at the helm of the training school, which was officially labeled the Bureau of Instruction and Training.

Seelen started by saying he understood that I had been an instructor in the army. I explained that was true, but only for one summer at West Point teaching cadets guerrilla warfare subjects. I mentioned that I also had served as an advisor in Vietnam for a very short time. After he added that he had heard I was doing a commendable job, I told him what a great job it was, and that I did my best. *Where could he possibly be going with this? This can't be the ultimate joke. Deputy chiefs don't call young firefighters to pass the time of day.*

He got to the point, explaining that the firefighter position at the school was opening up and he had heard that I might be the right guy for it. Some names had been batted around there, and it was suggested he call me first.

I didn't know what to say. I was honored, but I reminded him that I had only two years on the job. "Experience counts for a lot," he said, "but there's much more to it than that." His mention that the school was a busy place and that they did a lot of different things really hit some notes with me. The icing on the cake was his comment about the school really opening one's eyes to how the department works. Few people get the opportunity. He ended by suggesting I think about it, talk it over with my wife, especially since it meant a different schedule. I was to call him my next work shift.

When I cradled the phone, I looked up at Lt. Jendrzejek standing nearby. He was grinning like a proud papa. "Just what you wanted, hey?" he chimed.

"Yes, Loot, just what I wanted."

4

Back to School

My wife, Pat, and I talked about my going to the school. My excitement about the opportunity was obvious. Pat was more interested in the eight-hour-per-day schedule, which allowed me to be home nights, weekends and holidays — like "normal" people. I was never sure about her true feelings for the job, but I knew she didn't like being alone, especially taking care of a two-year-old. We on the job knew that if something was going to happen on the home front, it would happen while we were committed to a 24-hour shift. My zest for the profession made it critical that I balance job and family. I don't believe Pat thought that was happening, and it made for rough road. Nevertheless, I was certain that how I applied myself to my job could only benefit my family.

The school turned out to be a magnificent experience. It was common knowledge that anyone assigned to the school had it all together and would climb the promotional ladder. The school staff then consisted of a deputy chief, a captain, three lieutenants, a firefighter, and the motor vehicle operator instructor. Sharon, the long-time secretary, not only was a joy to work with, she was so efficient that we said she actually ran the place. Of the three lieutenants, two were recruit instructors, while the third oversaw public relations training, although duties commonly overlapped. When I first met with the staff, I made it clear that my central goal was to work with recruit classes, and everything else would be secondary. They agreed, and my first action was to rename the position assistant instructor, which I proudly wore on the front-piece of my traditional leather helmet. The fact that I was back on good terms with my dad and that he bought the expensive helmet enhanced its significance. Chief Seelen insisted that I wear warrant officer rank insignia to garner respect, but I stubbornly resisted, believing that respect could be earned other ways.

The large northwest-side facility had been a high school before it was purchased by the city to serve as the police and fire training site. Much to my delight, I was allowed to set up shop in a large room at the end of the hall, opposite the main offices. Since I was responsible for all the photo work, and

Located on Milwaukee's northwest side, the Fire Academy includes a main building for both fire and police training, a five-story training tower (shown here), and the activities building, which resembles an actual firehouse, complete with an engine and ladder truck.

indulged an interest in history, the room slowly began to fill with fire department material I had found scattered throughout the building. Everyone at the school brought with them their own ideas, which they presented every morning at a conference table where we started the day with bakery goods and coffee. I made a habit of running laps and working out in the police weight room even before this informal meeting. Besides reviewing everyone's projects, there was the usual firehouse banter, and periodically the police academy staff popped in. I enjoyed the exchange of information and gained even more insight to their operation. One of their visits, in fact, led to my suggestion for an impromptu class.

One of the police instructors mentioned that not only were officers on night patrol discovering more fires, some became trapped in burning buildings when they entered to rescue occupants. Although commendable, that left our fire companies with more people to rescue than was originally trapped. It made sense that if they were first on the scene, they should have a basic idea of what to do and how best to avoid danger. I volunteered to talk to their recruit class to offer basic information, which included fire behavior in buildings, the limits of moving through them, and precautions. The latter emphasized closing doors to contain fire spread, and explained the advantages and disadvantages of breaking windows. The young coppers were receptive to the session, and they came up with many interesting questions.

My first recruit class was slated to begin in late November 1978. After being sworn in, 12 recruits were ours to mold into firefighters over ten weeks. Only one of our Dirty Dozen gave us doubt. Part of learning how the department functions, I discovered, was learning politics. When we expressed to department brass that our problem child was best let go, their response was to ask if he could handle the hose, and an axe? Could he handle the ladders? Could he put on a mask, and did he pass the written exams? When we answered "Yes, but..." to all of the above, they concluded by saying that the city would counter by reminding us that we were not trained psychologists, so we couldn't fire him on attitude. "Put him on" was their final word. It rubbed against our grain to graduate the guy, but behind every cloud is a silver lining. Giving him a pass was akin to giving him enough rope to hang himself. He would do just that by getting in trouble down the road and leaving the job.

Since fires occurred in all types of weather, including Milwaukee's often harsh winters, training was conducted likewise, with no exception. Here, in 1978, recruits endure training advancing hose lines under the watchful eye of an instructor.

I was comfortable teaching and leading. Not only did I believe in what I was doing, having graduated from the course two years earlier turned out to be a plus since I had retained much of what I learned. The next class that came on board was 52 strong, including seven trainees from the county fire department. We would graduate 40 of them in June 1979. Having gotten my feet wet with the Dirty Dozen, I became involved with this group to the extent that often I worked alone with the class during tower operations. One day when the training lieutenants were tied up, I ran groups of trainees through a record 14 fires in the tower. I didn't wear a mask and had become quite adept at functioning in smoke, a "leather lung" in our parlance. The ill effects of smoke had become second nature, but driving to the school the next morning proved difficult since my vision was screwed up; emanating from every light was a gray starburst pattern. To say that was a red flag is an understatement. The recruits became intimately familiar with the five-story block tower, fighting countless fires, climbing its vertical cat ladder, and learning how to shut off sprinkler systems in heavy smoke. Drawing from a list of resources, we obtained material to burn for our many training fires. Goodwill Industries came across with used mattresses, some of which, when set afire, gave off noxious smoke that could gag a horse. We relied heavily upon Kunzelmann Esser Furniture Company on the south side for material used to pack furniture in railroad cars. The straw-like excelsior, although ideal for producing smoke and flame, we would later discover contained formaldehydes. When the results came back from the crime lab, I didn't want to think about how much of its toxic fumes I had inhaled. When Curtis Witzlib came on as an instructor some time later, his farming background resulted in unlimited supplies of hay to replace excelsior.

Another instructor came up with the idea of obtaining from the power company used line poles for recruits to practice on with axes. After recruits had chopped the poles into pieces, someone then decided we could burn the remnants in the tower's basement during sprinkler training to add realism. That seemed to be going great until one hot day when I was working with a group of recruits doing axe work. I heard yelling coming from the tower basement where my partner was working with a group learning how to shut off sprinkler heads in smoke. Recruits spilling out of the basement, followed by smoke, reminded me of rats being smoked out of their holes. Five recruits tipped over. Most disconcerting was the heavy-handed instructor emerging from the smoke, berating them for being wimps. Not only did the instructor later admit he went to the hospital the next day with chest pains, he was on the carpet explaining to the chief why rescue squads had been called to the school. The culprit was obvious: the used power-line poles, which had been treated with the wood preservative creosote. The stuff is toxic even when it's not burning. We should have known better.

I took full advantage of the free reign I was given with this group. A couple of things I had dealt with in the field had stayed with me, and now I had the opportunity to effect change. Remembering the run on which we lost the elevator mechanic, I established a class that dealt with elevator emergencies and tied it in with high-rise firefighting. I also enhanced a search and rescue evolution that had recruits negotiating the tower in smoke, while following hose lines and finding and removing victims. The decision had been made to outfit our ladder companies with rappelling gear, which meant that everyone in the firefighting division had to be trained in its use. The job fell to me, since I taught rappelling in the army, and I, in turn, trained a couple of trainers and taught our recruits. We first rappelled out of the tower's third-floor window, and then off of the roof of the five-story structure. I was able to cover the distance to the ground in two bounds, and was impressed when one of my recruits, Pat Balcerzak, matched the feat. Eventually, a safety net was erected, but that didn't spare my successor from a back injury when he staged a stunt jump.

I modified our physical training (PT) routine, which we experimentally lightened and moved from morning to the end of the training day. There seemed to be no point in tiring out recruits who would spend the remainder of the day in evolutions that demanded alertness. Despite a disciplined instructor–recruit relationship, I enjoyed the personalities and the enthusiasm of our recruits. I was always hopeful that they sensed my love for the profession and how much I loved teaching them. They made that obvious in a number of ways. Their favorite exercise during PT was the "Oh, Darlin.'" This was a four-count leg spread done on their backs. On the count of two, when they spread their legs wide, six inches off the floor, I had them moan loudly, "Oh, Darlin'!" They got a kick out of it, but I doubt that the exercise survived under later regimes that caved in to political correctness. My large class, on their long-awaited final day of training, were in their usual formation outside, waiting for me to lead them in PT. When I stepped outside, much to my surprise and amusement, they all wore red T-shirts with the words "Oh, Darlin'" emblazoned across the front. "What the hell is this?" I laughed. They refused to answer, much less budge, when I tried to start the session. Since I had never faced a mutiny by 40 fit people, my impulse was to run back inside. *Had I been that rough on them? Are they bent on revenge? I've made sure to be capable of doing and demonstrating everything I expected them to do. But they're up to something and sure as hell, I'm going to end up on the bad side of it.* A few refusals came out of their ranks and they still wouldn't respond to my exercise orders. They had made the grade and they knew it. Then they broke ranks and closed on me. I was surrounded. Oh, yeah, payback time. They pulled and ripped off my T-shirt and someone produced an "Oh, Darlin'" T-shirt. "Here, put this on!" There was laughing, and slaps and handshakes all around. I was one of them. Proudly, I pulled on the shirt, which brought the house down. I ordered ... okay, I suggested that we do a few laps and hit the cat ladder. Their joking and laughing told me there would be no point in being serious that day.

But there was one more thing I had to be serious with them about. Later, I herded them into a classroom, unbeknownst to the officers. This was firefighter-to-firefighter. This was my "reality class," during which I explained to them that they would not use some of what they had learned, and that we taught them nothing about how to deal with people, people of every age, people of every walk of life, people of every personality and character range,

Wearing SCBA and his valued leather helmet, Mutza briefs fire recruits prior to a major training burn in a vacant school building. Assignment to the training academy proved to be not only an eye-opener, but a valuable experience in the journey through a fire service career (courtesy Dale Mutza).

people who would like nothing better than to stick that authority up their asses, regardless of their skin color.

I went on to explain that regardless of their good intent, not everyone viewed them as angels of mercy. I told them to keep their eyes and ears and minds open, learn everything they could. It was important that they knew not to divulge personal information to the brothers, to mind their mouths and their manners with the public. They needed to be wary of violent people and stick together. I informed them that to news people, their shiny black helmets and clean coats said "Newbie," someone who didn't know any better and would blab what's going on. "Let the chiefs do the interviews." They were to remember that they were dealing with people at their worst, in their most troubled time. "They're relying on you." With utmost sincerity, I said that when they found themselves up to their elbows in gore, to remember that this was what they had chosen to do, and it was something few could do. "It makes you special. If something gnaws at you, talk to someone. You can't save the world but you can make a difference. You need to be able to look in the mirror and say 'I did my best.'"

In between recruit classes, I handled all department photography and worked with the school staff on myriad projects. Often that meant testing new equipment. Salespeople regularly came to us with their wares that ranged from tools to protective gear, which we thoroughly tested and evaluated. If we felt strongly about something, we turned it over to a busy company in the field to put it through the wringer. As I became familiar with the school's wide range of operations and became well-rounded in the scope of the fire service, I was given leeway to venture out on my own to research various subjects. And although the lowest rank on staff, I was respected and relied upon to complete various tasks. I reasoned that there was always a better way to do things, and it fell upon the think-tank at the school to spearhead new approaches, new strategies. One of the topics on which I focused was heavy rescue companies, which were common in large cities. I knew that rescue was one of the passions of innovative battalion chief Dan Lipski, so we bounced ideas off of each other. Although the use of rescue units was flexible, basically they consisted of a large truck crammed with specialized equipment and were manned by specially trained crews. They responded to major emergencies or could be specially called. Some cities used them as manpower squads at major blazes. I submitted the results of my studies to the chief, suggesting that a spare pumper truck be converted to save the cost of a new rig. Nothing came of it, but in later years, the department would address the need for special teams, and some of Dan Lipski's dreams would be realized. Lipski was an inspiration and worthy of admiration; I felt the city was remiss in passing over him when he threw his hat in the ring for the top chief's position.

People in the field sometimes submitted ideas. Seldom, however, were they acted upon or even answered, and seldom were they forwarded to the school. Not only did this affect morale, the talent on the job wasn't being tapped. Changes I tried to effect included the very name of our school: the Bureau of Instruction and Training. For whatever practical implication the name held, it didn't resonate. I often wondered what ran through the public's mind when they saw a red fire department vehicle lettered with "B.I.T." In fact, I had been asked numerous times what BIT meant. I felt the name Fire Academy presented a better image and explained better what we were about. Fire Academy, I felt, was simpler, yet sounded more professional. Chief Koleas, who would replace Chief Seelen, was so fond of the idea that he had the shop — incidentally, called the Bureau of Construction and Maintenance — re-letter our vehicles. Then I designed a patch, which remains in use, except that Fire Academy lettering conflicted with the traditional BIT designation, to which the school reverted. I felt that I had made headway, and later designed emblems for a couple of other department units, including our Hazardous Materials (Haz-Mat) Team. Was I into the job, or what?

Another area of interest was the use of helicopters, particularly for the evacuation of badly injured persons. U.S. Coast Guard and U.S. Army helicopters, although distant, were available, but no one knew how to safely and efficiently use them. Since I had experience with army helicopter operations, I felt responsible for undertaking the study. During the 1970s, the application of helicopters for fire and police work was catching on. Even our chief, William Stamm, was looking into an elaborate platform that was suspended below a large helicopter for high-rise fire fighting and rescue. Compelling me to press the issue was an incident we monitored on the department radio. Our rooms were wired to receive all radio communication, since school staff responded to all greater alarms to set up a command center.

On March 13, 1980, we were gathered in our lunch room when we heard an emergency response to a south side factory escalate into a major rescue operation. Two steeplejacks worked on a narrow scaffold attached to the outside of a 200-foot smokestack they were demolishing. A 500-pound chunk of stone they dislodged fell outward, instead of inward as planned, pinning and injuring one of the worker's legs. Engine 7's Captain Harry Tischer climbed a fully extended aerial ladder, finishing the climb using a makeshift ladder the workers had fastened to the stack, quite a feat considering the rungs were wet and unstable. "Car One," Chief Stamm, arrived and took over the operation, which, by now, had become quite the news grabber. The obvious solution was a helicopter, but snowy weather in Chicago prevented takeoff of a Coast Guard chopper. One was, however, able to get off the ground at the air station at Glenview, Illinois. I reminded Chief Koleas that Huey medical evacuation helicopters were stationed at nearby West Bend and we should try that angle. The chiefs at the scene — one of whom was a Coast Guard commander — were more familiar with Coast Guard operations and opted to stay on that course. Two hours had elapsed by the time the chopper arrived from Illinois and rescued the shivering trio from their perilous perch. I pursued the army helicopter connection as a resource, but old thinking prevailed. "Besides," they said, "what are the chances something like this will ever happen again?" That steered me into another project, which was to establish a list of agencies outside the department that could quickly provide specialized equipment, such as heavy power tools, cranes and wreckers. Although tradition, I felt, had a place in the fire service, as a mindset — moreover, as an identity — it stonewalled our efforts to improve.

I had gotten used to sleeping all night in my own bed, so periodic calls from the dispatcher for greater alarms in the middle of the night, especially in the grip of winter, tested my sense of dedication. If a fire went beyond a third alarm, all the school staff were notified. At the scene, we managed a coordination and control point called "Car 100." Since we had department cars assigned, periodically I went to major fires or unusual incidents during work hours to take training photographs. One of the least shining moments of my career occurred at one of these fires. I recognized the address for a fire given over the radio as being just one block from the school. Mention of an apartment building warned of a potential life hazard and a spreading fire. I ran out to the car I used and pulled up along with other rigs. As companies made quick work of the blaze, I walked around the building. When I came around to the front, I heard yelling; an officer I knew and admired, Jerry Ballering, jabbed a finger at my car and yelled, "Wayne, is that your car?" Puzzled, I answered, "Yeah, why?" And before he could answer, it became instantly, sickeningly clear. On the gurney in the rescue squad was a burned kid and my car blocked the rescue squad. The key was in my pocket.

After I moved my car and the rescue squad peeled out of the parking lot with the victim, Ballering said, "Christ, Wayne. I know you know better." I was sick. As much as my mistake stuck in my craw, so did Ballering's abiding faith in me, despite his anger. Obviously, humanity was the cornerstone of his character.

Having my own vehicle paid dividends one day when I heard on its radio a med call to my dad's rooming house. The dispatcher coolly cued me by telling that paramedics were responding and the name they were looking for on the mailbox was spelled M–u–t–z–a. I flipped on my lights and siren and got there in time to be alongside my dad while our meds expertly treated his heart attack.

The school was largely responsible for the department's public relations, fire prevention, interaction with the media, and institutional training. The Bureau of Fire Prevention had long been the victim of budget cuts, which left fire inspections to city building inspectors. Fire company officers were on their own when it came to becoming familiar with buildings, and especially hazards, in their first-in area. Public relations was a haphazard affair, with speaking engagements doled out to those in the field who showed interest by signing up. School staff could pick and choose assignments among requests received by schools, civic groups, etc. During Fire Prevention Week, things got busy. When Chief Tom Konicke came on board, he and I established the Public Relations Corps, which offered a more organized, better trained, and better prepared group of speakers, whose assignments were more equitably scheduled. The Fire Academy had long been committed to training the public and private sectors, particularly industry and hospitals, in the use of fire extinguishers. The fact that nurses comprised the majority of these attentive audiences enhanced the assignment's popularity among school staff.

Chief Seelen's introductory words rang true: we did a lot of different things. Never was I bored or lacking for something to do. I felt like I was in a library and I could select any book that piqued my interest. Speaking of libraries, one of my favorite pastimes was getting lost among the school's library holdings, which I organized as I researched various topics. Periodically, the research was at the request of an attorney for use in a case. The library proved to be a gold mine for the historian in me. The treasure trove of dusty historical material, coupled with the numerous artifacts that showed up on our doorstep, fed my desire to establish some sort of archival section to preserve the department's history. Fire service memorabilia are popular collectibles, and an excessive number of artifacts were ending up in taverns and department members' rec rooms, some of which, virtually, were fire department museums. One of my goals, then, was to gather everything into a locked room. Now if I could only convince the department to set aside some space to display this history.

Chief Gus Koleas, after he took over the helm from Chief Seelen, shared my views about the importance of preserving our history, and his exuberance led to a plan to convert two conjoined classrooms at the academy into a museum. The plan dissolved in the wake of a territorial battle between Koleas and Milwaukee Area Technical College, which used our facility to teach EMS and fire technology courses. After I left the school, I lost control of the archives, but, thankfully, sense eventually prevailed and the Milwaukee Fire Historical Society was established, even occupying the old south side quarters of Engine Company 23, complete with refurbished apparatus.

I especially enjoyed working with the media. What better way to boost our image in the public eye and promote the fire service. We had a great rapport with all the local news agencies, doing our best to keep them informed and include them in many of our activities, both official and social. At one of our big awards events, one of the TV stations obligingly showed a film of their bloopers the public would never see. It was great entertainment.

I worked with a Milwaukee Journal/Sentinel staffer on a fire department series, and I was a guest on Howard and Rosemary Gernette's *Dialing for Dollars* noon show on WISN-TV. Actually, I was there on behalf of the Milwaukee County Historical Society, where I would be speaking about the history of firefighting at their first demonstration day. After spending time with them off the air, it was easy to agree with public opinion that Howard and Rosemary were Milwaukee's favorite married couple. After on-air introductions, Rosemary's opener was: "Wayne, why *do* firemen wear red suspenders?"

Careful, Wayne, this is not the place for a smart-ass answer. I gave it to her straight: "To hold their pants up."

Cool as a cucumber, she asked, "That's it?"

"That's it, Rosemary."

Even more memorable were two programs requested by local TV stations. Fall was approaching, not to mention Fire Prevention Week, which prompted a request by WISN-TV to work with them on a special feature about fires during the heating season. Their choice of subjects was sound because heating appliances headed the list of causes of residential fires. Dick "Kogee" Kovatch, one of the training lieutenants, and I got the assignment. Discovering that we would be working with Channel 12's Bunny Raasch was a bonus. Bunny was Milwaukee's first woman news anchor and reporter. Besides being impressed with her professionalism and how she firmly managed her camera crew, we agreed that she was quite attractive.

When we met with Bunny to plan the project, she said that her goal was a dramatic presentation centered on an actual house fire. Our claim that we were just as proficient at starting fires as putting them out bought us her pretty smile. We checked with housing authority to find a vacant house slated for demolition. The building they gave us was ideal since it had no "exposures," meaning other nearby buildings to which our fire could spread. When Kogee and I checked the building over, we had the first-due engine company meet us to eye the layout. Since we expected to give Bunny a good fire, we'd need Engine 28's crew to get it under control.

The day of the shoot, Bunny showed up in a skirt and heels. We spent a good deal of time in the basement since we would set the fire next to the furnace. Kogee and I flashed each other typical boy grins every time Bunny's great legs went up the stairs. As the main camera was set up on a tripod and the engine crew suited up and laid a charged line, Bunny insisted that she be with us when we set the blaze. Her intense interest and curiosity about our profession was obvious. She was as much into her work as were we, which made her a joy to work with. She wasn't dressed for a basement fire, but we couldn't say no. We did warn, however, that we'd have a good sense of the fire's travel and how it would act. So we stressed to Bunny that when we said "Go," she had to get out immediately.

"Okay," she agreed, grinning. I sensed her trust in me.

"We'll give you a good show, Bunny, just stay next to me," I implored.

Kogee lit the cardboard cartons we had stacked near the furnace, knowing flames would devour the dry, dusty wood framing overhead, and spread laterally. Bunny knelt next to me and watched my movement, as I had asked. I was more interested in watching her facial expressions as the flames grew and crackled, their light reflected in her eyes. She turned toward the cameraman behind us. "You getting this?" By the time dark orange flames began rolling across the ceiling, she was mesmerized. With her clutching my sleeve, we duck-walked backwards as the heat intensified. The cameraman backed up to the stairs. As we had warned her, one of the dangers of basement fires was fire seeking air and rising, its path being the stairwell, our only way out. The name of the game was beating the fire to the stairs and staying below the heat. Watching the flames eat their way toward the stairs and brown smoke rolling up the top of the stairwell told us it was time to go. It got hot fast and the fire was near full bore, ready to devour the first floor. "Out now," Kogee snapped. The cameraman bolted, in a crouch, almost leaving his camera behind. He had been kneeling, unaware that his camera, just two feet above his head, was being damaged by heat. And up went Kogee. Bunny hesitated, as though knowing there were seconds remaining to the point of no return. "Bunny!" I yelled. "We gotta go. Now!" She hesitated again, looked at me, spun and went for the stairs. I loomed protectively over her as she scooted up the stairs in a crouch, the flames at our heels; heat stung the back of my neck. Kogee had been at the top of the stairs, eating smoke, wondering where we were, hoping something hadn't gone horribly wrong, sending him back down into that hell. Dashing outside, Bunny quickly masked her exhilaration, composed herself, grabbed a cameraman, stuck a mike in Kogee's face and nailed him with a question. She caught him red-eyed, tears, spittle and snot running down his face, off guard, coughing and sputtering out an answer about the dangers of heating appliances. In the background was 28's crew going in after our fire. It was perfect. She wanted drama. She got drama. I know why she hesitated in that basement — I had told her to stay with me, to watch me, and she read me like a book. Smart, tough broad, that Bunny. She was great!

A similar request from a TV station during the holiday season had Lieutenant Dennis Michalowski and me burning Christmas trees to dramatize their flammability. We gathered all types of real and artificial trees and ignited them by various means while being filmed and photographed. This too was an impactful safety lesson driven home by scenes of some trees literally exploding in flames. In the tower we added sobering realism by placing drapes and furniture nearby, along with gifts and dolls, all of which burst into flames. That had to make an impression on a TV audience.

Dennis' gruff characterization was offset by his wealth of education. The scowl he often wore on his serious face could easily break into a grin. Like everyone who served a stint at the school, Dennis brought with him his own ideas about doing things. He proposed changing our schedule from a five-day work week to four 10-hour days. I was the only one opposed in view of the fact that 8-hour days were actually 10-hour days, and 10-hour days would become 12-hour days. Post-work time was spent critiquing recruit performance, readying equipment, and shuttling our engine and ladder truck back to firehouses. Construction of a firehouse-type utility building on site would later provide storage of our rigs and equipment. Although I often told Dennis I thought he had a death wish, in view of his liberal use of gasoline to start training fires and his maniacal driving, we got along well; his sense of humor helped. Only once did we butt heads. A recruit was struggling with weekly written exams, but he shined on the fireground, displaying great fortitude and a positive attitude. It was obvious when someone was putting out 100 percent, which made it easier to overlook a slight weakness in one area that they made up for in others. This was one of those rare times when I was reminded that I was not an officer so my slant on the issue did not carry equal weight. To my dismay, the ambitious recruit was let go. It didn't help that I knew his girlfriend, who told me how much he wanted to be a firefighter.

Another interesting project Dennis and I worked on was at the behest of the police department, specifically their budding special tactics team, popularly called SWAT, for Special Weapons and Tactics. Months earlier, we had helped them prepare a large civil defense truck, one of a few crammed with disaster equipment and quartered in firehouses before they were declared surplus. We were intrigued by their inquiry about various types of glass after they dealt with a difficult incident in which a man held a young boy hostage at gunpoint in a car. Not knowing if a shot through the car's glass would be slowed or deflect only complicated the tense standoff. The incident ended with the boy spared, but the coppers were now bent on finding out how types of glass reacted when impacted by ballistics and tools.

Motivated by their sincerity and the sheer importance of the project, Dennis and I began research and collecting samples of every type of vehicle and building glass we could find. We talked to glass experts. Our findings would also give our people an edge in forcible entry techniques and removing glass during fires. We already knew from vehicle extrication experience that front and rear windshields were completely different than side windows and reacted in markedly different ways when struck. This we passed on to the police immediately. This triggered my memory of a fire in a downtown slum-lord's dump, where I was surprised that my axe bounced off of a large window when I took a swing. The clear panel reminded me of Plexiglas used on air-craft, but this was tougher. It wouldn't give. Someone said it was a new product called Lexan, which couldn't be broken. Now was the chance to find out more. I found that Lexan, or polycarbonate resin thermoplastic, is highly impact resistant. Ah, technology! We attacked our many glass samples with a vengeance, using every tool we had, along with various applications of fire, photographing as we went. Then the police tried various weapons on their range. So successful was the project that they were elated with the findings that would affect their tactics, and we developed a slide training program for firefighters. We tried to time these projects in between recruit training, which demanded much of our attention.

What about women fire recruits? It is a question that not only is still asked, but despite the passage of time has retained its sensitivity in some cir-cles. During the time that I was assigned to the academy, women had yet to establish a presence in the male-dominated profession. The Milwaukee Fire Department was no exception, although Chief Stamm was under the gun of a federal court order to hire women. Stamm stood his ground, his refrain being that he wasn't against women on the job, only unqualified women. Adding fuel to the already controversial subject was the fire chief of Madison, Wisconsin, who claimed that his department had the highest percentage of women because they were measured by more realistic standards; in other words, modified physical requirements that focused on overall strength and agility that more accurately reflected the demands of the job. And capping that was Milwaukee's Fire and Police Commission assertion that our firefighter training not only placed too much emphasis on upper body strength, it also was of boot camp mentality, which hindered the hiring of women. Add to this a female applicant's assertion that she was "out to bust the male ego" and we had a volatile mix. The media had a field day.

I was on school staff when the first female candidates came through, which was the only time I was content to be relegated to my firefighter rank and let the officers deal with the political fallout. Our paramedic program was in its infancy and was being eyed as a means of getting women on the job. First, however, they had to qualify as firefighters, which meant passing our rigorous training. The most controversial female recruit, who had a pen-chant for staying in the news, made repeated attempts. Female candidates were allowed to recycle into the next class if they washed out. During her third attempt, I was at the vacant building we burned where she was given three attempts to perform ladder raises to ventilate the building. After failing all three attempts, the senior instructor called her over and then called me over as a witness.

Aware of the importance of verifying that she couldn't perform the ladder-raising evolution, the instructor asked her if she understood that her three failed attempts meant she was terminated from training. All was very cut and dry as she acknowledged that, along with having to sign papers back at the school.

It all seemed simple enough, but back at the school, the first thing I saw her do was to ask the secretary for a fistful of change and she went to the pay phone to call the media. They couldn't help her now. Changes were in the air, but with the monkey on his back, Chief Stamm temporarily assigned her and another female paramedic hopeful to one of our rescue squads. That didn't sit well with the brotherhood or the union because squad members, like paramedics, had to be firefighters. But Stamm was "the man," he gave the orders, and his back was against the wall.

In light of prevailing attitudes, both on the instructors' and on the woman's part, a wall of discontent went up between them. Certainly, a discrimination suit filed by the woman laid the foundation for that wall. Training evolutions and equipment suspected of hindering the woman were scrutinized by the commission; their findings resulted in demands that certain aspects of the training be changed, and that heavier versions of identical ladders not be used. That these evolutions and equipment were used by instructors who connived to drive out the female was never proven. Baffling, though, were men obsessed with keeping women off the job, but years later, saw them as darlings. Female adoration and male machismo go a long way back.

In contrast, I worked with another female recruit who came close to graduating but couldn't cut the mustard, as they say. She didn't come with a chip on her shoulder and she declined to talk to reporters when she was dropped. Shame, because she told me that she found us instructors fair and the training tough, but necessary.

Bailing out Stamm, in a sense, was the person least likely to do so, his adversary, in fact, union president Joe Ruditys. Amidst the hand-wringing and head-scratching over how to get women into the department, Ruditys submitted to the Justice Department a pay compromise that followed on the heels of a 1978 federal ruling that the city could not require women to pass firefighter training in order to become paramedics.

History was made, finally, in January 1983 when Milwaukee graduated from the Fire Academy its first female firefighter, Debra Pross. Joining Pross a year later was Christine Welk, who also praised the fairness of her instructors. And, oh, was Stamm happy. On one occasion I recall Stamm coming out to the school to hear personally why the instructors were going to drop a female. His response was, "I don't care. Put her on!" The instructor refused, arguing with the chief.

My feelings about women firefighters? Someone's sex or race mattered not, as long as the person was qualified; more specifically, was able to do everything I was required to do to get the job. With regard to hiring, the inevitable was upon us, and my impression was that all of the agencies involved stepped on their dicks dealing with it.

Not all was bliss, as some of the women found firehouse life a tough go. Sometimes, there was outright vehemence between the brothers and the gals. At the firehouse where new paramedics trained, a firefighter who thought himself campy mooned the girls, buying himself a transfer to a slow house, then considered a form of punishment. At another house where the female was washing dishes, someone slipped a dildo into the suds. Not missing a beat, she washed it and put it with the other dishes to dry. The list goes on. When the media spotlight was turned off and the fire guys learned to share their bathrooms with females, the novelty of women in firehouses wore off and we got back to business.

It seemed that no recruit class could go the ten weeks without something noteworthy occurring. Often, it happened during training fires at vacant houses. We tried to select vacants that had minimal exposures and wouldn't disrupt traffic, and proceeded when weather was stable. Not only did we use the derelict buildings to practice every aspect of firefighting, I began teaching recruits building construction, often by dismantling parts of the structure.

"Don't just smash through things," I told them; "look at how something's built, and then methodically take it apart. Work smart and conserve your energy." Usually when we left a vacant, there was little left, even for vandals and scavengers.

During a vacant burn on a relatively calm day, we noticed brown smoke billowing behind a house on the opposite side of the freeway. I grabbed a couple of recruits and drove over to find a 20-foot boat in a yard fully involved in flames. I called for the rest of our group and our rigs to handle the blaze. We hadn't noticed that the wind had gotten stronger, and it carried embers from our training blaze across the freeway, onto the boat. The owner had no hard feelings, the city picked up the tab, and we were on the carpet explaining how this could have been prevented.

Creating realism was seldom a problem, as overzealous instructors commonly had fires get away from them. Often, our dispatcher radioed to ask if we were burning because the alarm bureau was receiving numerous calls for a fire in our area. Periodically, ladders were hastily abandoned on roofs when fires got away, leaving the instructors to explain the unusual number of req-

On a vacant house set aflame for training purposes, fire recruits demonstrate a standard roof opening made to vent heat and smoke, which buys time for trapped occupants and allows firefighters to advance inside. In unison, the two pull back roofing material after having made horizontal and vertical cuts.

uisitions for new ladders, or other equipment. For one of our classes we selected a vacant school to burn, which raised many eyebrows. We had the entire first-alarm assignment in the area come in to check out the place in case we had to call for help. When the guys pulled up, they looked at the large building, then at us, and said, "You guys are nuts." Burn the place we did, and the class did a bang-up job of attacking the impressive blazes we set.

Every now and then we got a call from an officer in the field saying that he was impressed with the recruit we had sent him, and the job we were doing. That was high praise. To this day it is a joy to see on the news a chief being interviewed about an incident and be able to say, "He was one of mine." And hopefully, they remember.

School staff was top shelf and I enjoyed the professional interaction, which was matched only by our social interaction; any event was an excuse for a party.

I worked with four recruit classes from which we graduated 95 firefighters. Despite the fast track I was on, everything I was learning, and the good things we were doing, I never could shake the feeling that to become fully rounded, and to take the lieutenant's exam, I needed more field experience. Besides, our daughter, Joanna, was now one year old, and Pat could better manage her through a 24-hour stretch. So I surprised everyone in the spring of 1980 by requesting a transfer back to the field. Okay, maybe they were right that I was crazy, but I had conviction. Chief Koleas, bless him, understood best. A perk of being at the school was that I could select my company. Garnering the most fire runs, with a fine reputation to boot, was Engine Company 5 in the center of the city. Yup, "Fightin' Fives" was where I wanted to be.

5

Engine 5

The three shifts we worked were color-coded red, green and blue. I would be a green-shifter. Trading a work day with someone from another shift was a privilege, as was overtime, which meant another 24 hours at your own house, or anywhere in the city. Working at another house, possibly on a different type of company, provided insight to their operation; good or bad, I learned from the experience. As much as I liked being at the academy, I had missed the firehouse, and the runs. The familiar smells of the apparatus bay wafting through the door invited me in to Engine 5. Summer's heat conjured up a heady cocktail of aromas: make mine wet hose, smoke, and leather, with a touch of warm oil and gasoline.

Being in the poor, black inner city, Engine Company 5 competed with a couple of other engine companies for highest number of runs. Engine 5 didn't log the highest number of total runs, but it edged out the others in fire runs. It was obvious by the growing number of vacant lots that Fives couldn't hold the record much longer. There were simply fewer buildings to burn. The area where we said "the hot bricks flew," sometimes literally, fell under various names, depending on one's outlook — it was the inner city, the ghetto, and to some, simply, the hole. Engine 5's high run tally was a bleak indicator of the area's poverty level and high crime rate. We could talk about the reasons for such blight till the cows come home, but our job was simply to go out and pick up the pieces, as best we could.

Engine 5's house was a modern building comprising three sections on one level. Flanking the roomy apparatus bay were living quarters, with the kitchen and offices opposite. The practical layout was tucked into a small side street with roundabout access to major streets. Like some single houses, we were partnered with a rescue squad, Squad 8.

I was part of a good crew, level-headed and reliable. The other firefighters were Bob Bett, who had been one of my recruits, and Myron Hooks, the cub. My boss was Dick Kovatch, who went to Engine 5 when he was promoted from lieutenant to captain while at the school. His position as house captain was one of the reasons I requested Engine 5. This was the third time I worked with Kogee, and we had become close friends. He ran a tight ship and was known for his dedication, efficiency and aggression. Some viewed him as a risk-taker. Admittedly, he didn't have an "off" switch, but I viewed his attributes as enormous pride. We were of the same grain, even joking that we were both stubborn Bohunks. However, I didn't share his enthusiasm for some things and I set my limits lower. For example:

In the middle of a bitter winter night, we responded to an alarm at Mt. Sinai Hospital. This was one of our routine runs, with our part being to mask up, pull a large hose pack off the rig and stand by while first-due companies checked the complex to find what set off the alarm. Rarely was there cause for alarm, the culprit instead being an over-sensitive system. I never say "never" because one of these innumerable calls turned out to be a basement fire. The chief could not give the order to "pick up" until we were positive there was no emergency. While waiting for word from companies inside, and trying not to think about the numbing cold, the radio came alive with a report of a fire with people trapped. It was in our area; in fact, when we looked toward where the address was, a yellow glow against the low cloud deck left no doubt that fire companies would be working till daylight. Since we were committed, we heard the next due companies being called off. When the dispatcher radioed additional information about people trapped, we knew it was bad.

As expected, Kovatch instantly chomped at the bit, a virtual fire horse kicking at its stall. That was our "first-in" and he wanted it. He even radioed the chief to ask if we could go back in service. "Negative," was the response; "we haven't found the problem here yet." Kogee wore the anxiety and frustration on his face. Through tightened jaw, he hissed, "Dammit." He paced. Looking at the ominous glow, he said, "We gotta get in there." We three firefighters didn't say a word, but gave each other knowing looks when Engine 13 radioed "fully involved" on their arrival. I reasoned: *All right, other crack companies are there, they're doing the job, sometimes the system can't be disrupted, what if Engine 2 finds something here in the hospital?* Finally, Engine 2 radioed the "all clear" and we were 10–8, or back in service. Kogee instantly called the dispatcher to see if we should go to the fire, but they were handling it. By the end of the shift, we heard that the fire was a vicious battle in the sub-zero temps, and two kids were dead. I was all right with not going home wasted, and especially not being burdened with the horrible loss. *Better them than us. It's how the dice fall. We'll get our turn. We'll damn sure get our turn.*

And get our turn we did. Accounting for a large portion of our runs were false alarms, the result of perpetrators activating alarm boxes on street corners. "Pulling the hook" brought a response of five or six rigs. Sometimes kids were on bicycles, pulling hooks as they rode. It was dangerous. With sirens wailing, fire trucks criss-crossed intersections throughout neighbor-hoods. Sometimes, people who had a problem with order waited with rocks and bottles. Sometimes, unsavory items were left in the boxes, or the boxes were even booby-trapped. Sometimes we pulled up to a box to find a gunshot or stabbing victim. In their world of uncertainty, the one thing upon which residents could rely was pulling that hook to get help. Eventually only one company was sent to a box alarm, and if, by chance, they had something, they radioed, "Fill out the assignment," and then had to go it alone until the cavalry arrived. In 1978, 113 voice fire-alarm boxes were installed in north side high crime areas. They proved a miserable failure, and were pulled during 1980. Enough was enough, and a few years later, all the boxes were pulled. Officials knew that the one thing everyone had, even in the ghetto, was a phone.

Busy companies and their response areas were good classrooms; experi-ence came quickly. I began to learn the area — the location and layout of hous-ing projects, known and suspected drug houses, taverns, areas where we were more welcome than others, the dumpsters that burned daily, and large build-ings where hazards lurked. The area was a patchwork of vacant lots, burnouts that we jokingly called "another one of our saves." Among the litter strewn about empty lots were mattresses that kids used as trampolines and often set afire. Sporadically, in stark contrast to rows of dilapidated houses, cyclone fences hemmed in the small grassy lots of tidy homes that had become shut-tered outposts of people who wished only to live in peace. It was a game of survival. Sometimes, if the sun was positioned just right, a street glittered with broken glass. "Canners," black men weathered beyond their years, pushed shopping carts laden with huge trash bags filled with cans, hoping aluminum drew a good price that week. Here and there, elderly men hovered over jacked-up cars that had seen better years. Their less productive contemporaries hud-dled in doorways sharing a brown bag. No buildings, especially dilapidated garages, were immune from gang graffiti that claimed turf and challenged rivals. It seemed that nearly everyone was armed with something, if only a stick — even kids. I began to recognize the addresses of our regulars. Most were alone, destitute, scared, or didn't have the ability to function. Runs to industrial sites scattered throughout our first-in area provided welcome changes of scenery.

Fires. We got our share. Sometimes more than we could a handle. One summer a group of "torches" must have had a bet going to see how many places they could burn. Maybe it was a gang initiation. We'd have two or three workers going in one block. First-in companies would knock one down, then drag their hose to another one. When relief companies came in to mop up, the first-in crews were sprawled out on their equipment, totally spent.

Such scenes reminded me of soldiers after a firefight. We found ourselves spread exceedingly thin one day when we responded alone to an alarm. To our amazement, we passed two separate building fires, blocks apart. The boss called them in, while we continued, per the rules, to our original alarm, which turned out to be a fire also. A man was trapped on a second-floor porch. The crew split — I took the line into the fire, Bett raised a ladder to the man, the boss and the cub went in to search, and the MPO got water. The first fire we passed grew into a greater alarm.

That no two fires were alike challenged the best tacticians. Prudent tacticians kept their thinking flexible and quickly weighed the strategies available to them. They also had to speedily factor in data such as building size, construction and use, occupancy, exposures, time of day, weather, water availability, and their own resources, to name a few. Often, first-arriving officers had to make snap decisions, regardless of how ludicrous they seemed. One day when I was acting lieutenant, we pulled onto a street where three houses were "going wide open." The buildings were built so close together that those adjacent to the original fire building easily caught fire. The narrow street was blocked with cars so I told the crew we'd supply ourselves from a hydrant. This was a reverse of our normal supply operation, which had the second arriving engine supplying the first. Engine 5 was known for being innovative, and we had practiced the forward lay often. One guy jumped off and wrapped the line around the hydrant for the hook-up. Now how to get down the gridlocked street to the burning buildings — I told the MPO, "Take the sidewalk." People scattered like a movie chase scene, while our hose played out of the hose bed. We now had an unlimited water supply, plus our rig and all of its equipment was at the fire. We ended up using our rig's deck gun to stop the fire's spread. After the ash settled, our unorthodox tactics drew a lot of comments.

For some months, a rash of neighborhood grocery store blazes added to our busy workload. Word on the street was that Blacks didn't like Middle Easterners dominating neighborhood businesses. So grocery stores burned, some completely, while other fires set by amateur firebugs fizzled. While responding to one of them, we almost struck the wide-eyed fleeing torch, who still gripped a gas can. Sometimes, after these fires, our pockets were stuffed with treats to stock our commissary. But we had scruples; we took only smoke-damaged goods we knew the health inspector would order trashed. Our booty was nothing compared to the antique treasures some companies "rescued" from run-down, tax delinquent buildings slated for demolition. I was impressed once seeing one of our ladder trucks rattling down the street with an old claw-foot bathtub nestled into its aerial ladder. If not us, the goods went to scrappers and thieves. I didn't care who got the meager remembrances of the once-grand homes, as long as they weren't destroyed by fire or the bulldozer.

I never ceased to be amazed at the human psyche, people's actions that triggered dramatic changes in their lives, often tragic. Take, for example, a house fire where a man was killed. When we pulled up, he was out of the burning home, on the front lawn, safe. But to our amazement, he dashed back in to "save" his television set. The next time we saw him, he was a grotesque, charred form on hands and knees, just feet from his TV. Myron, our cub, was shocked. We just shook our heads and said, "What the hell was the guy thinking?" Sad, very sad.

Myron was a super cub. His baby face and gentle eyes belied the power in his massive bulk. He used his imposing size to good advantage. Not only did he work like an ox, his physique was intimidating enough to make someone with violent tendencies to think twice. When we crawled into a nasty fire, it was comforting to know that Myron was back there humping line and not letting anyone past him to block our egress in case we wanted out in a hurry. Complementing his strength was his pleasant manner and the way in which he approached the job. Being black, it seemed to hurt him when on runs people gave him a hard time for being "one of them." Thankfully, there were times I could see in kids' eyes awe and admiration as they gazed up at hulking Firefighter Hooks, impressive in his turnout gear. Myron earned his keep and we were proud of him.

Myron's first EMS run is easy to remember because of how it affected him; he was conscientious. The call came in as a shooting, and when we pulled up, there was pandemonium, which often was the case. Since the police pulled up with us, we ran down the alley to the victim. I found it humorous when a young black cop running next to me huffed, "I sure am glad you guys are here!" I laughingly answered, "Are you serious? You see this ugly crowd? I'm glad you're here." We couldn't save the 18-year-old, who had been killed over 50 cents. Some in the crowd swore vengeance, and more police were called to disperse the angry mob. For Myron, the growing, agitated crowd, and the trauma of doing CPR on a young man with blood pumping out of his chest were overwhelming. Back at the firehouse, I found him leaning against the rig's bumper, staring out the door, misty-eyed. We talked about dealing with death and violence, which seemed to help him sort things out. But even Myron, eyes wide open, would steel to the carnage.

Other notable instances where people brought their lives to a sudden end included a fire in a downtown apartment building, to which we responded when it reached greater alarm proportions. A tenant decided to end his life by turning on his gas oven and burners, then lay down and expected to be put to sleep. *Painless enough*, he thought. Some time later he awoke to discover that, in fact, he hadn't died. We wondered if he was reconsidering when he went to the bathroom, sat on the toilet and lit a cigarette. The explosion blew out the walls of his apartment. The crew of Rescue Squad 1 arrived first to see flames roaring out of third-floor windows and a woman leaning out of another, screaming as heavy smoke pushed out behind her. The squad crew called for a second alarm and ran into the lobby where they ran into the guy who had wanted to die painlessly. He was in shock, all his clothes were burned off and his skin hung hideously in shreds. He died a few days later, the hard way. Luckily, no one else was seriously hurt. It remained a mystery to us how the guy got from his third floor apartment to the lobby.

We witnessed up close the frailty of the human mind when disaster struck. I've encountered people whose brains were so short-circuited by trauma that they could not remember their own names or how many children they had. For example: we were sent alone for a fire in a sofa outside of a building. As we headed toward the intersection of Tenth and Wright streets, we strained to pinpoint the source of gray smoke that hung in the humid air. A collective "Ah, shit!" came from us when we saw that it was indeed a burning sofa, but on the porch of a huge corner flat. Thick brown smoke now boiled from the first-floor windows of the pale yellow building.

The boss radioed, "Fill out the assignment, we have a working fire!" as Bob Bett and I jumped off the rig. Immediately a man grabbed two fistfuls of my heavy coat, panic and anguish in his saucer eyes, pleading, "My baby, ya gotta save my baby!" Stealing a look over his shoulder at bright orange flames bursting through a window, then locking my eyes on his, I demanded, "How many? What floor?" He stared through me with those wide panicked eyes, sobbing, "My baby, my baby."

There was no time to waste. Peeling his fingers from my coat, I could only offer, "We'll try. We'll try."

Working in single-company mode, Bob and I took a hose line into the building, while the boss and the cub ventilated and searched for victims. Spotting orange-yellow tongues of flame licking upward on the old wood siding, I knew that anyone on the first floor wasn't coming out alive.

We grabbed the line, not taking the 30 seconds to don masks. My focus on what we had to do was exceptionally sharp. As we stretched the line, I shouted to Bob that this had to be fast, and hoped the cavalry showed up soon. It was a long stretch to the back door so I yelled at two young gawkers to help us stretch the line. I was surprised that they snapped into action.

Laying lines to the back door was common practice since access to all levels of a house usually was at the rear. The back door was open. Crawling below the heavy brown-gray mass rolling out the doorway, I took a quick look and listened. I was peering into the yellow depths of hell, watching the devil's victorious dance. Knowing that Bob was dutifully behind me, I turned my head to tell him the first floor was a write-off. A tug on my coat jerked my head the other way to see the aide's face inches away. As the chief's second set of eyes, he was checking on us. "You okay?" he yelled into my ear.

"Yeah," I coughed. I told him to remember that we were in there, and that we might have victims.

Slapping my back, he yelled, "Water's coming," and disappeared.

I felt it important to turn and look into Bob's eyes. "Ready?" He nodded, "Let's do it." Crouching, we groped our way up the stairs, the smoke daring us, stinging our eyes and throats. At the top, thankfully, the smoke continued its thermal climb, allowing us to see into the upper floor. The eerie haze at floor level, the dull red glow ahead, the tremendous heat, and Satan's crackling laugh told us the fire would soon blast through this level. The man's face loomed ... "My baby, my baby."

As we crawled, a thunderous rumbling rolled from the front of the house. The sound was familiar, but before it registered, a wall of searing heat hit us. We flattened, faces pressed against warm linoleum. "Jesus Christ!" The pain around my ears and neck was unthinkable. I knew the troops had arrived and were working a large powerful hose line through the front windows, pushing the scalding wall onto us. Someone hadn't gotten the message. I knew personally the chief in charge and that he wouldn't order that move if he knew that a crew was inside.

Thankfully, our hose line snapped to life. As I sprayed a protective arc of water into the darkness, we scrambled for an adjacent room. Feeling and stumbling our way through the smoke-filled room, we felt in and under everything, pushing through constricted throats the words, "Anybody here?" As we moved, I sprayed intermittently overhead to cool the room. My mind spoke to the anguished face suspended in the darkness: *We're here. We're in your house. We're near your baby.* The face commanded my arms and legs. It controlled the mechanical push-pull of my lungs. I turned my head and the whole world exploded in my face — a paralyzing flash of light and a thousand pinpricks of pain. I tried to focus, recognizing the beams of a ladder jutting through the broken glass. Using a ladder to ventilate an upper floor was a good idea, just not at the instant my face was inches from the window.

As if things couldn't worsen, the hose in my arms went limp. Bob's subtle "Shit" told me he felt it too. It was our life line; *his baby's* life line. We were exhausted and punch-drunk from the toxic smoke. I was certain that I was blinded to some degree, my eyes and face having been shot-gunned by glass. With no water, and hearing shouts muffled by breathing apparatus, I reluctantly gasped to Bob, "We gotta go."

With Bob leading, we slid down the stairs, squeezing past cursing firefighters tripping and struggling to pull hose lines upward.

Ignoring my injuries, I let guilt wash over me. *His baby* was still in there, certainly dead by now.

Clenching my sleeve to guide me from the building, Bob pointed out why we had lost water. Squinting through lacerated corneas, I could make out multiple geysers of water spraying from our hose line, a new synthetic, single-jacket hose we were testing. Obviously, embers burned through it easily. Ah, technology.

Spent and dejected, I slid my helmet off my head, the thunk when it hit the ground sounding as though it were miles away. I plopped onto the curb so that Tom Heine of the rescue squad could check me over. Kneeling to face me, he winced, reminding me that my face was burned and bloody. The cold, wet towel someone placed on the back of my neck made me flush with a sense of kinship. Shaking his head as he gingerly daubed my face, Tom sighed, "Another ride to the hospital, Wayne." As he led me to the squad, through gray blurs I spotted the man who had lost his baby. He stood alone in despair, wringing his hands, waiting to hear, not grasping the obvious. I knew that anything I said to him now could not ease his pain.

The fire was under control and the usual process of overhaul had begun. Objects the fire had transformed from personal possessions to charred scrap were thrown from windows and shoveled into unrecognizable piles. Clunk — a bent and battered bird cage landed atop the smoldering pile. Inside the cage was a tiny blackened object with a hint of yellow. The man spotted it and threw up his arms, running toward it and wailing in agony. "My baby! My baby!" Seeing my mouth drop open, Tom asked, "What?"

"Nothing," I grinned, "let's go."

I got the impression we were in a fort in hostile territory, immune to the despair of the inner city, venturing out on missions when order gave way to chaos. Sometimes trouble knocked on our door, literally. It wasn't unusual for victims of crime to make it to our door for help. One sunny afternoon, three of us stood outside, shooting the breeze, when two cars careened by, each with passengers hanging out the windows shooting at each other. I found the similarity to the Roaring Twenties hilarious, but we ducked inside anyway in case they came back. Either these gangsters were bad shots or they made it out of our area, because we never got the expected call for a shooting victim. I took more seriously the distant shots I heard one cold night, two days before Christmas, when one of society's dregs shot and killed two cops. I had met the young officers, who were friends of a cop neighbor, weeks earlier. Thirteen months later, another cop, whom I knew from high school, was shot and killed serving a warrant at a pool hall not far from Engine 5.

Periodically, on runs we faced guns. On a call where we and a med unit worked on a PNB, or pulseless non-breather, a guy hovering in the background wore a shoulder holster. I wondered who among us noticed the butt of a weapon protruding from the holster. His silence was unnerving. Intermittently, he muttered, "Get up, Bob. Why isn't he getting up?" Kovatch had seen the gun and radioed the code for police assistance immediately. It seemed that the guy caught on. I didn't work on Bob, feeling it more important to keep an eye on our armed friend. When one of the paramedics announced that the defibrillator wasn't working, the guy surged into high gear, touching the gun butt and demanding to know what we meant that something wasn't working. *Jesus H. Christ, things are tense enough and you blurt out a hint that his pal Bob isn't going to make it.* Someone wisely stepped in and said they'd put in a new battery, so after fiddling with the machine, which was as dead as Bob, the med wisely exclaimed, "Hey, we've got pulses! Let's run with him." We couldn't get Bob on the stretcher fast enough, and tossed him into the rig. Of course, the part about pulses was all B.S. Kovatch later gave the three paramedics a piece of his mind about their communication blunder; I suggested we work on some sort of code system to use when things turned ugly before our gunfighters showed up. I don't recall being afraid of the jerk or his gun, only pissed off at his show of intimidation. I was content not knowing how we would have reacted had he pulled the gun.

We pulled up in front of a house where a man was burning insulation off of copper wire he was stuffing into a barrel on his front lawn; scrapyards wouldn't accept the precious metal still sheathed with insulation. Black, foul-smelling smoke rolled from the barrel, obviously irritating neighbors. No sooner did we tell him there was no open burning allowed in the city than he went into a rage, ranting that he would get his gun and shoot us if we didn't go away. Someone dragged a reduced line off of the rig to show him we meant business, so he upped the ante, stomping toward his front door. By the time he reappeared, waving a pistol, we were back on the rig, with our hose trailing in the street behind us. The bluecoats would have to explain the ordinance to him.

We were victims, to a much lesser degree, in our own firehouse. We caught on quickly to kids who kept us occupied in front of the firehouse while their partners slid through the back door to rip us off. We didn't catch on quickly enough because our lockers had been rifled and an expensive watch disappeared. *Why'd he bring that to work anyway?* Returning from a run, I pointed to an empty space in our lot and asked Greg Davis if that was where he parked his car. Accustomed to our ribbing, he didn't bother to look, just waved me away. "Greg, I'm serious. Isn't that where you always park your ride?" And a nice ride it was. He was sick. It was so stripped when found in a vacant garage a few blocks away, he was sorry he got it back. "They should have burned the thing," he fumed.

I tried to stay ahead of the game by buying an old beater station wagon that was built like a tank; painted dark green, it even looked like one. After I bolted a crude hasp and padlock to the hood, I took a good deal of ribbing — until one early morning we came back to find the hood of everyone's car raised. It looked like a classic car show at a drive-in. Everyone's battery was gone — except mine. "So," I whimsically asked the seething group, "anyone need a ride?"

Through firehouse life, we coped. Not everything at Engine 5 was doom and gloom. Kovatch held to a strict housekeeping and maintenance regimen. Stripping and waxing floors seemed to be his passion. Between floor work and crawling into fires, my knees felt like those of an old hooker. He organized the boss's office and kept it neat as a pin, even tending to his plants that hung from the ceiling. Visitors told us we had the sharpest looking firehouse in the city. Pride abounded. Even our rig reflected our pride. I applied a large patriotic eagle decal to the Mack's blunt nose, and our MPOs painted the wheel lug nuts silver. During the holiday season, Christmas tree lights framed the cab and a wreath adorned its nose. There was something eerily renewing and serene about fresh-fallen snow blanketing the run-down area, proof that nature is the great pretender. In the middle of the night all was quiet except for the clinking chains hugging our wheels cutting fresh furrows in deep, virgin snow. Ghostly vacants, whose dark shadows contrasted with white, beckoned to tell us stories about better days. I wanted to hear.

Nights like that reminded me that for all the ugliness in our work, there was also beauty. You see half naked black kids playing in the spray leaking from your hoses on a July afternoon, and their innocence makes you smile. You see an impassive full moon glowing defiantly behind gray smoke drifting aimlessly across the peak of a roof. In the dark of a January night you stop to take in the splendor of one of your rigs no longer red but sheathed majestically in ice and splashed with red and white lights. You let the smile of a pretty girl springing past your firehouse steal your heart, if only for a moment. You admire the symmetry of ladders and white hose streams angled toward a building, as though supporting it. And you marvel at the beauty of rolling yellow flames. You hate the fire but your eyes capture its powerful beauty.

Time between runs was spent training, working out, watching TV, reading, working on pet projects or hanging around the kitchen solving the world's problems. Other companies and cops stopped by periodically to chew the rag, have a cup of joe, and compare notes on what was happening in the streets. Less frequent visitors were fire buffs who, for various reasons, admired firefighters, their apparatus, and the sheer excitement of fires. For reasons that escape me, we had labeled them "farkels," after the Farkel Family comedy sketch of the popular *Rowan and Martin's Laugh-In* TV show. Not intended to be derogatory, the term stuck. Firefighters, in fact, called each other farkels, lest they take themselves too seriously. I often said that we all had a bit of farkel in us, or we wouldn't be on the job. In actuality, buffs were, and remain, public-minded citizens who provide services to emergency personnel on and off the fireground. The Milwaukee Fire Bell Club has long stood out among the many support groups across the country.

Of course there was the usual horseplay in the firehouse. It didn't take the boys long to get bored and contrive some way to work on some hapless soul. The pranks pulled in firehouses would fill their own book. Some were time-honored foolery, while others were ingenious. Lines were often crossed and tempers flared. One morning a guy in a frisky mood tried to wake Myron in a most unsavory way and I ended up, literally, between the warring parties. Myron almost took the kitchen doors off the hinges when he chased the guy, who was pleading for help. We let the chase go on for a while since we liked Myron and the offender needed a lesson. Given his size and power, Myron was the last guy I would think to provoke. Like Myron, I had limits. One doesn't fool with someone's personal belongings, including turnout gear. Some pranks, such as stepping into your boots and feeling an egg break, or opening your locker to find its contents covered with flour, just weren't funny. Nor was it tolerable getting hit with a bucket of water in winter and getting a hitch immediately after. Water fights in the summer were a different story. With rival companies, they were endless. Some engine crews actually kept handy atop their rig a short hose line, called a Lipski Loop, that could quickly be charged from the pump when another company came near. And it wasn't unusual for a company to launch a water attack on a rival firehouse. We planned such a raid against our archrival, Engine 30. We would hit them at lunch, the sacred noon hour, when, according to firefighters, "the whole world eats."

We plotted carefully, for this would be the mother of all raids, the one they would talk about for years ... all right, months, maybe. We coasted onto their apron, our arrival masked by traffic noise. As expected, it being a hot day, their overhead door was open and they were in the kitchen at the rear of the building. The MPO quickly activated the pump and we dashed into their firehouse with a hose line. By the surprised looks on their faces when we appeared at the kitchen doorway, they hadn't heard our rig go into pump gear. They were trapped. As water snapped into the line, we nodded at Chief Warzala. He grabbed his plate full of ribs, corn and potatoes and dashed through his office side door, slamming it. Everyone in view, that tantalizing meal, the entire kitchen, got hosed down. During our quick retreat, we helped them with house cleaning by washing down their apparatus floor, and their rig, inside and out. And we snatched their prized pressurized water extinguisher, so often used against us.

It was laughing and high-fives on the short trip back to our cave, but the line had been drawn and we would tread softly whenever in Engine 30's sights. We returned the extinguisher, but not before its chrome finish was brightly painted with salutations.

Hot summer weather also meant being sent to turn off fire hydrants that citizens had opened to create their own neighborhood rec area. Placing a tire over the hydrant and wedging a board into it at an upward angle produced a powerful spray. It was a costly and dangerous game. Hydrants not only produce tremendous flow, some up to 100 gallons per minute, their spray can obliterate intersections, playing havoc with traffic. It took precious time to shut one down, remove its rig, and hook up to get water onto a fire. Of course, the kids didn't appreciate our shutting down their personal water parks, which often led to threats, mobs and violence. We spent so much time at open hydrants that the job was turned over to the water department, who ended up calling for police protection more often than we had.

An especially hot fire on a day when the temperature neared 100 degrees comes to mind, not because of the heat, but because of a person at the scene. The one-story wood building converted to a church was a yellow fireball when we pulled in. As we laid our lines to the rear of the building, staying low, waiting for water, we heard, "Hi, guys!" Out from the bushes behind us popped a guy we recognized as a farkel we had labeled Soda Man. Although not affiliated with our Fire Bell Club, he had followed our fires for some time, always parked nearby with a trunk full of cold drinks in the summer and hot coffee in the winter. Some gladly took his offerings but we kept our distance, not only doubting his authenticity and sincerity, but also suspecting he may have started some of the fires, especially those with highly suspicious origins. We asked our chief to have the police check him out. Although he came up clean, I believed that he knew we were on to him. When he didn't show up any more, we heard that either he was in prison or driving a truck cross-country. I was glad to see him go, and I welcomed the drop in the number of large, suspicious fires.

I used to say, "You can get used to anything. Even a dog can get used to being kicked every day." In our area, where violence was ever-present, that wasn't a stretch of the truth. As in war, which I called "the ultimate human experience," being assigned to Engine 5 again affirmed my belief that we are characters on a stage. But this show was extreme and spoke volumes about the hate and despair that seemed pervasive. Love comes in many forms, but hate is one-size-fits-all. We saw too many examples of that, often in cases where perpetrator and victim not only knew each other but were related. The disease had even permeated the inner city's young. No one wakes up thinking, *Today I'm going to be a hardened criminal.* It starts with the young, with small crimes, becoming experienced and desensitized until they view others merely as weak targets to exploit, regardless the risk. It bothered me greatly to have to rescue from a sewer puppies that kids had gleefully shoved through the grates, or finding an elderly man in a field beaten so badly by kids with pipes that he was drenched in blood. Such disregard for human life bothered us all, profoundly. Knowing what little value some of them had for life, even their blood kin, we knew our lives to them weren't worth spit. We acted accordingly and warned our cubs. Those that had never experienced the inner city looked on in amazement, then faintly, and then no longer cared to look. Their experience wove an emotional tapestry until one event became another, with the realization that it was never-ending.

One of the subsidized projects in our area proved to be a particular vexation; any trip in there guaranteed trouble. Within its boundaries, more than anywhere, some residents had figured out the system. Sympathizers within the complex told us that word had spread that to maximize the "free ride," one had only to say "trouble breathing." And supposedly to get us there more quickly for even a minor fire, one should say "people trapped." What they didn't realize was that we didn't play the "cry wolf" game — we responded the same, every time, without fail. Often when we backed into the project for a dumpster fire, we were barraged with large rocks. On the blue shift, one of those bricks found its target, striking Engine 5's windshield, blasting the MPO's face with glass. When I saw him after he recovered, he said he loved being at 5's, he loved the work, but this had turned him around and he wanted out.

That same project was known as a gang stronghold, which warranted an extra degree of caution from us and the police. Gangs had their own sense of justice, and we sometimes had to clean up the results. As acting lieutenant one day, I warned a young black cop not to straddle a gang teen lying on the ground after he had been shot in the knee. The kid swore vengeance and when the cop got near, the kid kicked, calling the cop a "nigger Uncle Tom motherfucker." I kept my distance, asking the kid if he wanted help. He didn't answer, and when we approached with bandages, his good leg again came up. When we backed away, he screamed, "You gotta help me, honkey motherfucker!" "Yeah? Watch!" I snapped back. I turned to the cop, "We're outta here. He's all yours. You can call a private ambulance after you place him in custody." The kid was more bothered by our presence than by the bullet in his knee. We knew that after he recovered, there would be a retaliatory shooting; I only hoped it happened on my day off.

Dumpster fires were daily occurrences — go in alone, cub brings the hand pump, someone grabs a drag fork, remind the kid to turn his face away when he's spraying because sometimes there are surprises in there, stir up the putrid mess, dump the can's remaining water, all the time watching the people around us, then the boss takes a final look with his light to make sure it's out and there are no bodies in there. Sometimes, when kids taunted us at trash fires, fire guys would respond with, "Sheeit, you call this a fire? You amateurs don't know how to start a *real* fire." Then to set up the oncoming shift, they'd add, "Bet you can't start a good one tomorrow." I avoided such exchanges, knowing the damn kid would take the dare, which could backfire and lead to a horrific outcome.

Once, a kid proudly displayed the lighter with which he had lit a dumpster. One of our guys grabbed it, admonishing him. That pissed the kid off, and we went home the next morning dead tired because the all-night runs to that same project were evenly spaced. Some things were best left alone.

Car fires too were dime-a-dozen; same basic procedure, which included checking the interior for surprises. But they usually required that a line be laid. Sometimes vehicles were burned to hide crime evidence, such as having been stripped after being stolen, or someone was trying to make out on an insurance claim scam.

We logged countless vehicle accidents, some of which became tricky affairs if we had to extricate victims. Heavy extrication with power tools fell to the ladder company. The worst I remember at Engine 5? A Volkswagen hatchback chopped in half by a car being chased by police. A man and a woman were killed. On a par with that one was a call to the police station at Fourth and Locust streets. The dispatcher mentioned that vehicles were burning; one was afire when we pulled up in front of the police station. Instantly grabbing my attention was a badly burned body in the gutter. People were standing nearby, avoiding it, not helping, gawking at the wrecked vehicles. We laid a line and charged it.

I went to the burn victim, while my partners helped cops trying to remove victims still trapped in the vehicles. The man's clothes were burned off; only his wallet and shreds of his pants stuck to his charred flesh. He was conscious and lucid, unsurprisingly because full thickness burns destroy nerve ends. The body has so many amazing methods of responding to pain receptors. Thankfully, paramedics were on the scene quickly, but I covered the man with a wet sheet to preserve his dignity, more than to medically treat him. I wish I could recall the dialogue I had with him. He told me the cops from the station had pulled him out of the burning car. He was a pastor, and I was moved by his abiding faith in the face of death. I don't know if he made it, as I vowed not to follow up on victims, lest I feed an emotion mill.

EMS runs, better known as squad runs, or to the lesser enthused, puker runs, accounted for more than half of our run totals. These runs seemed evenly divided between legitimate medical emergencies, obvious abuses of the system, and shootings and stabbings. We kept a list of reasons why people were shot or stabbed; our favorites were these: 50 cents, taking a cigarette out of someone's pack, a pair of socks (a guy shot his own brother over that one), and the usual boyfriend-girlfriend thing. I remember at a shooting a cop asking a guy in cuffs why he had shot his girlfriend. His response: "I loves the bitch." It was touching. You only hurt the ones you love. Our busiest paramedic unit, Med 5, in their quarters kept tally of shootings and stabbings by placing colored markers at the wound site on a human target silhouette. Guns and knives each had their own color, while miscellaneous weapons were differentiated by other colors. It turned into quite the colorful artwork, but by year's end, they gave up because the paper couldn't hold so many markers.

One of our shootings had an interesting twist. At a Fond du Lac Avenue tavern we often visited to patch holes in human flesh, a patron with a bullet in his thigh was spitting fire and screaming for revenge on the punk who had shot him. Later the investigating detectives told us that the guy had been shot accidentally by a cop. It seems the cop was new at undercover work and quite nervous; so nervous, in fact, that he kept his hand in his pocket with his gun, finger on the trigger. His drunken, obnoxious victim, sitting next to him, made a sudden move, which spooked the cop, making him pull the trigger. The bullet went through his coat into the man's thigh. The undercover newbie bolted out the door and didn't show up till later that day, owning up to his supervisor how it all had gone down. I wonder if the guy ever found out who shot him.

Just weeks later, our crews responded when someone pulled the hook outside that tavern. They discovered at the notorious false alarm box a hooker with a screwdriver lodged in the skull portion of her eye socket.

Cops were central figures with whom we shared the stage. I didn't envy their frustrating, dangerous work, especially in the inner city. Watching them with shotgun at the ready, creeping through the shadows of a darkened house hiding a dangerous suspect, underscored their work. But then, one of them would tell me we were crazy to scale a burning roof when rats were jumping from the eaves to escape. We all had our jobs to do. They, more than we, seemed to live in a black-and-white world where they saw only good or bad. And they, like us, were bent on making order of chaos, but they had more authority to do so. Firefighters seemed to live in a grayer world, where underlying chaos festered. And since we often muddled through our efforts to make order, we compensated on the home front, being good citizens, for example, striving for morality in family. It intensified our complexity.

Only a couple of times do I remember being at odds with Milwaukee's Finest. After a tough fire in an apartment building, where we had a fatality, we were slogging down the wet, blackened hall to take a breather, when in the dim light I saw a detective daintily making his way toward us to see the victim. He tried hard to tiptoe in the debris-littered water and not touch the smoke-blackened walls. I had seen him before and I recalled that he was known for his expensive suits. I could appreciate his impeccable attire, but his bitching about the mess *we* made — never mind the fire — rankled me.

When he got near I closed the gap, leaving him a choice of brushing that imported suit against my soaked, sooty coat or the sooty wall. He chose my shoulder and gasped when he looked down at his smudged suit. As he blabbered with disgust, I drew close to him, making him recoil as though I was going to kiss him fully on the mouth, black phlegm and all. "Nasty mess after a fire, ain't it?" I hissed. I hoped he had enough sense to throw coveralls, boots and gloves into his car, because this wouldn't be his last fire fatality.

Many people thought that our jobs were similar, but we, along with our brothers and sisters in blue, knew better. Despite the differences in job descriptions, we usually got along, and helped each other — until labor issues gave rise to the disturbing exception.

At the heart of the issue was that despite a judge's 1980 decision that firefighters did not have pay parity with police, he refused to allow firefighters to renegotiate their contract. Fire union president Smokin' Joe Ruditys then recommended that we strike. And strike we did, not once but twice, illegally. The political clout of the fire union, which was in the mayor's camp, averted punishment by the courts and by Chief Stamm. Task forces comprising chiefs and a couple of non-strikers ran out of three firehouses, and the National Guard was activated.

Despite almost total participation in the walkout, there was division in the ranks. Not all of us echoed the booming chorus of union diehards, who, with chins tucked in and chests out, proclaimed that we were "brothers of the barrel." Striking, for many of us, was a moral and emotional tug-of-war. The silent majority were afraid of losing their jobs, believing there had to be better ways than allowing the power and political self interests of union leaders to control their livelihoods. But the glue of the brotherhood, resolute en masse, held firm.

The picket lines at Engine 5 grew silent when we received word there was a fire in our area, evident by smoke rising to the west. Peering into the firehouse at our big rig in darkness, all of its power stilled, made me sick that we weren't going. I felt even sicker when we heard that a guy jumped from an upper floor to escape and was critically injured.

Inflammatory remarks made to news reporters by firefighters about cops didn't help, and it set the stage for a bitter feud. True, I believed that we should have pay parity with police, but I never thought I was better than them. Shame on those among our ranks who thought they were. But the die was cast, and it would take a long time to shore up the rapport we had with police. But before that happened, some police watch-dogged our picket lines, daring us to get out of line. Some went nose-to-nose with us — one confrontation between police and fire supervisors at a fatal traffic accident made front page news — while some were only too happy to write a ticket when they discovered they had stopped an off-duty firefighter. No longer did showing your badge get you off the hook.

Only on one occasion did I vent my frustration. At a fire in a large flat, there seemed to be a larger group of cops than normally covered a fire. After the blaze was knocked down, we went outside to dump our masks and get tools for overhaul. The cops razzed us, and being hot and exhausted, I didn't appreciate it. Two of us went back into the attic to begin overhaul. Looking out of a small window toward the street I noticed the cops were still in a cluster, obviously having a good time, knowing their large presence rankled us.

On the floor, among the debris in the attic, lay a hose line used on the fire. I eyed the line and then my partner. He shot me an, "Oh, you're not thinking that" look. I dragged the line to the window opening, aimed toward the blue mass on the street and opened the nozzle.

Within a minute the chief was in the attic asking if I had blasted the group of cops with the line, which lay at my feet. I put on my best confused face, shrugged and answered, "Just wettin' down, Chief." Knowing me and that it was all he was going to get from me, he said, "Oh, okay, I thought so." I saw his grin as he turned away. My partner had taken a powder.

When things got back to normal, we got back to the business of fighting fires, and not each other. And business was good. At a major fire, in fact, we rescued cops who had gotten trapped trying to rescue trapped occupants. However, tension between us and police flared anew after we reported overhearing a young cop tell her partner that they could say they were in there too and be heroes and get some time off. The tension was short-lived after she admitted the ruse, which was a slap to the heroic cops who went in.

Although rescue was paramount, and the department did its best to recognize standout rescues, most of us agreed that it was simply part of our job. Some of us shirked recognition, content with the satisfaction of having saved someone. Taking independent action was discouraged because it violated the team concept, and company officers were accountable for their crew. I once broke off from my crew at a major blaze at a three-story downtown apartment building. I was wrong and I could have ended up dead wrong. After dashing into the building and searching for victims, I found a couple nearly overcome

Engine Company 5's gang with their trusty Mack pumper in 1984. From left to right are Firefighter Jim Washcovick, MPO Don Sauberan, Captain Dick Kovatch and Firefighter Wayne Mutza (courtesy Dale Mutza).

and frozen with fear, cowering at the end of a hall blocked by fire and smoke. I got them out but received an ass-chewing from Kovatch so horrendous that I thought his neck veins would burst. And then it was the battalion chief's turn, although he started his fire and brimstone session by saying what a great job I did getting those people out. That the couple lived to tell about their experience made it easier to sit down after all that ass-chewing. My superiors' sincerity and masked worry, plus my gaining more experience over time, helped pull in the reins. Most memorable was when our MPO, Don Sauberan, leaned into me and muttered, "Remember, this ain't the movies and you ain't John Wayne."

We all benefited from the experience Don had amassed during his early years with the busy Second Battalion. When things were slow and someone cockily said, "Let's get a good fire!" Don always countered with, "There is no such thing. The last time I said that I was at Ladder 10 and we lost three kids."

Rescue had its light moments. Struggling to get a hose line up stairs to the second floor of a burning house, we passed our cub Myron and another firefighter bringing down an obese woman. She was nude and as they struggled, with Myron grabbing her legs, his face was buried in her crotch. Later discussions about the rescue took the expected perverse turn with Myron stating that now he wasn't sure he could ever have oral sex. Poor Myron, who had consistently evaded the question about whether he "tasted the fruit of the loins," had no idea how much he would regret saying that.

When rescues went bad, they went very bad. The image of one incident, in particular, remains as clear as the day it happened. The fire was in a run-down two-story that stood alone on a nearby Walnut Street corner. Downstairs was a vacant storefront, with a separate, enclosed stairway leading to second-floor living quarters. When we pulled up, flames leaped from the blown-out store window. Bob Paul, a red shifter, who was part of our crew that day, had the nozzle and kicked in the door leading to the second floor. That sudden blast of air gave the fire new life and the stairwell erupted in flames. It was impressive to see Bob knock down the flames and fight his way valiantly up the stairs, with us backing him up every inch of the way. After making the top landing, we fought our way through smoke and flame down the stretch of the narrow building, finally ending up at the rear. With the building vented and the smoke lifting, we could make out a body lying on the floor. The fire hadn't extended that far so, the body wasn't burned. Just then someone opened an outside door just a few feet from where the body lay, bathing it in sunlight. I thought, *My God, we just fought our way through this place, from one end to the other, and there he lies, just a few feet from the door he was probably trying to get to. Jesus, all we would have had to do was run to the back, go up the rear outside stairs, and open this door. We could have reached in and grabbed him.* The victim was quickly dragged out onto the outside landing and CPR was begun. He was carried down to the ground, where a med unit on scene immediately went to work.

We were sick. We kicked ourselves in the ass. It would have been so simple. Why did we focus on the front and not send anyone to check the back? One of our paramedics came over to where we sat, heads down, dejected, and told us the guy didn't make it, but that he was probably gone when we pulled up. "Ya gotta let it go. You did your best," he consoled.

But we didn't do our best. Never again did we pull up to a fire and not check the back at the first opportunity. Often, the rear of a building was where you could find Engine 5, with all the fire they could handle, and sometimes pulling people out of windows. Our boss, Dick Kovatch, became a battalion chief and one of the best tacticians on the job, and he always made sure someone was checking the rear of a building.

That fire didn't end there. It slipped into a psychological dimension filled with self-doubt and denial. *It doesn't bother me. Win some, lose some. His number was up.* Denial is temporary and sucks for the long haul. The emotions will come out, but not always in a positive way. We wanted answers so badly that we supplied some even when there weren't any. And we got angry; at ourselves, at the meds, at our leaders, at everyone, even at the dead guy because his place burned, because he didn't get out that goddamned back door, because he didn't give us another chance to save him.

The dead guy didn't do anything wrong. The fire may have been an accident; not his fault. He didn't want to die. So how could we be mad at him? It was an accident, a random event in a world where things go terribly wrong, a world that doesn't forgive — but we can.

Given the oft professed sense of family in the fire service, as in any tightly knit organization, one of the most difficult things to cope with is something bad happening to one of our own. It happened one night in a nasty fire in a block-long complex of two-story businesses on Lisbon Avenue. A large second-story printing business had been burning unnoticed for some time. In the fire service there is a theory that if a building has been burning out of control for 20 minutes, the structural integrity of that building must be questioned. Adding to the significance of this fire was that I ended up in dire straights.

We were deep into the place dragging a line in blackness. I had a bad feeling, which worsened when we heard a loud *karump* and felt a rush of air. The roof had come down. Just then a mask warning bell sounded and we each felt behind us to feel if it was our bell vibrating.

"It's mine," I yelled.

"What do ya wanna do?" one of my partners asked.

"I'm okay," I answered. "I'll make it back all right. You two stay with the line."

"Careful," I heard behind me.

I crept along, feeling the hose line. I was taking smoke and becoming disoriented, and became confused when I felt multiple lines crossing. I was lost. *Damn, I should've been out by now.* I heard a horrible scream, but something didn't seem right, as it came from above, not behind me where I thought my crew was. I was familiar with the effects of smoke inhalation, but that didn't make it any easier to function. *Maybe the scream wasn't above me.* I got to a sitting position and tried to reason this through. Although I tried to rely on my senses, especially what I felt and heard around me, my mind narrowed from lack of oxygen. Although sheathed in blackness, I knew my vision was failing, and my brain, overwhelmed by the smoke and deadly gasses coursing through my bloodstream, could no longer make rational decisions.

I felt a wall and followed it, eventually feeling fresh air and hearing the sweet, familiar clatter of diesel motors and pumps humming out on the street. I could feel the vibration of those red and chrome behemoths. I tumbled down the stairs, reveled in the blurry lights of our rigs, and sat down, sucking clean air. When someone got an oxygen mask on me, I prayed for its revitalizing effects to come quickly. My crew spilled out of the doorway, looking as bad as I felt.

The scream I had heard came from Mike Sweet, Ladder 9's cub. After they swung their aerial to the roof parapet, heavy smoke obliterated Mike's view of the top of the wall. When he stepped off the aerial into space, his leg hung up in the rungs and snapped as his weight took him over. Veteran truck man Clarence Kuehmichel engineered a tricky one-point suspension, using the aerial as a crane, and lowered Mike to the street in a Stokes basket.

Mike was one of my star recruits, gung-ho about becoming a firefighter, and now his career was ended abruptly by a misstep and a shattered leg. It was a real downer.

No matter how calculated were the risks we took, the amount of experience we gained, or how much we honed our skills, injuries were commonplace. We accepted that they came with the territory. We were without our boss, Dick Kovatch, for a few months after he fell into a burning basement. One moment he was directly in front of us as we felt our way through a smoky, vacant house, and the next moment he was gone. No noise, no warning. We felt in front of us. We yelled for him. Gone. When we felt the hole's edge we realized what had happened, and crews went into the basement to bring him out, dazed, white as a sheet, and with a damaged shoulder. When the smoke cleared, it became apparent that occupants had cut a hole in the floor as a makeshift garbage chute to the basement. *And yet another place scratched from the list of potential covers of* Good Housekeeping *magazine.* Helping cushion Kogee's landing were mounds of garbage, which had been set afire. True to our character, when someone asked how it happened, we said that one of us shoved him to put an end to his relentless floor stripping campaign.

A serious injury to my hip traces back to a basement fire in one of our projects. Basement fires are bad enough, but when they're confined to small areas of a block building, their heat buildup is tremendous. We were going down the stairwell, which had become a chimney. The smoke rolling out of this basement was ink black, indicating some form of hydrocarbon accelerant. Our team was Kovatch, Jim "Wojo" Washcovick and me. We stayed low on the stair landing, donning masks, waiting for water in our line, as the black poison rolled over our heads. The heat was incredible, so the name of the game was to get beneath it, on the basement floor.

No sooner had our line become rigid with water pressure than Kogee and Wojo slid down the stairs. I should have been on their heels but I hesitated when my mask face-piece snagged. In the few seconds it took to get my face-piece partially squared away, they were gone. I was weighing backing them up wearing a mask with a lousy seal against backing out, when the searing pain of my ears blistering sent me down the stairs ass over tea kettle. When I rolled onto the basement floor, I tried hard to concentrate on backing them but the pain in my back and hip had my full attention. Wojo easily took down the fire, while I lay there, useless, sucking acrid smoke, ears stinging, with jolts of pain firing through my hip. An angry tenant, it seemed, had used gasoline to set fire to stacks of tires in a basement storage locker. The asshole didn't realize the extent of the damage he had caused, to me and to people who lived in the building. The vindictive side of me wished he had gotten trapped when the 80 octane he splashed around blew.

Wojo came to us from busy Engine 32, where he had learned the art of handling the pipe under the tutelage of ace firefighters Jim "Griz" Greely and Lieutenant Gene Frankowski. Wojo not only was a dynamic firefighter with boundless energy, he was a good friend. It never ceased to amaze me how he could get up for a run in the middle of the night after a busy day and be rarin' to go. There was no limit to our humorous conversation, much of which isn't fit for less than an R-rated audience. Wojo's quick wit fit his boyish looks on a thin frame, which he topped off with a toothpick perpetually wedged between his teeth or behind his ear.

Some fires went "textbook," while at others everything that could go wrong did. My best example of the latter, which I called a cluster-fuck, occurred, of all places, in a cluster of buses. It went bad from the start. When we first pulled in to a storage facility for city buses, black smoke was visible. Since the construction of buses made them a witch's brew of synthetics, chemicals and countless other flammables, they were dangerous enough when burning, much less in a tightly packed grouping. We couldn't find a way into the storage yard, which gave the fire more time to gain headway. Once we did get in and found a yard hydrant, its low pressure did us little good. The buses were so close together that we got on top of them to pinpoint the fire. But they were high and slippery, and if we fell into the chasms formed by the tight rows, we'd never get out. While trying to get water from a street hydrant and laying lines, we heard the sirens of next-due companies circling, trying to find a way in. Meanwhile, the fire grew and more black smoke shrouded the area. We ended up dumping water on the buses with a large "open butt" hose from a railroad bridge. When we finally did get lines laid to the buses, we couldn't get in them and the fires were tough to put out. Even their windshields wouldn't punch out when we tried to break them. We thought we were good at adapting to different situations, but at the bus lot, we looked like a fish trying to ride a bicycle, a cluster-fuck of the highest order. Nothing went right. At least no one got hurt. Shortly thereafter, we arranged with the transport company to provide a bus and teach us what we needed to know, and it opened their eyes to changes they needed to make.

Another run that proved especially troublesome involved a young boy with his arm caught in a gap of a monstrous concrete porch. The boy was calm but his mother was distraught. We looked closely at his pinned arm and exchanged a few ideas about how best to free him. All the pulling and tugging on the boy's arm before we arrived had made his arm swell, making the seal tighter. We leaned into a large steel pry bar and someone produced a can of motor oil, but nothing worked. We went through a mental inventory of the tools carried on our ladder trucks, but cutting or busting the concrete would cause injury to the boy. Then someone said, "What about Jaws?" This was the nickname for the relatively new Hurst power tool with tons of power. We had only two, which were carried on two ladder trucks, one on each side of the city.

So we called for a Jaws-equipped truck and talked to the boy while we waited. The special call brought a chief, and then a med unit to monitor the boy, who stayed remarkably calm. Mom, however, was becoming agitated, and a crowd gathered. What had started as a seemingly simple call turned into a large production. We were hoping the news media monitoring our airwaves wasn't having a slow day and hunting for a story. Eventually, the ladder company arrived, and Jaws worked as advertised, easily separating the concrete. The boy was none the worse for wear and we were glad to end that run.

"Textbook," on the other hand, was a fire where flames lapped freely from every window of a huge two-story flat. For the first time we decided to try using a two-and-a-half-inch line. This was a common tactic, but we were going to take it inside, up to the fire as a hand-line. Given the difficulty in handling the bulky line and its back-pressure, this simply wasn't done at a house fire. Seeing us take the line in and knowing our reputation, Chief Arnie Heling came up behind us, sternly advising, "No circus acts, understand?" "Got it, Chief," we smiled. Once we positioned the monster line at the top of the stairs and held on, we swept the line from one end to the other, boring through walls like they were paper, effectively knocking down every bit of flame. It was amazing. We were off the scene in record time. Chief Warzala exclaimed, "Impressive as hell!" There were doubters and head shakers, who, of course, said we were nuts.

The most flame I ever saw was during my stay with Engine 5. It was a nighttime greater alarm downtown on Plankinton Avenue. A seven-story building being demolished was totally wrapped in bright yellow flames. We manned one of countless large lines set up outside the heat and collapse perimeter. For us it was no big deal, merely a monstrous rubbish fire, void of the challenge of crawling in on a smoky, snotty mattress fire. But the media loved it.

Credit for some of our most challenging runs goes to man's best friend.

At a garage fire, I mistakenly walked through a yard where I surprised a huge dog standing guard on a porch. He stood alert and froze, his wolf-like eyes boring into mine. He had the advantage as we faced off feet away. I felt naked not having a tool in my hand, not that I would ever want to harm an animal. I slowly backed away, talking quietly, while our eyes stayed locked on each other. I was on his turf, but he gave me a pass and I breathed a huge sigh of relief as I closed his gate behind me. I was not so fortunate in a smoky basement fire where I felt an incredibly sharp pain in my ankle. The new mom made no sound when she sank her teeth into me after I stepped on one of her newborn pups. When the smoke cleared, my anguish over having killed the pup made me forget about the pain in my ankle.

The dispatcher said he was on the phone with a guy having chest pain when the caller no longer responded. We saw through windows on the front porch a man down on the floor with the phone near him. It was obvious he had made the 911 call before he went down with a heart attack. Forced entry wouldn't have been a problem if a large dog hadn't been guarding him. We had to get to the man, and knowing how protective dogs are of their owners, we had to come up with something quick. Luckily, the place had a fenced-in yard, so we forced the rear door and let the dog loose, allowing us to get in the front and tend to the man. He went to the hospital, the police secured his home, and the dog was taken by the Humane Society. Had we not been able to remove the dog, my choice would have been to blast it in the face with a carbon dioxide fire extinguisher. The extremely cold gas would only have stunned the dog and, hopefully, kept him at bay. In extreme cases we would have the police dispatch the animal, but I didn't even want to think about that. That would be the absolute last measure I would take. Imagine doing that and having to tell the owner, if he recovered? *Good news, bad news. You made it, but your dog didn't.* I had hoped never to have to dispatch an animal, but I did once.

One sub-zero morning we were called to a fire at a known drug house. The place was locked up tight. Brown smoke chugging from every crack told us the place was heavily charged with fire. We heard barking and when we busted open the door, a pit bull lunged at us, stopped in mid-air by his heavy chain. There was no way around him. Trapped occupants were the priority so I told a cop the dog had to go for us to get in. It took two rounds to bring him down. Drug house, pit bull, it didn't matter; I felt shitty about it. I was sure I wouldn't feel remorse had we found the owner's body in the fire.

At a raging attic fire, when we finally got up the steps, on the landing were two pit bulls, chained, dead from the fire. The doorway they had guarded dutifully to the end led to the drug lab where the fire began. When the smoke lifted, sweeping a light across the attic floor revealed that it was covered solid with dog feces. I hoped that somehow, somewhere, punishment would come to the subhumans responsible. Every time that we brought a dog or a cat out of a fire, and it lived, I felt that we had, in some small way, atoned for the one I had to put down. In the black, steaming ruins of an attic fire, a huge white cat caught my eye. I was amazed it was still alive but knowing the resiliency of felines, I opted to leave the dazed animal. I thought of my sister-in-law, who adored her big cats, and thought, *What the hell,* and brought it out for oxygen. Diane's face lit up when I told her that.

Having a few years at Engine 5 under my belt, fires were routine, but I never let my guard down. Periodically, something came along that was unusual and brought with it a lesson. I took great interest in the science of fire behavior, which helped feed my desire to investigate fires. I never lost sight of the fact that fire was a living, breathing animal that demanded respect. Accordingly, I studied it and marveled how it moved through buildings, accomplishing its insidious task. For example: at a fire with Engine 13, a motorcycle leaning against the side of a wood frame house caught fire. Fire ate its way through the siding, got into the wall space and traveled upward, all the way to the attic. Many of the houses in our area were older wood-frame dwellings with "balloon construction," which meant their wall spaces were open from top to bottom. Fire could travel unimpeded and break out where one least expected it. Hence, we had an outside fire at the first floor level, which also presented as an attic fire. It was important to think ahead of a fire, trying to figure out its travel in hidden spaces. While Engine 13's gang checked the interior of the first floor, we went to the second floor with a hose line. We felt short "knee walls" with the more sensitive backs of our hands, but that was a mistake. Knee walls are set farther in from exterior walls, in which the fire actually is racing upward. At the front end of the second floor, Myron poked a hole in the ceiling with a pike pole. A flame belched downward through the small hole. *Uh oh.* This fire had bypassed the second floor and an attic fire raged over our heads, virtually undetected. Before any of us could say a word, flame again dropped down through the hole and a fireball rolled across the super-heated ceiling. We dropped the line and ran, diving into the stairwell just as the entire second floor lit up behind us. What had appeared as a fire about to be put under control, ended up burning the roof off of the place. Another lesson learned.

Much worse than a fire burning freely was a fire confined, starving for oxygen. The very worst confined fire I ever confronted played a large part in ending my fire service career. It happened at King Furniture, a foreboding, three-story structure with a furniture store on the main level, apartments on the two top floors, and a full basement and a partial sub-basement. Inspecting the old place told us it was ripe for disaster. It was only seven blocks away and every time we rolled past, we didn't wonder if it would burn, only which shift would get it when it did. One Sunday morning in February, five rings for a fire sounded in Engine 5's quarters. We recognized the address and I muttered, "Shit, King Furniture." I wouldn't hear the outcome of the fire until days later because I would be in a mechanical resuscitator at St. Luke's Hospital even before it was declared under control.

Thick gray smoke rolled from the basement we knew was segmented into a maze. Don got us water fast, and we masked up and knelt at the top of the stairway, which was now a flue. The only way for the smoke and heat to escape was our only way down. Somewhere, deep in the belly of this monster, a fire burned. We had about 15 minutes of air to find it and beat it, or we would be lucky to get out of that maze alive. Kovatch had called for a second alarm, mainly to search the myriad living quarters above the furniture store. It weighed heavily on our minds that above us was a floor loaded with furniture that could come crashing into the basement. This was a nightmare.

Down we went into the dark. As we crawled it got hotter, but the crackling we hoped to hear and the glow we hoped to see never came. We crawled slowly and methodically, feeling our way along, trying not to become disoriented by the many walls and rooms. The blackness in smoke plays tricks on you, when your brain can no longer stand the nothingness. Only your partners, your breathing, the nozzle you grip, the hose you drag, mean anything. Sound amplifies. Things you bump into have no names, no identity. They can be anything and must be moved or surmounted. When splinters of yellow or cherry red crack through the blackness, it's beautiful, yet deadly, and some fear subsides knowing you've finally found fire. But flames didn't appear. It remained black. We heard only the sounds of our mechanical breathing and the shuffling of our bodies along the floor. Fear squeezed. Our mask alarm bells went off so we backed out, using our hose line as a life line. Back in daylight, as others quickly changed our air bottles, I found it odd how smoke and steam rose from our bodies. Back down we went, following the line we had left, finally reaching the nozzle. It was hotter than before. The fire was winning, having gained headway. It was eating its way through the building and we still hadn't found it. *If this bastard gets air from somewhere, it'll backdraft and they'll find our bodies down here.* For once, I was grateful there were no basement windows for outside crews to ventilate. That prevented the beast from getting the air it craved.

My mind fogged over. I remember little from this point forward, except that I imagined I was clumsily paddling on top of boxes floating in black water. I faintly remember people walking past me, talking, in half light. And then I was in a paramedic unit, like a giddy drunk making light of the concerns of the people jammed in there and fussing over me. I felt like I had separated from my body and watched the commotion from above.

Crews ended up cutting large holes in the floor of the furniture store to fight the fire from above, a dangerous tactic. Engine 5's crew went back down a third time, too proud to allow any other company to finish what they had started. Examination of my mask revealed that when I changed air tanks, a large cinder had lodged in the exhalation valve, blocking it open so that I was breathing the poisonous smoke in the basement. When I returned to work, our arson investigator, Lieutenant Brian Wachowiak, stopped by with a list of the various materials that had burned in the fire. They included electrical equipment and rubber clothing that gave off deadly gasses when burned. My lungs would never be the same.

One month later we responded to a nasty basement fire in a big building, on the same street as King Furniture, and just a few blocks west. Again, I was certain the angels had come to close my eyes. This one was nearly as spooky. Reputable Fightin' Engine 13 had a mixed crew that wasn't as aggressive as their usual bunch, and they were scared. We backed them up when they went down into the basement, and shortly we heard one of them screaming, "I'm burning!" Man, that was creepy. We tried to sort it out, to help them. They backed out and it was our turn in the barrel. We weren't any braver, just more afraid of being cowards. We found an extremely hot, confined fire, which we beat by a slim margin. Four of us went to the hospital with burns and smoke inhalation. Thinking about the way 13's make-up crew handled themselves reminded me to carefully eye the partners beginning a shift with me.

Sometimes we questioned not only each other's judgment but that of our leaders, especially if we smelled danger. Such was the case at a fire in a small two-story house at Fifth and Reservoir, where a younger, newly promoted chief was in charge. The fire had had possession of the house well beyond 20 minutes. In fact, the second floor had already burned through. This should have clued him to alter his tactics. But, for some reason, it seemed important to him to get someone inside to fight the fire. The place was a write-off and we knew it; it should have become a surround-and-drown. The old shack was ready to topple like a house of cards, but he ordered Engine 5 to take a line to the attic. To the chief I implored that this joint has been going for some time and maybe we should stay out of it. "Besides, it's a vacant." But he insisted we see what we could do in the attic, so we three reluctantly dragged a line up the rickety stairs. Once at the top, Lenny Brandt, being the senior man and an aggressive firefighter, had the pipe and I backed him up; our third guy humped line farther behind us. And then came the familiar, sickening rumble.

The chimney toppled, along with part of the roof just ahead of us. I dove for open air on top of the fallen roof, but Lenny was trapped beneath me, under the roof. I yelled for help as the fire now burned freely around us. No one came so our third man and I clawed and strained to pull up pieces of shattered roof to free Lenny before the fire got to him. We helped him down the stairs and off he went to the hospital. When I passed the chief, he stood with his mouth open, in a daze. I glared and blurted, "I told you that goddamn dump was unsafe!" Despite his error, and our complaints, nothing came of it and he remained unaccountable. I wondered if his conscience ever bothered him. At a similar blaze just days later, Lenny experienced a similar predicament; he never returned to work and left the job on disability.

A typical day at Engine 5 had us coming in early — before 8 A.M. shift change punched through the "joker stand" — as a courtesy, to relieve our counterparts, and then tell them, "You're down." Then it was check over the rig, especially your mask. Get the straps positioned just so for quick donning, charge the system, make sure the bell rings, and place the face-piece against your face to make sure air is flowing and it seals well. Then bleed the air, making sure the bell rings when the gauge shows 500 psi. Everyone ends up in the kitchen, except the cub, who stays busy somewhere else. Some of the off-going people are there too, often wearing the long night on their faces; sullen, red eyes, their skin darkened from stubborn smoke stains; dirty hands wrapped around bulky, worn, steaming mugs of coffee. Smoke odors blend with those of the strong coffee. Staring into his cup, a guy murmurs, "Man, this mud is strong!"

"Hit it with a line," another offers.

The boss adds, "Are you kidding? This is wiener water."

The bakery someone thoughtfully bought on their ride in is opened. If it's rolls from Sciortino's on the east side, or Miller's Bakery, it is soon gone. I take in the aroma of the roll before slathering on soft butter and peanut butter. "Man, this is orgasmic," I coo. I lean through the door and yell onto the apparatus floor for Myron to get in here and have one of these before they're gone. The cook is rummaging through the frig and cabinets planning the day's two meals, served at noon and at five. "The whole world eats at noon and five." If no one volunteers to cook, we rotate the job. Some of our cooks are masters and we look forward to their offerings. Throw a few bucks on the table and you'll probably eat like a king. Bad meals will be rewarded with, "This was fit for a king. Here, King, here, boy," feeding an imaginary dog under the table. No mercy. The off-going crew wearily drifts off, leaving us to go over the day's agenda. The cook scoops up the pile of greenbacks and asks, "Any requests?"

"Liver," I answer.

At the end of the long table, someone adds, "Chinese."

I look over the top of my paper and end it with, "You're cooking. Surprise us."

Conversation runs the gamut. It ranges from talk about our kids' education to whatever is in the newspaper being shuffled about the table. Often, it's a bitch session focusing on department policies or perpetual union-administration squabbles. "Hey, how's Lackovic doing?" He's on Ladder 9 in our battalion and is on injury leave after accidentally dipping his circular saw into his leg on a smoky roof. The spinning blade neatly sliced open his thigh, down to the bone. "He's doin' fine. Comin' back soon," someone answers. Approving nods all around. Wojo says, "Good truck man, Lacky. It can happen to anyone." More nods.

Invariably, talk turns to women, with Don grinning through his dark, perfect moustache, cupping his hands and forming a heart in front of him explaining that his favorite is a gal with a heart-shaped ass and "with tits that stand out to here," moving his hands out from his chest. "With 'nipplus erectus,' those babies stand out like two young lieutenants standing at attention at Engine 2." I had heard it before, but I lowered the paper, feigned a surprised look and said, "Why, Don, I didn't know you could speak Latin," snapping the paper upright before he could answer. The conversation veered toward the differences in labial shapes when the boss interrupted, shoving papers at us: "Okay, okay, enough. Here's the latest notices. Initial them after you read them." Someone curses, taking offense at the notice that cautions, "Be sure overhead door is opened before pulling out of quarters." It had been issued after a ladder truck was driven through an overhead door when someone inadvertently hit the "down" button.

Our battalion chief came around in late morning on his rounds, dropping off department mail. He usually ended up in the kitchen for a cup of joe, dispensing important news, sometimes just sharing hunting or fishing stories, or golf tips to anyone who gathered around. Don didn't come in for that, saying that those who did were "knob gobblers" and "tit-takers." Sometimes, I thought he was right. Chief Don "Warzy" Warzala ran the neighboring Second Battalion on our shift. He said that Engine 5 was his favorite house. I liked Warzy. Half of our fires, if not more, were in his battalion. He was a good tactician, personable, and much respected. He revealed to me one day that since he was losing his aide, he would like me to drive him. That was great honor, and I looked forward to the step up, but the union pressed to have the chief's aide position eliminated. That added to my growing dissatisfaction with the union. Every time Warzy popped in, and I was cooking, he stuck his nose into pots steaming on the stove, tasted its contents, and added — when I wasn't looking — whatever spice he thought it needed. He not only visited us for meals, he joined us on the tailboard for a smoke after a fire was knocked down. Warzy didn't hide his disapproval of women on the job, and when Debbie Pross, our first female firefighter, was assigned from school to Warzy's beloved Second Battalion, he kept her out of his house as he had vowed, assigning her instead to Engine 21. But Warzy would mellow, and he really changed his tune after our female paramedics tended to him when he suffered a heart attack. Under the tutelage of a tough, fair boss, Fred Kasierling, Debbie made the grade.

An hour after shift began it was housework, which included everything from cleaning the rig to mopping the floors. All equipment was doubly checked. Before lunch, we were back in the kitchen, enjoying the smells wafting from the cook area, and maybe helping the cook prepare the meal. The noon meal often was the larger of the two; meat and potatoes, veggies, salad, and maybe desert. Often heard while digging into the feast was, "I wonder what the poor people are eating today." I kiddingly asked Don if he left the lock off the cabinet so the wife and kids could get at the saltines. In between runs we practiced hose layouts in a nearby field, inspected hazard sites, had young members practice driving, or hooked up with nearby companies to train. Kovatch frowned on TV watching during the day. Normally, after 6 P.M. was our time. Some days we didn't turn a wheel until it got dark, and then the calls came in, sometimes not stopping until the early morning hours.

If it was daybreak, often we didn't bother slogging back to the rack. After a fire, there was work to do and we were too wound up to get back to sleep anyway. Sometimes, we critiqued the fire. If it hadn't gone well, we might be at the table getting our asses chewed. By morning, we were the sullen, weary faces at the kitchen table, dirty hands clutching the cup of steaming mud, waiting for our reliefs to walk in the door. And when they did, they knew they'd hear, "We're not hiring."

I was grateful for the long drive home, which allowed me to make the transition from work to family mode. When I arrived home, I covered only the highlights of my shift to Pat's half-ear and really got into being with my kids. If the weather was kind, out came the bikes and it was off to the park. Sometimes just holding the kids, feeling their soft skin and smelling their hair, was all I needed. I didn't realize then that those moments wouldn't last forever, and that our worlds would change so dramatically.

Being partnered with Rescue Squad 8 meant that engine guys would, in rotation, fill the slots of squad men on their days off. No one relished "the puker," so no one volunteered. Those regularly assigned to the squad had their reasons for wanting the assignment, which I didn't question. Some were content not to daily face flames, eat smoke, or work at heights or in darkness. Better them than me, nevertheless. But if I drew the duty, I made the best of

Often more challenging than greater alarm fires was the basic dwelling fire. Milwaukee's Engine Company 13 had just pulled up to this "worker," and firefighters moved quickly to enter the home to rescue occupants. Despite their efforts, a woman died in the blaze.

it. The right partner could even make for an interesting day. Sometimes I fought the craziness by four-wheeling through barren fields or playing tunes with the various settings of the electronic siren. I was getting quite good at it and it got the attention of drivers who had become conditioned to sirens as usual neighborhood noise.

A day on the squad guaranteed a sleepless night, meals when you could grab them, and confrontation with some of our pillars of society. Trust in each other was vital since there were only two of us, versus five, and we carried no heavy tools into dangerous environments. Only once do I recall a partner placing us in jeopardy, when a young woman with a bloody hand and two fingers missing ran out of a house screaming that she had been stabbed. Hysterical, she ran back inside, and my partner dashed in after her. "Bob, no!" I yelled. "The cops are coming." Luckily, the knife wielder had split, and the cops showed up as I ran in after him. Later, I asked, "Bob, what the hell are you doing?" I was astonished when he answered that since he was black, they'd listen to him. He said he could reason with them. "Christ, Bob," I fired back, "you saw what a black guy did to a black woman. Now what do you think your life is worth in there? You with a uniform, representing authority, and riding in with whitey?" He turned sheepish. I liked Bob and didn't want to scold him, but the run could have taken a bad turn.

So many runs by our busy rescue squads had taken a bad turn that engine companies were sent with them. Something had to be done, especially after Squad 4's crew had been ambushed in a dark hallway, and one of our squads was stolen on a run, killing a woman when it crashed into her car. Seeing the woman speared by jagged metal infuriated bystanders who pulled the thief from the squad and beat him. He admitted he thought there were drugs in the car. Paramedic units had drugs, and their vehicles were identical to squads. The number of tense, often violent, confrontations between inner city companies and civilians rose dramatically. Something had to be done. Bureaucracy got in the way of quick, sure-fire solutions, so word spread among our crews to call for a ladder company if things got ugly. A band-aid solution, maybe, but it brought a bunch of guys with big tools. So our number of runs increased, and our squad crews felt safer in numbers.

One of four babies I delivered while on the job was with Bob Bett on Squad 8. One night we were to meet the police in the intersection of 20th and Vliet streets. All we saw when we pulled up was a taxi in the middle of the street and a police car nearby. *Looks pretty calm; shouldn't be a big deal; the cabbie probably got rolled.* Peering into the cab with a light, I saw sprawled out on the back seat a young, very pregnant woman, knees drawn up, while the cop knelt in the front seat leaning over into the back with a flashlight. He looked up at us and said, "She's having a baby." I quipped, "Can't get anything past you, huh?" The cab driver sat motionless, staring straight ahead as though waiting for his fare to pay and get out.

Mom was calm and said very little except answers to our questions. She told us she was 18 and this was her third child. Her pain was moderate. Her quietness was unnerving; not what we expected from a woman pushing out a child. When she had called her doctor, he told her she had time and to take a cab to the hospital. Now the baby's glistening head shone in my light, so there was no time to waste. Bob hurriedly gathered from the OB kit items we would need, and none too soon. Out slipped baby into my hands. When I exclaimed to mom, "Hey, you have a little girl!" she said nothing but just smiled weakly. I guessed this was a routine event for her and it meant only an uncertain future filled with more struggle and heartache. We suctioned the baby, laid it on her belly, and tied and cut the cord. Then it was wrapped and we dashed to the hospital, her original destination. I asked the cop to follow the cab the few blocks to the hospital so we didn't have to take time to move the woman.

A nurse I knew grabbed me at the hospital, wrinkled her nose when she looked at my messy hands, and ordered, "The baby's fine. You come with me.

Let's get you cleaned up." Another nurse came over to say it looked like the mother had an STD. This whole bringing-a-baby-into-the-world thing was losing appeal fast.

Typically, the regularly assigned squad person rode in the back tending the patient en route to the hospital, and the fill-in drove. I was especially grateful for that arrangement the day Greg Davis and I had a lady who had blistering burns from her shoulders up. Most of her hair had burned away when it ignited as she leaned over a stove. The stench of burned hair and skin, along with her constant screaming the long distance to St. Mary's Burn Center, nearly caused me to crash into a light pole.

The life of a squad man, and later a squad woman, to me was a special calling. I saw numerous examples of difficult situations they dealt with. One with a humorous note, to us at least, happened when Tom Heine worked his regular spot on the squad. When their rig backed in, I noticed the driver's rearview mirror was shattered, and there were huge scratches in its white paint. Tom climbed out looking flustered, a look we seldom saw on mild-mannered Tom. His partner explained that their patient turned out to be an M-O, which meant requiring mental observation. When they stood on her porch and knocked on the door, she burst through the door waving a huge knife. Tom went over the railing and his partner cleared the steps in one leap. She focused on tall, handsome, ripped, blue-eyed, blonde-haired Tom.

Waving that big knife and screaming, "I want you, you blue-eyed devil!" she chased Tom down the street as he yelled "10–54" into his walkie-talkie. That ten-code meant "need police assistance immediately." He doubled back to get to the squad and his partner, with his admirer on his tail, still screaming. Around the squad they went, with her attacking the vehicle with the knife. She forgot about Tom for a moment and got inside the rig. At least now they knew where she was, but the wide back doors flew open and out flew medical kits that shattered and spread their contents when they hit the pavement. "Ah, shit," was all Tom could say. Anything else not secured came out too. She jumped out and went to work on the squad again, giving Tom a few more spins around the rig, squealing that she'd get that white, blue-eyed devil!

The cops rolled in, drew their guns and talked the woman out of the knife, and off to the hoosegow she went, certain to end up in a secure observation ward. Tom didn't say much about the party, and we helped as best we could to get their rig back in order. We took our time so they could wind down before hitting the streets again. We're far enough along in this book for you to guess the ribbing Tom took about being the object of affection of his newfound girlfriend.

Tom's wild episode was one of countless runs that supported my statement, which held that while riding the squad for six months, you will see every type of crime committed with every type of weapon imaginable, and every type of injury. I also said that every politician, every judge, every juror, and toss in most liberals, ought to experience that six months on the puker.

Over time, I felt that I was becoming a pretty good judge of character when dealing with civilians. It became easier to tell if they were sincere, what their game was. Figuring people out didn't mean that you could confront them with your discovery, as that often invited trouble. I remember, for example, after a long night on the rescue squad, being part of an emergency response to a jumper on the 35th Street viaduct. We held back on one end of the viaduct so all the commotion didn't panic the person. On a railroad light tower, which was next to the viaduct and rising above it, was a young man standing on the tower railing talking to a cop below him. The railing hemmed the tower's square platform and it was only four or five inches wide. But the guy actually seemed comfortable standing on it.

Initial attempts to find out his problem and talk him down failed. He seemed to make a grand show of his lofty perch, even walking it like a guard walking a perimeter. Obviously, he reveled in the attention. His deftness at height impressed me, but that's where my admiration ended. I knew he wasn't serious about ending his life; he would have done it quietly, sans fanfare. Swearing at the cops and firefighters below, and throwing light bulbs at them, he reminded me of a tyrant controlling his subjects.

I watched amused for a while. When a priest was summoned, he swore at him and lobbed a couple of bulbs. Everyone, it seemed, took their turn talking to him. It only encouraged him to go on. His sister was brought to the scene and that really set him off. *Aha, trouble in the family. He's sending them a big message.* It went on for hours, the talking, cops trying to make their way up the tower. This is stalemated, I thought. Most of us knew he wasn't serious, just needed to be M-O'd. Since we had a long night and now it was way past our shift end, I told my partner I'd be in the back, getting some shuteye on the stretcher. "Wake me when he jumps or comes down. There are only so many light bulbs on that tower."

After a short nap, I asked my partner, dozing in the front seat, if our friend was still up there. Peering upward, he droned, "Yeah, nothing's happening." I'd had enough. I climbed out and said to the weary cops, "Mind if I have a word with this bozo?"

"Be our guest," one said with a sweeping wave.

My heavy soles crunching on broken glass, I got within light bulb range and hollered up to the guy: "Hey asshole, see this mess?" Boredom had brought me to the point of telling him to end his stupid game, that everyone, including him, is tired, that he's tied up traffic so bad that people were late for work, and that he probably got more attention than he counted on.

"Fuck you, man," he answered half heartedly.

"Yeah, fuck you too. What's got you so pissed off? You think some of us haven't been where you are?" The police supervisor standing near me with arms folded nodded in agreement.

"You think you got problems?" I went on. "We see people with problems every day." I told him to give it another shot. Then I yelled to him that he wasn't serious, but if he wanted to jump, to do it so we could scoop up his body and get on with our day. My anger was genuine. He looked surprised, then relented and sat on the railing. That was a risky judgment call on my part, but no other approach had worked and eventually, he would tire and fall. He climbed down into the arms of Milwaukee's Finest. The chief sauntered over, grinning, and said, "Mutz, I don't know who's crazier, him or you."

"Sometimes bein' crazy helps, chief. And who's to say what crazy is, anyway?"

Craziness was what Bob Bett described one day when he returned from a run with Squad 8. They were tending to a huge woman who had brawled with family members, when in the middle of the chaotic scene the woman casually told Bob that he should take a look at the guy in the next room too. Bob peered in to see a guy face down on a bed, a large knife sticking out of his back. He was dead. Now that's craziness.

Despite such craziness, my most indelible image of working in the ghetto came not from a heinous crime scene, or from the charred skeleton of a burned-out building, but in a dimly lit, broken-down house where four little kids stood quietly, wide-eyed, looking up at Myron towering over them, black like them and made even larger by his bulky turnout gear. The kids were dirty, wearing only faded, torn underwear. Each held a bowl in which were pieces of bread, nothing more. Radiators in the old shack clanged and hissed as they competed against winter drafts blowing through broken windows.

"Look at that," one of our guys said, shining a light on the kitchen wall, making legions of roaches scatter; "moving walls," we called them. Roaches too freely traversed the rumpled, dark-stained sheet atop the bed on which the four little ones slept. Despite our indifference to the squalor, we had social services intervene, knowing it didn't make the adults any more responsible.

We told our cubs never to lean against anything in a place like that, and to shake their clothes out well, stomp their feet, so they didn't take home any unwanted pets.

I had passed the five-year mark at Engine 5. I suppose to a degree I was desensitized. One had to be. And I had developed rough edges. I stood my ground with people whose sole intent was to give us a hard time. I knew my job. I knew my limits. The more the stress of a situation ramped up, the calmer I got. It was a weird defense mechanism. I was told I could command authority without being authoritative. It was a great experience, but it was time to go. My cohorts were beginning to say I was insensitive. Wojo ribbed me by echoing something we were told on a run: "Ya'll ain't got no compassion." They were kidding, but I figured the mere mention had foundation. Confirmation came at a house fire where I tried to break in the door, at which I shined. Three tries, with a well-placed mule kick or an axe, and we were usually in. This door wouldn't give no matter how hard I put the head of my axe to the lock section. A scruffy guy at the bottom of the stairs taunted me. "C'mon man, you gotta get in there." I ignored him as I re-aimed. Wham! Still no give. My friend kept it up. "Hey man, what's wrong wit ya'll?" Wham! Nothing. "C'mon mista fi...." I spun around and snapped, "Here, asshole. You take a try!" and slid the axe down the stairs where it landed at his feet. He was stunned. Our MPO, Stan, put his hand on the guy's shoulder and shooed him away.

Back at quarters, Stan came in the kitchen where I sat alone, smiled politely and said, "Wayne, I think it's time. You need to take a ride."

I felt like a quitter when I answered, "Maybe you're right," but Stan was right. I was committed to my family, and maybe I wouldn't have to try so hard to maintain balance. I was so up to my ears in the job that I had become critical of things I didn't feel were beneficial to us. One of them was the "warming bus." Someone on the third floor worked out a deal with the transport company for them to bring a bus to a fire, especially in winter, where we would be tied up for a couple of hours. Typically, the first-in company at a fire was last out. That was simply how it worked and it made sense because that rig was stripped of lines that were committed. Later-arriving companies that used less equipment could get back in service quicker. Besides, a company likely had transferred into our quarters to cover our area. And that crew didn't leave until they had helped us get back in service.

So at a house fire on a winter night, the bus came. I was told to take a break and go warm up. Sitting in the bus only made me feel that we were dragging this out needlessly. It was better to stay working, keep the momentum, and not rest or warm up for a long period because that only made it harder to get back in the game. Sitting there, watching other crews work, I knew that we were losing focus; that sense of newness dulled. The bus was a terrific idea for people left homeless by fire, until the Red Cross arrived and got them to shelter.

Many of us noticed policy changes, which included overkill at alarms. More people and rigs than ever stood idle at fires. The silhouette of all these firefighters standing there leaning on pike poles reminded me of a group of shepherds. And if that didn't look bad on the nightly news, I didn't know what did. It's bad enough that most news images of firefighters at a scene show them standing around, as though they've been summoned merely to give their assessment. The truth is that either they managed the incident before news hounds arrived, or others are working where you can't take cameras.

My last day at Engine 5 was on Squad 8. I was teamed with John "Radar" Konetz. Radar knew his way around and we made a good team. We hit 20 runs, which was nowhere near record. In the vestige of darkness, we were sent to a stabbing, which wasn't our first of the shift. We arrived at the projects and lugged our medical kits to where we saw a group of people. The scene was typical: a group of cops, onlookers, a victim, and nearby, the evildoer in cuffs.

As we drew closer, we noticed a woman sitting in a chair. When a cop stepped in front of us to say she was in bad shape, it didn't make sense that she was sitting upright, conscious, and not saying a word. When we closed the distance all we saw was red. She was covered in blood. The lap of her dress formed a bowl that was filled with it. She held a small blood-soaked towel to the side of her head. We leaned in and I said, "Let's have a look." When she pulled the towel away and the cop shined his light on her, I sensed the other cops looking away. We were amazed to see the entire side of her head split open vertically, in front of her ear, down to her jaw. White sinewy tissue glistened in the light. Now I understood why the other cops were keeping their distance. It was a ghastly sight. The woman was stout, but considering that wound and her blood loss, she should not have been conscious.

The helpful cop then shined his light onto something on the ground nearby. "That's what he used." I recognized a commando knife, also called a trench knife; a long, slender blood-stained blade, its handle a wide menacing arc of finger holes with large points on the outside of the arc. In the military this was a fearsome close-in combat weapon. Nearby, surrounded by cops, stood handcuffed the huge, shirtless monster: the boyfriend. Given his size, he didn't need the knife to inflict damage to the woman. *But why take chances? What if she fought back?*

After we used all the trauma packs we had to pack the wound, Radar told me to get the couple of sanitary napkins in the bottom of the kit. Good idea. We heard the med unit's siren, ever so thankful they were coming in to take over with their advanced skills and equipment. Bone-tired like us, they plodded to where we were and I described to their team leader the incredible wound, asked the cop to show them the weapon with his flashlight, and added that we'd get their cot. She stunned me with, "Are we 10–8?" meaning off of this run and back in service. After a moment of paralyzed speechlessness, I blurted, "What? Are you shittin' me? Do you see that blood? She's lucky she's alive." Incensed, I demanded that they run with the patient. With a look of disgust and resignation, she turned to her crew and said, "Okay, go get the cot."

Looking again at the angry face of the monster in cuffs, it struck me that if in war I could kill an unknown enemy, I could kill this animal.

During the ride back to quarters, squinting through dry, tired eyes at the sun's rays stabbing through pewter clouds, Radar and I shared x-rated opinions about the monster criminal, the med officer, and the depravity of the entire godforsaken area.

Stan was right. I needed a ride.

6

Scary Stuff

Next to my name on the transfer list was "Engine Company 33," on the south side's Forest Home Avenue. I hoped I didn't find the street name a literal description of a tranquil resting place. Pushing nine years on the job, the south side seemed like a good place for a respite, and no more. I would be spared the long ride across town and be in a more hospitable neighborhood. But Engine 33 got few runs, and the old house was smelly and one of the most cramped. Sharing the old dump with the five-person engine was the Third Battalion Chief and Med Unit 3.

The few benefits of being on the south side were offset by the cold, hard fact that our job was intervention in people's lives when they most needed help. I accepted that much easier than I accepted the regimen, and the very character, of the old house. Granted, a slower company meant a slower pace, but complacency had long been in residence there. My crew comprised old-timers. When I asked how the night watch rotation worked, I was told I wouldn't have to take watch. My curiosity was met with, "Because the boss's wife doesn't want him sleeping in the same dorm with women, so he takes permanent watch." And that was only one of the indications that this was a separate fire department, unlike that from which I had just transferred. Antagonism between the female paramedics and the old-timers on the engine hung in the dank air. Soon it became obvious that this place also housed chief's pets, pathetic brown noses who shadowed the old chiefs and laughed too hard at their jokes.

Since I was big on goals, my new goal was to get out of that place as soon as possible. In the meantime, I told my chief, Stanley Gumm, who I thought was the best of the three Third Battalion chiefs, I was his to do with as he wished. I offered that I was eligible to serve as acting lieutenant, I would happily fill in as the EMT on the med unit, and, since I could drive any rig in his battalion, I would serve as acting MPO; anything to avoid having to spend the entire shift sitting around with the old farts; anything to feel productive, anything to avoid falling into the pit of boredom and complacency.

I interacted most with those assigned to the med unit, simply because they were younger, and they too took a dim view of the sexism and improprieties that permeated the place like its bad odor. A number of people watched my arrival with interest because I would be working in proximity with one of the females whose presence stirred controversy when women first came through the training school. But she and I, for the most part, had moved on and we got along fine, even working together on the med unit, where she was in charge. When I later discovered that one of the older guys had kicked her, I urged her to press charges against him. Beside the ritualized interaction around which male firefighters wrapped their masculinity — interaction characterized by razzing peers to remain self-assured — this house practiced ignoring females in such rituals. The boys took umbrage at the fact that their firehouse no longer was a haven for all-white male conversation. As a unit, they fed each other's bitterness. Many of us do it to some degree.

The meek engine boss had long since relinquished his authority, even deferring to the cook, who every afternoon announced, "Goin' for bread, boss," which translated to "Goin' for nookie" or "Goin' for a few beers." There was no reason for the cook to go out shopping twice during the shift. In his defense, however, he did return two hours later with a loaf of bread; it was usually stale and came from the bakery two doors from the firehouse. When the guy was off, the paramedics asked me to cook, knowing that I enjoyed it and didn't do a bad job of it. I was happy to oblige and show up the regular cook, who fumed when he heard I gave everyone their money's worth. Sometimes the meds "carried," which meant they were watching their beltlines, or simply refused to put money in the cook's pocket. The latter meant a stop at nearby Leon's custard stand.

I saw numerous examples of the laxity and unprofessionalism that prevailed. The old house fronted the street, separated by a sidewalk often used by elderly residents visiting the nearby cemetery. One day, one of our oldtimers heard noise I was making with a shovel, scraping up broken glass and high weeds growing through the cracks of the walk. He admonished, "What are you doing?" I answered that one day one of the old folks was going to trip on the trash, and besides, it looked bad. I was astonished when he replied that doing things like that would only make the bosses expect it all the time. He had me at a loss for words, and I could only come back by telling him to get the hell away from me if he wasn't going to help.

The worst example came in the middle of the night, when we were awakened by five rings for a fire. Acting on reflex, in one fluid motion I sat up, swung sideways, planted my feet into the boots and bunker pants next to my bed, and hoisted the suspenders over my shoulders, which brought the bulky pants up as I stood. Then I ambled to the nearest pole hole and slid to the apparatus floor. Within those 20 seconds, information about the fire came over the house speakers. I threw on my coat hanging nearby and climbed up onto the rig. Silence. No one was coming. I heard no commotion, no movement. *Am I going nuts? I did hear the alarm come in, didn't I? Where the hell is everyone?* Then, finally, movement. A couple of the guys came down the stairs, not bothering with the pole, scratching their asses, yawning. My driver came out of the bathroom, zipping up. I couldn't believe what I was seeing. They clambered aboard the engine as though we were going out for a practice drive. When we got back, I said to no one, but loud enough for everyone to hear, "If I see that again, I'll write up this whole fuckin' place!" They looked hurt. Even worse was the slow drive to the address of the fire. My driver was known for dawdling so that "those young bucks" on other companies could be first in and lay out their hose. Only once did he drive the expected speed with lights and siren to an address of a reported fire — it was his address.

The activity, challenge and excitement I longed for came from working on the med unit with two paramedics. I drove while they worked in the back on patients. Since there weren't enough med units to adequately cover the city, we often filled in for north side units, which meant a dash across the 27th Street viaduct. We got our share of vehicle accidents, trauma, cardiac cases, and the usual business from the knife and gun club. Suicides in our area were significantly lower in number than other areas I had worked in. In fact, I recall only one — a call from a concerned neighbor took us to a south side apartment where we found a lady seemingly in repose on a bed. Clutched in her hand was a rusty, battered .38-caliber revolver that looked as though it shouldn't have worked. But the hole in the woman's temple proved that it was, indeed, capable of firing. On the kitchen table was a note to her husband saying she couldn't take the pain of cancer anymore, and how much she loved him. He was due to arrive from work soon so they could have lunch. She was 49 years old. I hated reading suicide notes.

While some firefighters preferred not to have a med unit in their house, I usually enjoyed the paramedics' company and was grateful for the learning experience when I worked with them. Especially interesting was the variety of approaches and bedside manner they used to manage their patients. Unlike some of the boys who stuck out their chests and defended their territory and their manhood, I didn't feel threatened by the women. And they didn't wear negligees in the dorm as some of the wives seemed to think. I especially enjoyed watching the reaction of wives who came to the firehouse to visit their husbands. I swore I could read their minds as they gave a female paramedic the once-over: *So that's so and so; so that's what she looks like.* Our women held their own and did their jobs, the same, if not better, than some of the boys. Some were proud combatants in the protracted sexual revolution and came on strong in opposition to sexism. That tended to widen the gap rather than bringing about a solution; nevertheless, theirs were voices that had to be heard. The wind of change was blowing, and we had to lean into it and move on.

While many shied away from acting positions to fill in for MPOs and bosses on off days, I jumped at every opportunity, more for the challenge and experience than the few extra dollars on my paycheck. With the position of MPO came awesome responsibility from not only driving the big rig with five people on board, but operating the pump to get water. Firefighters, who drove ladder trucks complained that although they too had great responsibility, theirs was not a promoted position and they didn't get an extra dime for it. The union responded by pushing for a new position called heavy equipment operator, or HEO, which encompassed drivers of both engines and ladder trucks. Most of the MPOs bristled at the concept because they could now be assigned to a ladder company and end up on a burning roof, and not at a pump panel, somewhat out of harm's way. Having had enough of fighting fires often was the reason some aspired to become MPOs. But the union, which wasn't known for representing factions such as chief's aides, MPOs and paramedics, got its way and everyone had to adjust.

During shifts when I acted as MPO, I was in a higher state of alertness, replaying in my mind street directions and procedures for getting water. I remembered well the sting of once not being able to get water when I was acting MPO on Engine 5. I was exonerated because I hadn't been shown the trick to bypass a step when the old spare rig refused to go into pump gear. Being cleared of responsibility didn't matter because our cub, Myron, got burned waiting for water at the top of the stairs to the burning attic, and Captain Kovatch was in my face demanding to know if it was my fault. Myron, bless him, didn't hold it against me.

As acting MPO one day on Engine 33, all of my conscious efforts went out the window when my boss ordered me *not* to do my job. We were second-in on a house fire on South 16th Street. I saw Engine 23 pull in on the narrow street and I knew the MPO would stop near the burning house and drop off the crew that would lay out lines. Seeing me at the other end of the block, he knew that I would turn around and back down the street to drop off a large line and lay out to a hydrant to supply him. If I did my job right, Engine 23's crew would have all the water it needed. But when I began my sweeping turn, my boss barked, "No!" I thought I heard wrong or was about to hit something I didn't see. Tapping on the brakes, I snapped, "What?" I had heard him right because he said, "Don't back down." This was no time for discussion, and knowing his dull character, I didn't think he had just thought of a brilliant alternate tactic. "Are you serious?" I yelled that they were waiting on us, that they need water, that I *had* to supply them. I couldn't believe he then told me to pull forward down the street and our crew would assist Engine 23. I slammed the rig into park gear and ran to help Engine 23's MPO drag a large line to a hydrant near them, explaining through short breaths to the fuming guy what my boss had ordered.

Dodging procedure as we did caused a serious time delay, giving the fire time to gain headway. *Christ, I hope there's no one in there.* As I watched the fire break through the roof, Chief Gumm came up to me, looked me in the eye, then up the street to where my rig was parked, then back into my eyes and said, "Wayne, what's this?"

Looking over his shoulder to see flames chasing Ladder 14's crew off of the roof, I fumed that *this* was what I had been ordered to do. Adamantly, I went on that I would grab the first chance that came along to get off of the south side, because it was just too scary for me.

He surprised me by lowering his hooded eyes and saying that he didn't blame me, and he'd help where he could.

It wasn't any better acting as a boss. Few of the guys with time on the job would act, I believed, because they didn't think their pals would take them seriously; and they didn't want to get eaten alive by the old-timers, some of whom were so intimidating they were called "acid tongues." In any workplace, being a boss to older, more experienced workers is a challenge. It means walking a fine line, respecting their experience, yet carefully exercising authority. I equated a few of the old-timers to the wolf that is capable of sensing the weakness of its prey. Thankfully, there were more who remembered where they came from and showed respect if you treated them fairly, and they were happy to share their expertise. Usually, the dedication and professionalism of even the gruffest old-timers shined through when they realized you meant business. It was a mind game. For example:

Engine 10 on the southwest side was nicknamed "the country club," and for good reason. Not only was it a large house nestled into a quiet neighborhood, it was said to be a repository for friends of the chief, many of whom were golfers. For those who desired to sit back and wait for retirement, it was said to be a gravy assignment since Engine 10, and its partner Ladder 17, rarely turned a wheel. My reputation as a "black cat," meaning I brought work to slow companies I visited, held true one day when I was acting lieutenant at Engine 10.

The day had the usual start: first, tell the boss who I was relieving with the phrase "You're down," meaning I had replaced his turnout gear with mine, then ask if there was anything I should pay particular attention to, and check my mask — but before the 8 A.M. punches came through the joker stand, I had already disrupted routine at Engine 10. When the warning bell on my mask sounded, two guys poked their heads from the kitchen to see what the noise was. I grinned, knowing this could be a long day. At least the bell didn't have them running for the phone. *My mask works fine; theirs had better.*

After I checked the daybook to see who my crew was, I went into the kitchen to meet them. The words I first heard gave me more reason to worry: "Hey boss, relax. Nothing ever happens around here. We'll take care of you today." The morning went okay, with everyone going about their usual routine. After a great lunch of fried bluegill and homemade coleslaw and potato pancakes, someone yelled, "To the beds." He wasn't kidding. At what workplace can you sit at a kitchen table and have coffee and bakery, chat and read the paper, and then eat a big meal at noon? In the afternoon, it's wash your car, nap, work out, work on hobbies, and then get called to supper. Then it's TV, go to bed, and maybe get a run, or God forbid, a fire. Gravy. *But a black cat is with you today.*

In the middle of the night, snoring in the stuffy dorm was stilled by five rings for a fire. We got out of the barn in good time and I kept my ear to the radio for first-due Engine 29's report. *Damn, they should have been there by now.* I called the dispatcher because maybe in the excitement, 29's boss forgot to radio "10–23" (arrived at scene) and a few words describing what they found. Dispatch hasn't heard. *Shit. Something's wrong.* I radioed Engine 29 on fire-ground frequency, but no answer. *They must have their hands full.*

When we pulled up, I quickly gathered in some of the sights to form a quick picture of what might be going on. In my view was Engine 29's rig with no one around, a few people, including a young girl, nude, except for a short nightie that went only to her navel. The teen was dazed, not aware of her dress. That meant something had traumatized her. And I smelled smoke. *They're in that building and something's up. Now to sort it out.* I radioed to the dispatcher and incoming companies that there was smoke in the area, and possibly a working fire in a three-story apartment building. Again I radioed Engine 29. Nothing. I'd had enough. I snapped at my crew, "Goddammit, something's up. Get masks on and get a line in there!" One of my crew, who I would discover later had a severe alcohol abuse problem, not only pulled the wrong hose pack off the rig, but dropped it in a pile. He was one of the cocky old-timers who, at the beginning of the shift, told me what he'd do if something happened. I sternly corrected him by saying that instead he would wait for my word. Now, he was loaded and as useless as the heap of hose that lay at his feet. I ordered him to stay outside and to get the girl covered up.

I ran the steps looking for the fire, finding smoke on the third floor. Up we went, humping a line. At the end of the long hall was Engine 29 in a cluster-fuck. Visible in the smoke was an elderly woman down on the floor. I ordered two guys to get her out of there. The dispatcher had wisely sent a med unit. We got the line into the burning apartment, and as soon as we knocked down the fire, I went out into the hall to find 29's boss. I pulled him around the corner, got in his face, and read him the riot act. You can fill in the dialogue. Then, back at quarters, I went after my drunken fireman, in private. Incensed, I told him that his selfishness put us one man dangerously short! "Get help," I insisted. "Do something about it, because if I ever work with you again, I'll lay you up." I would work with him again, and it created a shit storm of controversy.

Alcoholism was a problem on the job. Not only was it going on in some firehouses, it was said that some chiefs hid their drunks in slow houses, where they only drank more. Most of us could name the drinking houses. Veterans told me that some actually had cocktail hours, when someone's trunk in a secluded parking lot opened to reveal a portable bar. We heard too of both firefighters and bosses becoming so incapacitated that they were left on the rig at fires. I saw it one afternoon when a fill-in boss on our ladder company couldn't be wakened for a fire. One of the guys finally slapped his face, hard, but his loud snoring never missed a beat, so we took off without him. We gave him an earful when we returned. *Since our schedule allows two days off and you still needed to drink on duty, you have a problem.* And we had only one guy handling the relatively new Employee's Assistance Program for thousands of city employees. A small part of the solution came from the chief's new city-wide transfer policy, which was intended to equalize the age and experience of fire companies. It created uproar among old-timers who felt betrayed because they felt they had served their time in the hole and were entitled to ride out their last few years in a slow house. Nor did it sit well with young, aggressive firefighters who preferred to serve in busy companies. But young and old switched places across the city, quelling the pervasive old-timer attitude in outlying areas. It was rumored that one of the desired effects of the policy was to rid the department of some of the old and dead wood. It did prompt more retirements, but I was impressed with many old-timers who found it in themselves to rise to the task, performing admirably in busy houses. Some even seemed to revel in the opportunity to get back to where the hot bricks flew. Some, in their entire careers, had never been there.

Seeing how the various battalions operated not only gave me perspective, but also bolstered my appreciation for the positive aspects of the job. Within the gloomy confines of the old house during the long shift, it was sometimes difficult to see the glass as half full. Patrice Ripple, a paramedic I had worked with on the north side, helped the hands of the clock move. Often, while I retreated to a cramped corner of a second-floor hall to read, "Rips" sat on the floor using a locker as a backrest, and we gabbed about an endless number of topics. Patrice, to this day, clearly recalls her med unit following our engine to a fire in a three-story apartment building where I broke through a floor, but didn't fall completely through. Such calamities must have become commonplace, because I barely remember the incident.

On the plus side, despite being mentally tired from the long shift, I didn't have to fight the effects of physical exhaustion to enjoy time with family. Jeff, at ten years old, was active in baseball and I was thrilled to watch him play. My darling Joanna, at seven, was the apple of my eye. Joe was a playful five and Jason's arrival to the world was on the horizon. They made it easy to separate job from family. And there were always improvements to be made to the house, which I had expanded to a two-story. Jeff's interest and skill at model-building and his involvement with scouts provided more great father-and-son opportunities.

Because of my commitment to family, I limited myself to occasional fire department social events. Year-on parties (to celebrate completion of a probie's first year) and bowling sweepers (annual tournaments) were well-attended events. So much liquor flowed that some of the fire guys put aside their contempt for women on the job, freeing their hormonal inner selves, igniting many a hot rumor. Some women, however, felt duped after playing kissy-face with firemen, only to return to stone-age thinking back in the firehouse. Union meetings too sometimes proved a good excuse for a night on the town. Periodically, on a warm evening, the union prez mockingly raced through a meeting format, slammed down his gavel, calling it adjourned inside of 20 minutes, causing a rush for the door to get to the next "meeting place." I found it hilarious one summer when a few of the wives got together, with one commenting about the many issues that must have made a recent union meeting last so long that her hubby didn't get home till late. Reportedly, one of her friends finally piped up, "Honey, there are no union meetings in the summer." Taking first place in the "putting one over on the wife" category occurred when a few of the boys told their betrotheds they were going on a hunting trip, and then stashed their guns and gear and boarded a plane for Vegas. The jig was up when a bride discovered that hubby hadn't found the surprise she put in his gun case.

The opportunity I was seeking, to move on from the boredom and complacency, and that odor, of Engine 33 came in the form of a phone call. It was Jerry Frank, who was an up-and-comer, and who I had worked with at the academy where he was assigned as a captain. Jerry, I knew, looked after me, and now that he made battalion chief, he asked personally for me. This was a high honor. In Jerry's battalion was Engine 13, one of our busiest engines. When he asked how I liked it "down there," I didn't mince words about my desire to get off of the scary south side.

All business, he continued, "Okay. Maybe I can help. I'm looking for an experienced first pipe on Engine 13. The job's yours if you want it, and I could use you."

I couldn't believe I told him that although I was honored, that would be my fourth engine, and I had really been planning to submit a request for a busy ladder company to get truck experience. Jerry said he understood and then asked if I had a particular truck in mind.

What the hell, he asked and he has the power. Is he just curious or will he act on this?

"Ladder 9," I answered.

"Good choice, Mutz. You take care."

"You too, Jerry, and thanks."

I didn't make anything of it until about two weeks later when one of the old chiefs from another shift sat at the end of the table, brown-noses at his side like court jesters. He rumpled the transfer list as he squinted to read it. I tried to ignore him because I didn't care for him or his pets. My resentment for the old guff stemmed from his past comment that my friend, Ken Grabske, was a malingerer for lying up with health problems. That was just prior to Ken's massive fatal heart attack. "Who's this Mutza guy?" he stammered. A couple of people glanced at me and grinned but before anyone could answer, he babbled on that he didn't know I was getting shifted to Ladder 9, as though it had to be cleared through him, especially since he was friends with the chief of the department. *Yeah, you old prick. I've been in your house for months and you have no idea who I am.* His attitude riled me and I rose to say something, but halfway up, the guy next to me grabbed my arm and pulled downward, whispering in my ear, "Uh, uh, don't do it, Wayne. For once, shut up and let it go. You're getting a ride outta here. Don't blow it now."

He was right. I sat down and shut up.

7

Truck Man

Department manpower staffing held that a ladder company should run with a crew of five: an officer and four firefighters. Thankfully, the union vehemently opposed reorganization plans periodically proposed by chiefs, and rumblings from City Hall that not only would reduce ladder company manpower, but would eliminate ladder companies themselves.

Ladder company operations at a structure fire were based on the five-person crew. If a roof opening had to be made to vent the fire, three firefighters climbed either the aerial ladder or a 30-foot ground ladder, lugging two roof ladders and a power saw to the peak. Over the fire, perched on roof ladders hooked over the peak, two of them cut a large square opening, pulling back the shingles and roof boards with axes to vent smoke, heat and flame. The officer and youngest member, meanwhile, went inside for search and rescue, took out windows, or forced entry. The third firefighter operated as a swing man, helping either pair or working independently.

After engine crews knocked down the fire, ladder crews brought in a generator to power a large exhaust fan, or to power portable lighting. Everyone then worked to overhaul. If the fire had extensively involved the roof, it fell upon the ladder crew to "skin the roof," no easy task as it involved stripping off all shingles and even roof decking that flames had reached. Overhaul was a thorough process, removing most burned material and opening spaces where flame might be hiding. The tiniest flame that survived hidden deep in a corner, under debris, or between shingles could, hours later, have the place rolling again. The embarrassment and harassment that came on the heels of a rekindle usually was enough to motivate crews to do a thorough job the first time.

Ladder 9 shared quarters with Engine 32 and the Fifth Battalion chief in a west side neighborhood that reflected changing demographics; a steady increase in the number of alarms was a signpost of a declining society, rife with changing values. I was reminded of Engine 5, where sometimes it had seemed that we were in a war where lives and property were destroyed, and where the enemies were not only fire and human frailty, but hate and apathy.

The author poses with his mount while assigned to busy Ladder Company 9. The truck was a fast and powerful, unique flat-faced Mack equipped with a rear-mount aerial that reached 100 feet (courtesy Dale Mutza).

This was hardly a place where people hummed McCartney's *Ebony and Ivory*. Between the three rigs, some days the doors were open more often than closed. Such was life in neighborhoods where bad guys ruled and "mother" was only half of a word.

Throughout the area huge flats stood shoulder to shoulder, some so close together that we could jump from one roof to another. Narrow gangways not only ruled out the use of ground ladders, but also allowed fires to spread easily to adjacent buildings. Apartment buildings that lined the streets on the fringes of downtown provided plenty of action, and there was enough industry in the area to provide variety in alarms.

Ladder 9's rig was a straight-frame truck with a flat-faced Mack cab; nothing fancy, just a dependable workhorse. Its rear-mount, 100-foot aerial allowed it to be driven straight in to the fire building, eliminating the jackknife maneuvering of tractor-trailers necessary for stability. At the control pedestal, the driver quickly brought the "big stick" out of the bed, raising and extending it to the target. Our one-of-a-kind rig was known for belching huge clouds of black diesel smoke from its exhaust. Before air quality in our firehouses became a health concern, the walls of Engine 32 and Ladder 9 wore the dark stains of a busy house. Thankfully, the house was newly constructed, with living quarters relatively sealed from the apparatus bays. The firehouse-turned-outpost featured a parking lot surrounded by barbed wire. When break-ins and theft from our cars continued, and even loudspeakers were torn from the building, the enclosure was fortified with additional barbed wire. Some simply relented and left their cars unlocked so they could be rifled without windows being broken. Once, we were lured to the fringes of our area by a report of a fire with people trapped. Suspecting we'd been had, we hastily returned to quarters to find a young man trying to separate our TV from the bulky stand to which we had bolted it. He easily outran us.

I showed up early for work my first day at Ladder 9. When I approached the big rig, I discovered that someone already was clambering about, checking it over. It was Cindy Kuzminski, who had come from our paramedic ranks. Our introduction was cool but I expected nothing less. Although some played the seniority game to the hilt, and I had five years on Cindy, I listened to her few pointers about how they did things. I knew the ritual — regardless of knowing my way around the job, I would have to be accepted. I had to learn their organizational culture. It didn't take long to realize that Cindy was a non-participant in the boy-girl problems that plagued the department. She easily carried her own weight and did her job well. And she seemed to have the respect of her coworkers. Her slender frame belied her strength. She worked out with the guys regularly but she didn't go in for all the horseplay. Cindy wisely kept her private life just that, always maintaining a moderately low profile, warming to you only when you had earned her trust. The boss was Lt. Pepie Du De Voire, a friend and fellow ex-looper who loved the job as much as I did. Dennis Clay, who had been one of my recruits, drove the rig. The remaining firefighters were Mike Payne and "Country Joe" Kardach. Joe died at a young age, and the others rose in ranks ranging from lieutenant to assistant chief. Having six assigned to Ladder 9 meant that someone was either scheduled off or relieving someone on another company, usually within the battalion. We didn't fit the image of a typical truck crew, brutish hulks that engine men liked to say had strong backs and weak minds, knuckles dragging along the ground. Nevertheless, this was a young, solid crew that worked hard as a team, got along and had fun. It felt good to be there.

Fires were abundant and our rival was Ladder 12, which long held the lead as busiest truck in the city. Competition between the two often was so intense that drivers spared nothing to beat the opposition to the fire. That competitive spirit, unfortunately, sometimes caused accidents. Like the engine company that got the line to the fire, it was a matter of pride for the ladder company that "got the roof." That illustrates the uniqueness of the fire service; companies — teams, if you will — vied for the opportunity to do the toughest, most dangerous work. Yet, within the same service, in stark contrast, were individuals who not only were content to yield to the competition, but worked hard to avoid work.

Strange as it sounds, few jobs offer the opportunity to work to the point of exhaustion, yet to be grinning, feeling good about yourself and your teammates and what you accomplished. If things were slow, or someone was feeling pent up, we often joked that we needed a good knock-down, drag-out fire where we could vent, bust up a building and get our asses kicked. If someone was sick with a cold or hung over, we said that all they needed was a good snotty, pissed-up mattress fire. We got them often and they were, indeed, nasty. The routine was to crawl in, find the flaming mattress, knock the flames down with a hand pump, roll it up and get it to a window to toss outside. The danger lay in the smoldering bundle erupting into flames when it popped open and got air. Once, when we found a huge smoldering mattress on a second floor, we had to wrestle it down the stairs to get it through a doorway to the outside. We stumbled on the stairs, and the thing partially opened with me straddling it. There could be no better reminder than that flame impingement never to get in that position again.

Also high on the list of common, yet especially nasty, fires was "burnt meat." Food left cooking on a stove, when it burned to a char, gave off smoke that attacked and cut off one's airway. The name of the game was to remove it from the heat and open the place as fast as you could. You knew that the sting in your throat and bitter taste of a burnt meat fire would last all day.

To me, the only inhaled substances worse to deal with were tear gas or the refrigerant sulfur dioxide.

Roof openings — our stock in trade — unquestionably, were a dicey affair. Dennis Clay and I proved a good roof team. Not only was he quick to get the aerial to the roof, he moved more quickly than I did and with more agility, while I could hang longer in the smoke. So he went up first, set his roof ladder and started the opening with his axe. I was close behind, and our swing person usually brought us the power saw. When the horizontal and vertical cuts were made, in unison we laid into the roofing material with the pick ends of our axes, peeling it back to vent heat and smoke. The roaring whine of our saw told engine crews inside that they would soon be able to advance and would not have to sweat a backdraft. The faster we moved on top, the better we made it inside for them. Working hard on a roof, above a blaze in summer's heat, while wearing bulky turnout gear was a true test of will. Winter's embrace wasn't any better, especially on ice- and snow-covered roofs. One advantage of winter was the distinct melt outline often made by the fire on the snowy roof, telling us where to make our opening. When the opening was made, observers on the ground usually saw two bodies on roof ladders, not moving, spent. But we soon rallied, as there still was much to do.

Sometimes the fire won the race and we ended up trapped on the roof, cut off by flames from our aerial or extension ladder. More than once I saw firefighters straddle a ground ladder and slide down the beams in hasty retreat. After a stubborn blaze where Ladder 12's Leo Harper and I got cut off and had to yell for help getting off the roof, I devised an escape rope and hook that fit into my coat pocket. It still comes in handy when cutting trees. Dangerous too was using a powerful circular saw in blinding smoke and darkness, while balancing on a roof ladder. More than once I found cuts from the high rpm blade in our ladders, and once even in the steel toe of my boot. Exhaustion often led to injuries. With Sean Slowey as my roof partner, we were fortunate to have gotten through a shift during which we opened five roofs, with the last fire coming in about 5 A.M. We were dead on our feet, going through the motions, relying more on our axes, thanks to a temperamental power saw that was difficult to start. With gray dawn peeking over the horizon while on the roof of our fifth worker, Sean gave up on the saw and went to work with his axe. Barely able to raise my arms, and calling the stubborn saw a string of inexplicable names, I gave the cold, dead machine one last pull of the starter cord and it roared to life, only to die a swift death. Dead tired or not, I came alive on that roof, my axe in good swing, sinking soundly with satisfying crunches into shingles and beaver board, like a seasoned carpenter's trusted hammer hitting the sweet spot. Being perched up there, under dawn's rising veil, eating smoke, wasn't what I was doing, it was who I was. While numb with exhaustion, driving home was a lesson in concentration. And I was numb to the personal achievement in staying power, my only emotion being regret that my family would see only a smoke-smudged, red-eyed zombie for most of the day.

Proof that bad decisions make good stories occurred on November 16, 1986, when we responded to a fire at one of the many apartment buildings that lined West Wells Street. We were one of three ladder companies sent since life hazard was high and the fire was called in by the police, who reported that people were trapped. Heavy smoke pushing from the many door and window openings greeted us when we pulled in. Since the building was multiple-occupancy, there was enough work for everybody. The chief had only to point at us and say, "Ladder 9, take the inside," which we knew meant search and rescue of trapped occupants. We grabbed masks and split into two teams, with another firefighter and I led by our boss that day, Lt. Jack Behling. In a narrow gangway we looked up to see four cops on an upper recessed porch hollering that they were trapped. We discovered later that they had entered the building to help occupants escape only to be driven out onto the porch by the quickly spreading fire. Now dense gray smoke rolled from the window openings behind them. We ran for a ladder and got them down, then masked up and crawled through the same window frames into the blinding smoke.

Staying in voice contact, we thoroughly searched, room by room. We checked everywhere: in closets, under furniture, even in dresser drawers and cabinets, knowing that panicked kids will hide anywhere. Out in a hallway we were about to enter a room where fire was breaking through the wall when the door opened and we were met by another search team. Through facepieces we yelled, "Did you check that room?" Their barely visible nods and muffled assents didn't convince me because I noticed by their helmet shields that they belonged to a less busy south side company, probably summoned by the second alarm. Behling, who was all business and heavy on experience, kept at them: "You sure you checked that area?" More nods; "Yeah, yeah, nobody in there." We moved down the hall to another room.

We went into extensive overhaul mode when elsewhere in the building a body of someone killed in the fire was found. But that death and our rescue of the four cops proved trivial news compared to the news that broke seven weeks later: a man's body was found beneath rubble on the second floor by the deceased's relatives. And did heads roll. The chief conducted an investigation, we provided written statements, and the media had a field day. The family filed a multi-million-dollar lawsuit, claiming we failed to rescue their son. In our defense, the body was charred and buried beneath charred rubble, plus we had little time left on our air tanks and had to keep moving. Although we were cleared of negligence, I felt that we had made a bad decision in trust-ing the other search team and not covering the same ground. Although the victim couldn't have survived the fire, had we found the body, the family at least would have been spared some agony. After the proverbial barn door was closed, second and third searches were ordered conducted at every fire.

Not long afterward, in a similar apartment building blaze in the same area, we found a charred body, although this one was at the top of a stair landing. Standing over the body, I told someone that we should get our cubs over to see it. The battalion chief came over, looked down at the charred form and snapped, "Get a blanket over him!" I retorted, "Who's gonna see it, Chief? Us?" *Besides*, I thought, *soon the police will arrive to photograph it, so what's the point?* I walked away thinking the chief's emotions were askew, and he might still have been feeling the sting of the body discovered seven weeks after a fire.

Notable was another apartment building fire in the same area, although this one had a bright outcome. Pulling up to the smoke-filled block on West State Street, we spotted a group of people huddled tightly together on a third-floor wrought-iron balcony. Drawing closer, a chill ran through me when I counted seven people squatting on the narrow framework, which was intended as decoration only, and certainly was not designed to support such weight. I called in a marker with the big guy, begging to keep that balcony attached to the building. Dennis and I had never moved so fast. He screeched the big Mack to a halt, vaulted out of the cab, leaped up onto the turntable, and swung the aerial up and over to the third floor. During agonizing seconds that seemed like a lifetime, things began to move in slow motion. Cranking my head upward, I yelled, "Don't move! I'm coming." I felt a knot in my gut as I watched putrid brown smoke envelop their heads, forcing them to lean outward. The metallic taste of dread hung in my mouth. I couldn't swallow. *Keep them there, please keep them there.* Like a runner tensed at the starting block, I coiled to spring up the aerial. As soon as Dennis locked in the aerial and shouted "Go," up I bounded. Dennis later said that I hit only every other rung. He had expertly placed the aerial's tip just under the balcony's metal frame.

At the top I faced seven adults, a row of wide-eyed, frozen faces. I felt the heat that gnawed at their backs. My first words to them were something like, "I know it's a nice view from up here, but you have to come down with me now." Thankfully, they didn't panic and rush the aerial. "One at a time. Don't move till I grab you." Extending a leg out onto the slender iron frame, feeling it move downward stole my breath. The best film director couldn't have added more drama. *What's holding this thing to the brick?* Their first move astonished me; a man extended his arm to me, his hand clutching a small black and white dog. I grabbed it by the nape of the neck, ready to drop it to the pavement below. "No time for this. We gotta go, now!" *What the hell am I doing? I can't drop this dog. Ah, fuck it.* I stuffed the mutt into the man's jacket and got him onto the ladder, wrapped my leg around the aerial and swung off so he could get by me. "Go down," I urged. "Hug the ladder." Then the others — pull them into me, push them down onto the aerial, swing out of their way, and urge them to hurry and stay low. I felt immense relief seeing them on the aerial, with Dennis and an HEO helping them off the rig. Last was an elderly woman I quickly helped onto the aerial, covering her body with mine on the way down.

But I wasn't done. My charges had told me that a man was still inside. I yelled to Dennis that I was going in. Back up I went, crawling through the window frame. I heard behind me, "You want a mask?"

"No time," I answered into the brown mass.

The smoke attacked my lungs and eyes. I felt the push of heat. Quickly clambering through the apartment, I found no one, but out in the hall, shrouded in the brown fog lay an elderly man, semi-conscious, propped up on one elbow, refusing to go down. *Spunky. I like that.* "What say we go get some fresh air, old-timer?"

"Yeah," he wheezed.

Half crawling, I dragged with him to the stairs, where another company wearing masks took him from me, and I followed them out. Out on the street, my lucky seven were being tended to but none of my comrades were around our rig. I put on a mask and went inside to meet up with them.

When the boss asked, "Where ya been?" I nonchalantly answered that I was just screwin' off. He gave me a sideward glance that said he knew better.

Later, I laughed at Dennis when he yapped about my bounding up the aerial to snatch the seven. He was enjoying himself and I gave in, thinking, *I guess eight saves isn't a bad day's work — I could get my arms around that— but I didn't do it alone.* I laughed again when the picture on the front page of the next morning's paper showed my ass coming down the aerial helping the last woman down. I closed my eyes in self-satisfaction when I saw in the background a familiar man holding a little black and white dog.

I hated flat roofs. Although flat roofs give the impression they are safer to work from, I never felt comfortable on them. Gable roofs are stronger. The older a flat-roofed building, typically, the stronger they are. Newer construction often relies on truss forms, and the number of firefighter deaths reported across the country caused by truss roofs that failed early in fires wasn't lost on us. Flat roofs comprising plywood and sheet metal, and then topped with tar and pea gravel, played hell with our saws and were a bitch to open. My qualms about the dangers of flat roofs became reality one hot August day in 1987.

The call came in as a tavern fire at 19th and Chambers streets. Still some distance from the scene we saw the dark stain in the sky, and the radio came to life with the obvious from the first arriving company: "We have a working fire." Exchanging knowing looks, we hung on as HEO Roger Semenske maneuvered the big Mack through traffic. Despite the oppressive late afternoon heat, we pulled on gloves, raised collars and securely fastened the straps and buckles of our heavy protective clothing. The siren's scream and the blast of the air horn drowned out our amplified heartbeats as we went through a mental checklist of procedures and equipment.

As we pulled into the chaotic scene, dense smoke obscuring the streets told us this was a nasty fire; we wouldn't have much time to gain the upper hand. We joined other first-alarm companies preparing for battle. Fireground din is like no other: diesel engines growl and pumps hum loudly, glass breaks, power saws scream, ladders clang and the fire itself crackles and roars, while shouts ricochet across the scene. The sweet, almost intoxicating smell of burning wood pierced our nostrils. Rigs were jockeyed into position, heavy hoses slapped the pavement as they were laid, and yellow-clad warriors scurried about in what we called organized confusion.

A delay. We argued with a man to get him to move his car from the tight spot where our rig had to be. Finally, Roger raised and extended the aerial to the flat roof of the three-story building. Dark smoke rolled from every opening in the upper floors, and crimson flames jetted menacingly through the dark mass, sending towers of sparks skyward. Embers floated downward like huge snowflakes, triggering curses when they found bare skin. The huge volume of fire along with the color and pressure of the smoke were telltale signs of an arsonist's work. Up the aerial we went, lugging equipment, me first, followed by Roger, Cindy, Lt. Jim Groth and our cub, Dick Kaiser. We knew that the summer heat, combined with the heat of the fire, plus working hard in turnout gear, would quickly sap our strength. I was already soaked with sweat. *I really need to beef up my workout schedule.*

On the roof, we split into two teams: I and two others broke out skylights and pried off scuttle covers, while two began a trench cut, which is made ahead of a fast-moving fire, forcing it to vent there, halting its lateral spread. The sound of thudding axes and breaking glass told us that our rival, Ladder 12, was doing the same on another part of the roof. Our efforts released billowing smoke that turned day into night. The fire raging below was taking full possession of the building, its intense heat and billowing smoke taking a toll on us. The roof deck had become spongy and we were slipping on melted tar — obvious signs that we had yet to turn the tide of battle, and we had to quickly get off of the roof. Our pride would take a backseat to this one. *Goddamn these flat roofs!*

In our haste to bail, we abandoned our equipment. I was last to climb onto the aerial ladder, and as I did, I took a last look back. For a brief moment, the billowing smoke parted and through shimmering heat waves I glimpsed a firefighter on the opposite end of the roof. I yelled to Dick Kaiser to get down the ladder, "now!" I told him I was going back to check on someone I spotted. Blindly, trying to suck air through my constricted throat, I searched for the guy I had seen, fearing that he was cut off from escape. At the far end of the roof was one of Ladder 12's guys, a seasoned truck man, making a final attempt to open a trench cut. Yellow, searing flames jetting from his opening made me recoil. Simultaneously we shouted, "We gotta get outta here! The roof's going!" Adrift in the dark sea of acrid smoke, we separated, so I headed in the direction of my aerial. Nearly overcome and disoriented by the blinding, toxic mass, I wavered and groped my way back in the direction of my escape from that hell.

Then it happened.

My next step was into space. Instinctively I lunged forward, smashed my chest against something solid, and caught the hole's edge with one hand. I dropped the axe I was carrying and my helmet was knocked off. It suddenly became a very private, almost spiritual battle. I refused to lose. I was no stranger to a standoff with fire, but I was pathetic, hanging there, spent, injured, alone. Hopelessness washed over me, but I wouldn't allow my life to flash before me. I felt my boots soften from the searing heat racing up the shaft. Soon, I knew, their thin black rubber would fuse painfully to my skin. Refusing to just hang there and burn as though I were on a spit, a cerebral backup system clicked on and thought processes stirred.

I guessed that I was hanging in a common scuttle opening. I knew that I was facing northward and remembered, from my initial size-up, a window to my north and another to the west. I would drop into the opening, hit the floor beneath me, hopefully be under the roaring flames, and dive for a window. At that point, a three-story fall seemed better than playing into Lucifer's hand.

Although I've survived tight spots, I believed I had finally exceeded my limits, used up all my markers, and that my plan was futile. The heat was unbearable, stinging my legs. My chest screamed in pain. Severe lack of oxygen and deadly gasses coursing through my bloodstream diminished my ability to think rationally. Muscle refused to function. I lost all concept of time. My grip loosened. Pain turned to numbness and I drifted into a welcome sea of gray, which brightened to the proverbial intense white light. I felt calm. Kaleidoscopic images of my kids and smiling family danced before me and I floated outside my body to join them. My right hand lost its grip and fell to my side.

It's over ... letting go ... God, forgive...

Voices. I heard voices. My turn had come to say, "Help me." Then I felt tugging, upward. It was Dick Kaiser and Roger Semenske, who had come back, in defiance of orders, because they sensed something had gone wrong, and giving up was not in their characters. Severely weakened, I was dead weight, but they reached down into the thick smoke and heat and pulled me out by a leather equipment belt around my waist. They pulled me to the aerial and we tumbled down. Moments later, the entire roof collapsed into the fire below. As my rescuers took me to a paramedic unit, the battleground seemed eerily quiet — a busy street scene in an action movie with the sound turned off. People looked at me like I was a ghost. *Maybe this isn't real.* Word had spread that I died in the fire.

Later, Kaiser and Semenske described their feelings of helplessness when they returned to the roof. People involved in traumatic events often recall vividly a single fragment of the episode; for them, it was spotting only my fingers clinging to the edge of the shaft when the smoke parted, only for an instant. Had they not listened to their humane inner voices, I would have died. The chiefs commanding the fire told me that had I let go, I would have plunged down a 30-foot-deep air shaft lined with protruding climbing spikes, into the fire. Even if there had been a floor beneath me, fire consumed that level. The window I had hoped to reach was blocked by a stairwell filled with fire.

My leather helmet was never recovered, but a ladder company gave me my charred and melted axe, which they found in the rubble days later. It reminded me of how sweet life truly can be. And so did Deb, my newfound love, who gave me a card showing a terror-stricken cat hanging by its paws, with the words, "Hang in there, baby." I don't remember filling my kids in on what had happened as my oldest, Jeff, was only 11 years old.

The chief's commendation letter for Firefighter Richard Kaiser and Heavy Equipment Operator Roger Semenske read, in part, "Their concern, at the risk of their own lives, for a fallen comrade is to be commended and held as an example for all firefighters." They received national recognition for their daring deed.

It took months for my brain to finally erase the slow-motion clip of me dropping into that blazing, smoke-charged shaft, being shredded on the way down, and burning at the bottom.

Every time I thought the angels had come to close my eyes, instead they got me through, and afterward I felt an indescribable awareness of every living thing, a gift I had valued since my Vietnam experience. *You haven't lived till you've almost died.*

After I recuperated, I logged the experience and regained my perspective. I learned to work smarter, to be more methodical and measured. I felt wiser

This photograph dramatically illustrates the dangerous conditions atop the three-story building at 20th and Chambers streets that nearly claimed the life of the author on August 5, 1987. It also speaks of the heroism of Mutza's teammates, Dick Kaiser and Roger Semenske, who risked their lives to save him. The cause of the two-alarm blaze was labeled arson (courtesy Chuck Liedtke Photo).

and seasoned in how I worked. I went back to work on a number of projects I had been involved with. More importantly, my life was taking a new turn. A few months earlier, I had met one of our new paramedics, Debbie Dutkiewicz. After spending a couple of hours at Engine 3's quarters incorporating my newly designed Haz-Mat emblem into metal signs for their truck, I stopped at Engine 5 for gas. It was a cold January day and out of the firehouse walked a female paramedic I hadn't seen before. *Well, check out this beauty.* She was polite and respectful, and I was fascinated, even excited, by talking with her. I was taken by her sincerity and humor. It didn't dawn on me that I had a department car and that cubs were required to pump gas when a chief showed up. I told her I didn't expect her to do that, since winter's wind was biting. Besides, I wasn't a chief, and even if I was, I'd certainly pump my own gas. She went inside and later, when I went in to chew the rag with the guys, I listened with one ear, more intent on seeing where she was. And on the sly, I rummaged through personnel files in the office to find out more about her. This is probably a good time to add that I felt my marriage had run its course and was on shaky ground, although I knew not to advertise that. Without taking myself too seriously, I made a point to stay at a distance when it came to fraternizing with our females. In addition, my troubled marriage had me believing that I wasn't good at relationships, and I had best avoid them. But I knew what I liked, and Deb's smile and brown eyes were intoxicating. And so I climbed aboard the emotional roller coaster and hung on. Most important was being true to my kids. They were my focus. I struggled with trying to be more open with my wife, but our home was a battleground. Resentment abounded and resolution seemed light-years away. And when I saw my son and daughter hugging each other in a corner, crying, their eyes wide with fear because their parents were arguing at fever pitch, I made a decision. It became all about protecting them and providing for them, and, finally, being true to myself. I should have been more open with my mother- and father-in-law, of whom I was very fond. Unfortunately, I lost sight of the fact that I was more than "their fireman"—I was a son they loved.

Through it all, I maintained job performance. Studying for promotion took on even greater importance. Whatever I accomplished on the job, I reasoned, would benefit us all. I put even more effort into being a parent and a firefighter; it was what I knew, and I did my best, although parenting is the toughest job I've ever had.

Six weeks after I had met Deb, I ran into her at a year-on party. Determined to talk to her, I broke from the Ladder 9 pack and we moved off into a private corner, where we talked for two hours. Again I was impressed, and soon we were caught up in refreshing conversation. I felt my emotions gaining a foothold. My admiration for Deb soon gave way to adoration. One of my cohorts must have felt a whiskey-fueled pang of jealousy, because he bellowed for all to hear as Deb and I left, "Sure, leave with the married guy." I'd deal with the fallout from that later. My nights on my mother's couch were ending and a new life was beginning. Coolly, wisely, Deb warned that I might be jumping from the frying pan into the fire, but as she chimes to this day, "Nobody tells Wayne Mutza what to do." I was used to heat, or maybe I simply hadn't learned, or wouldn't learn, to stay out of it, especially when following my heart. And she became my heart.

When I walked into the firehouse, I tried to leave my private life out on the doorstep. There was little room for clouded emotions or distraction in a line of work that often meant life or death. I believed that if one of us was having a bad day, that wasn't the place to have it.

One of the many bright spots during my tenure at Ladder 9 was having Jeff Venus assigned to us, straight from the training academy. U.S. Air Force–trained, crash-crew member Jeff Venus was gung-ho, yes-sir no-sir, dedicated, disciplined, and as dead serious about the job as anyone could possibly be. To have a cub of such caliber was a blessing. Despite his chiseled features,

complete with military-style haircut and hard physique, Jeff exuded an innocence that endeared him to the coarsest of souls. Jeff not only would climb
the ranks during his fire service career, but as a reservist would serve four
tours in our wars in the Middle East. He was the kind of guy you were glad
was on your side.

Both my boss and the engine boss were transferred, and I wasn't particularly pleased with their replacements. So I simply remained dedicated to
doing my job and stayed out of their way, unless they put us in unnecessary
danger. It was enough that risk was a condition of employment. Engine 32
was so busy with EMS, or squad, runs that we got our share covering for
them. Getting more than our share, we discovered, was by design. Our disdain
for the engine boss grew after the chief caught him delaying going back in
service until they pulled up to the firehouse. That was supposed to be done
at the scene of the alarm. Stretching his time out of service meant that other
companies would have to take runs normally his. His ruse could have had
dangerous consequences. Our boss was a surly character who seemed threatened that he never had us quite under control. It was humorous, really. Only
once do I recall him putting us at undue risk. At a reported stabbing, we
found a large woman sitting near the bottom of a steep staircase with a stab
wound. Her attacker, the live-in boyfriend, stood at the top of the stairs still
brandishing the large knife. We opted not to move the injured woman, because
I was able to convince the man to stay up there. We told him an ambulance
was coming and to just let us get her out of there. We had no truck with him.
When it dawned on him that the police were on the way, he wanted out. We
were content to have him out of there and to let the police find him, but his
only way out was the stairwell.

I told him that if he laid down the knife in plain view and quietly scooted
around us, hands in the air, as we shielded the woman, he was out of there.
I knew we could handle the scrawny bastard without that big blade. He agreed,
laid the knife on the edge of the step and scurried down. Just as he squeezed
past us, our boss poked a finger at him, sneered and snapped, "Hey, who do
you think you are?" *Goddammit! We almost had him out of here and you had
to open your smart-ass flapper.* They began to tussle, the woman screamed, we
shoved him out of the door and off he bolted. Thankfully, bailing out of there
was more important to him than getting a piece of our boss. Later, I brushed
past the scowling lieutenant and muttered, "Way to go, boss man." This and
countless incidents of violence against firefighters and EMS personnel pointed
to the dire need for a course of action. Having had enough of the violence,
I took up the cause, pouring my heart into it. I began gathering data from
across the country and talking with others in our department. My research
showed that the situation was worse than anyone seemed to realize.

Not only were the streets getting meaner, they were presenting us with a new hazard. My first known exposure came on a run where we milled about on a sidewalk looking for someone who had been assaulted. All was quiet and we were about to call in a false alarm, when a man turned the corner and walked toward us. He didn't look roughed up, but when he neared, we noticed blood around his mouth. *Doesn't look too bad, he probably got popped in the mouth during a scrap.* As always, we watched his hands and his eyes, trying to read his intent. "Are you hurt? Were you assaulted?" the boss asked. His response surprised us. Very calmly, he answered, trying not to gurgle on blood, "Yes, I was shot in the mouth." Opening his mouth and pointing inward, he said that he could feel it in the back of his throat.

Someone produced a flashlight from their pocket. Peering in we saw only red. He began to choke, so I told him to try to keep his mouth open while I carefully swept my fingers around inside his mouth. That seemed to help so I withdrew my bloody hand, knelt down and wiped it on the grass. We got a med unit on the way, sat him down, and began an EMS assessment. Although we told him he didn't have to talk since the police were coming, he was able to tell us that he was held up. The robber stuck the gun in his mouth while he handed over his wallet. The scum got what he wanted but pulled the trigger anyway and ran.

Someone used the hand pump to wash my hands. We made little of the shooting, just another senseless act. Back at quarters, an hour later, the hospital called to tell us that the man had AIDS. No-nonsense chief Bill Schaefer walked into the kitchen and asked for details of the run. When he heard where my hand had been, he was irate. His words were clear and loud for all to hear: "Mutza, if I ever hear that you handle someone again without gloves, I'll have you up on charges!" His sharp voice was piercing. He spared no one his hard glare. "Yes, sir, Chief." For once, I didn't mind an ass-chewing in front of coworkers and being the object of his lesson. It had the intended effect. Schaefer cared about his people. That was real leadership. I didn't know the man well, but I didn't need to. He carried himself in a way that commanded authority, leaving little room for questions or arguments, and that was enough for me.

The AIDS scare was on. It was even in the newspapers, and who doesn't believe everything that's in the news? The article headline stated: *AIDS has emergency crews scared: Rescuers want to know if patients have disease.* Thankfully, one of those interviewed was friend and paramedic Bonnie McFarlane, who, when interviewed, said, "I would not deny care to an AIDS victim, nor do I know of any colleagues who would." She went on, "I'll admit that when I started, I didn't take the precautions that I take now. It's something that you think about every day, that you could be putting your life on the line." In the same article, a fire officer admitted that AIDS had already changed the pattern of response, and that some members held back if they knew what they were facing. Even more dangerous, we were told, were hepatitis strains. I teamed with paramedic Pat Harris to develop a slide presentation about germs and infectious diseases, which was required viewing. The issue seemed to stir widespread moralizing and re-evaluation of placing others before our own safety. To me it was just another hazard added to the pile, so I heeded safety precautions and didn't let it affect how I operated.

Other issues came to the fore, overshadowing, if only temporarily, the AIDS issue. On September 30, 1987, an off day for me, a half mile from our quarters, companies arrived at a house fire, a savage fire. Chief Jim Rechlitz remembers:

> This was my most serious fire. Twelve people perished, nine were children. I will never forget Lt. Tom Glubka of Ladder 9 saying to me, "We don't have to ventilate the building, Chief, it's coming through the roof. We'll take the second building." Or the police officer saying to me, "There are twelve people unaccounted for." I told him I hope they got out because we did not have a chance. Fire was coming out of all the windows. Fire operations went smoothly and efficiently as a hydrant was right in front of the building, but it took us ten minutes before we knocked it down and entered. They were called to heaven before we got there.

Two weeks later, another fire just blocks away killed six people. And two weeks after that, when an elderly woman died in a mattress fire in her home in the same area, the department recorded 23 fire deaths for the year, tying a deadly record set 20 years earlier.

After the massive fatality, my friend Wojo, with hands shoved into his pockets and wide-eyed, said, "Me and Radar stacked the burned bodies in the squad, like fuckin' cordwood." He blew out hard and tried to describe, but couldn't, the smell that smothered them when they drove downtown to the sheriff's morgue. He could only look sideways and mutter, "Jesus Christ." Wojo's words were an acknowledgment of evil and sadness. The whole tragedy was right there on his face. Another friend, Clarence Kuehmichel, his hawk-like, angular Native American features emphasizing his candor, said with eyes locked on mine, "I was at both fires, first in." It wasn't a boast, it was just the truth. He fell silent, eyes never moving from mine, as though I could respond. There was nothing to say.

From the ashes came not only the rounds of expected meetings, pointed questions demanding answers, and political back-stepping, but something new to us: stress counseling. Credit for pioneering the concept, officially labeled Critical Incident Stress Debriefing, or CISD, is given Dr. Jeffrey T. Mitchell of the University of Maryland. As early as the 1970s, Mitchell, a former firefighter and paramedic, began looking at how emergency workers handled job stress. He found that people who deal with trauma for a living experienced one or more of a long list of damaging and even debilitating physical, cognitive, and behavioral symptoms. It became apparent that too often people who dedicate their lives to saving others seldom think to save themselves.

I didn't believe that you could train anyone to handle repeated grief and loss, exposure to danger and violence, or to pick up human remains. I did believe that people found it within themselves to handle mental chaos, shove it to the back of the pile, and move on. The only things that haunt you are the things you *let* haunt you. But for some, the stuff didn't go away; it only got stored and accumulated. It became the boogey man, the noise in the basement, the lurking shadow on a dark street. Some, as they amassed years on the job, began building walls around themselves, brick by brick, run by run, until it became a room, void of light, and it ended up having a door that they opened only to a few, if any. We saw how stress unchecked led to drug use, alcoholism, divorce and suicide. No one, not even his wife, knew why 29-year-old Firefighter Jon Smith called in sick before his shift at Engine 30, went into the basement, covered himself with a blanket, put a gun barrel in his mouth and pulled the trigger. A couple of the brothers told me that Jon had asked about our Employee's Assistance Program, but he wouldn't listen to their advice to get help for drug abuse. Jon had been one of my recruits, a star player with a beaming personality. I knew of a few others who died by their own hands. Suicides were, and are, more common than most people realize.

With only five med units in the city, some of our paramedics already were experiencing signs of loss of function after constant exposure, called burnout. Paramedics interviewed for a newspaper article dismissed the term as meaningless generalization, blaming emotional exhaustion instead on everyone else in the program. Some did, however, accept the term, one admitting that he started to see himself in his patients. The article examined why half of the paramedics trained since the program's inception had quit. Unhappy with the loss rate, the department began assigning those who quit to busy companies to dissuade others. Women hired from civilian status had no out, except to quit the department or take firefighter training. Chief Norm Wichman, who supervised the program, identified a heavy workload and stress as major causes for attrition.

Two years before the tragic house fires, Midwest Express Airlines flight 105 crashed into a forest preserve just after takeoff from Milwaukee's Mitchell Field, killing all 31 aboard. Illustrating the difference in how people respond to trauma was a conversation I had about the tragedy with Paramedic Officer Dave Tomasino. Despite the carnage that had lain before him, what stood out in his mind was a fierce jurisdictional battle between responding fire departments, and, most notably, a single deer killed by the crash.

So Milwaukee got on board and after the fatal fires developed a CISD team. People found it therapeutic, but as the department often did, it went into overdrive, with anyone who had handled a basic traffic fatality ordered to a debriefing. I thought that interfered with a natural resiliency we should be building, and it should be up to the individual how they handle it, how to maintain perspective. Often, it was enough to talk with someone you trusted. Eventually the department toned it down and participation became more voluntary. Such sessions helped to slow or stop the momentum of post-traumatic psychological deterioration and stabilize the cognitive and affective processes.

I had mixed feelings about another program instituted after the fires, called Project FOCUS, for Firefighters Out Creating Urban Safety. It had companies on the streets every day, on a rotating schedule, stopping at every residence in low-income neighborhoods to install smoke detectors, which had been donated by various firms. While it made many homes safer, it stripped the responsibility from people who knew better. It wasn't unusual to check detectors after a fire to find batteries had been removed so they could power toys or electronic gadgets. We were addressing only one small part of the problem. We didn't confiscate misused space heaters or matches left out in front of kids, we didn't rewire dangerous electrical devices, we didn't turn off stove burners left on for heat — the list goes on. Conversely, the most positive programs derived from the fires were Survive Alive House and enhanced public relations. Public relations ... didn't we start that a decade earlier?

Speaking of responsibility — I remember one cold, damp day being at a house fire in which two kids left alone died. *Un-fucking-forgivable,* I thought. During overhaul while walking down the block to my rig, a young woman approached, a huge boa around her neck and trying to balance on stiletto heels, a difficult task because she was stinking drunk. She stopped and wavered, squinting past me trying to make out the fire scene. I suspected this was mom. Not taking my eyes off her, I stretched my arm back, pointing toward the steaming, burned-out house, "You live there?" She confirmed it when her sunken eyes went wide and her smeared lips parted, trying to form words. Her shiny, coffee-colored complexion paled. Her narrow jaw went slack. She gasped and folded to her knees right there in front of me, grabbing my knees. The protracted pain of grief had begun. I peeled her hands away and hailed a cop, who pulled the now wailing woman to her feet and helped her stagger to her squad car. Her two kids she had left alone while she got cozy at the corner tavern had gotten cold and turned on the stove burners for heat, and then tossed papers atop the pretty blue flames. Their little friend next door said they had done it before. Maybe they were simply mimicking something they had seen an adult do. Kids do that.

Fires weren't our only stress producers. We took most EMS runs in stride and relied heavily on our paramedics to handle advanced medical care. Some cases were extreme.

When we pulled up to the intersection of 27th and Highland streets, I didn't immediately see the problem but blood running in the gutter really piqued my senses. At the curb was a car parked close behind a pickup truck. Too close. The car was wedged under the truck's tailgate, actually lifting it upward. I should've known by how distant the onlookers stayed that there was something ghastly here.

When I stepped alongside the mated vehicles, my breath skipped and I felt pinpricks along my temples. A body was pinned, inverted, between the two metal hulks. But for a strand of wet, fleshy material, the body was severed at the hips, the legs dangling sickeningly over the street. The image was of a rag doll, no longer recognizable as human. My mind flashed a snapshot of a body pinned in an ambushed jeep on a dusty road. The flashback was a rare occurrence, thankfully.

A young man had been loading items into the bed of his pickup when a woman in a big four-door careened around the corner and smashed square into the pickup. The impact drove the young man against the lowered tailgate-turned-cleaver, as though it were an ancient torture device. The car hit with such force that it wedged under the pickup, lifting it, leaving only inches for paramedics to work from below on the body. They quickly started an IV but we all knew it was hopeless. Although the guy had bled out, the meds felt a pulse for a brief moment.

It was our job as a truck crew to figure out a way to quickly separate the locked vehicles to free the body. Pepie, Dennis and I agreed we could run a rope up our aerial ladder and use it as a crane to lift the pickup. In what seemed like mere seconds, we had the rope over the rungs and Dennis was swinging the aerial over the mess. He nudged the ladder upward until the rope went taut and the body halves were released. Squatting, we tried to support the dangling severed legs and we plopped the two halves onto the stretcher. Now we waited for the helicopter that had been called. I latched onto some bothersome thoughts about bringing in the chopper, actually welcoming the shift in focus. *Flight for Life is fairly new. It's really windy. Lots of obstacles. This crowd has grown. We have no training in landing that thing and we can't talk with the pilot.* Scanning the intersection-soon-to-become-landing-zone, I shuddered at the sight of poles and wires, not to mention many people. I told the chief that we really needed to get these people way back; I volunteered to direct the pilot in, but he waved off my warnings. This was his show and no one, by God, was going to tell him how to run it.

When the chopper arrived, I wondered if anyone knew what the pilot's two slow orbits over the scene meant. I knew what he saw. *You see those too-close crowds, and the wires, and the poles, don't you? You feel those gusts, don't you?* I knew what he was thinking: *Damn, this looks dicey. It's gonna be tight. One try, that's all this gets or I'm outta here. Wish I had commo with them down there.* And down he skillfully brought the bird, fighting through the wind, bucking, measuring the distance from his rotor blades to those poles as his skids did the two-step on the asphalt. His ascent wasn't any easier. The target hospital was a straight shot west, five miles, no more — ten, twelve minutes, maybe, by ground with lights and siren, but this was much more dramatic, and sometimes our people became alarmists and got caught up in the hype.

I felt for the dead boy, and his family, beyond grief, which motivated me to offer my help in implementing a program for best using the helicopter. I had spent some hours in them and had seen a few things that might help. So did some other guys on the job. I talked to our EMS chief about it, but nothing ever came of it. I then pictured being TV's Gomer Pyle with that goofy look saying, "Surprise, surprise!" Whenever that chopper came in for an accident victim, I tried to be behind a tree because I'd seen what flailing rotor blades can do to bodies, and I'd seen enough hacked up bodies.

That call was exempt from our dark humor; it took longer to push it to the back of the cranial file drawer and move on. Easily qualifying as runner-up for worst run while assigned to Ladder 9 was one that came over the radio as we returned from a call. More unsettling than the call's vagueness — and being only a couple of blocks away — was that it was Mother's Day. Like Christmas, Mother's Day is an emotional holiday, and sometimes emotions go into overdrive. There is consensus among emergency workers that such days account for spikes in the number of calls. Statistics point to similar increases, both in fire and EMS calls, on nights of a full moon.

When we pulled up to the old flat, people were out on the porch, hysterical. Rather than run in, we yelled from a distance, "What's going on?" Hearing key words such as "shot" and "gun" had the boss on the radio checking on police response. We needed to know where the shooter was before taking another step. Finally, a more composed woman came toward us explaining that a family member had shot himself but reassuring us that the gun was no longer a danger. As we got onto the porch, we sidestepped in time to get out of the way of distraught people spilling through the door. Emotions, and tempers, were at peak. Despite the number of people inside, all stayed well clear of the dining room. The reason was obvious.

Draped over the seat of a simple chair was a body of a young man, facing upward, forming a perfect, but grotesque, arch of death. His arms bowed outward, palms up, as though pleading. Blood poured from a large hole in his temple, rapidly increasing the diameter of the red pool beneath him. Even through his shock of dark hair it was apparent that the bullet's exit had removed much of his skull. One hand still gripped the magnum revolver. I knew instantly there was no saving this guy, my focus instead being the gun, especially since tempers flared among the crowd. Trying awkwardly to avoid stepping fully in the widening puddle, we plopped him onto the floor. I quickly pried the gun from his grip and handed it to the first cop that walked to where we were. And that's as far as any of the cops would venture, taken aback by the massive red puddle, and its gaggingly rich iron odor.

While we hovered over the body debating whether to begin CPR, especially since there were no med units available—*of course not, it's Mother's Day*—we heard much scuffling and arguing between cops and the crowd. While the boss listened, Cindy insisted we do CPR because death had just occurred and the body could yield parts. I countered, pointing out that we couldn't get a med unit. Besides, his brain was gone and everything had shut down. The boss, glancing nervously at the crush of people in the house, proved the tie-breaker and mumbled, "Just go through the motions, if anything." The young man was clinically dead and before long would be biologically dead—dead dead.

By the time we got a rescue squad, a few people were in cuffs out on the porch and still others were arguing with the police, whose presence was growing. I wondered if the young man's mom was among the crowd. What powerful message was the dead guy trying to send, waiting for family to be gathered on Mother's Day, and then blowing his brains out in front of them? I didn't want to know any more. I was happy to get out of there. The fact that the guy waited for his audience bothered me more than his death, or his young age. More often people commit suicide when they are alone. And I didn't necessarily buy into "attempted suicide." What is that, really? They do it or they don't. Someone who truly wants to end it, will. Give me a snotty mattress fire any day.

Other things happened at Ladder 9 that summer to keep us honest. A high point, for me, at least, was trading in our rig for an older tractor-trailer type while our black smoke-blowing machine went in for overhaul. Like all tractor trailers, this one had a tiller position at the rear. Being a fire truck enthusiast, I admired the long rigs and thrilled at the opportunity to finally learn how to use the tiller. I enjoyed the challenge of maneuvering the entire trailer, trying to read the driver's moves. Backing into tight quarters was even trickier. The only danger, really, was allowing the trailer to "whip," which happened if you didn't steer back inside a turn near its end. A good driver remembered that you were back there and made your job easy. An exceptional driver could tell you to hold the tiller wheel straight and get the rig almost anywhere. Dennis was the latter. We became a good enough team to make bets that we could do a 180-degree turn on a standard-width street. Positioning the long rig at a fire on a crowded street took great skill. It had to be jackknifed in just the right spot so the truck's weight could counterbalance the extended aerial. With this old rig, when the jackknife was set, the tillerman — all right, the tiller person — had to quickly unbuckle, remove the steering wheel and shaft, and undo clamps to swing the windshield out of the way so the aerial could be raised out of the bed. Fun stuff.

Not so fun one night while high up in the tiller was hearing, almost sensing, something behind me. Jerking around, I was surprised to see a man climbing aboard the rig, looking like he was bent on attacking me. We had already started moving, but we weren't going fast enough to signal Dennis to make an emergency stop that would toss off my unwelcome rider. I opted for my heavy leather-and-metal spanner belt, which I swung at the guy as I called him every name in the book. He tumbled off and rolled into the street, got up and threw a fit as we roared off into the night. *What a fuckin' zoo,* I thought.

The type of runs to which we responded often were based on the season. To escape summer's heat, people flocked to their neighborhood park pools. That became a problem when the pools were closed and defiant types climbed the fence to take a dip after dark. On two of those nights, one week apart, we responded to calls to the Washington Park pool to find bodies of teenage boys at the bottom of the pool. On the first call, I wasn't sure what equipment to bring, so I grabbed our longest pike pole, a 16-footer. Someone else grabbed the bolt cutters. Rope and ladders followed. Peering through the chain-link fence, we could make out at the bottom, in the middle of the pool, a dark human form contrasted against light blue.

Not waiting for ladders to go up or locks to be cut off, another guy and I climbed the fence and jumped down onto the other side. My intent was to hook the body but he was too far away. To my amazement, the other guy, without hesitation, peeled off his shoes and dove in. My amazement had everything to do with the guy's reputation for cowardice at fires, shirking EMS runs, and generally being a weasel. But in he went, like a torpedo, straight to the dark form at the bottom of the pool. Unable to swim a lick, I yelled for others to hurry over the fence, and then could only watch and be ready to try to hook them. He got hold of the body and went for the surface where he began struggling, arms beating the water into a white froth. I saw then how large the body was. Luckily he was within reach of the pike pole. He grabbed on with one hand, towing the body with the other, and we pulled them in.

We rolled them out and immediately began CPR, not knowing how long the victim had been under. The meds rolled in and took over, but the kid's defiance had ended at poolside. His rescuer said that if I hadn't thought to bring that pole, he would've drowned. I complimented him on the dive, which I thought was ballsy and self sacrificing. What a lesson in humanity.

One week later we were back at the same spot, at night, fishing a teen's body out of the pool, except that he was smaller and in the shallow end. He too, found his final relief from the heat on the cool concrete at poolside.

Life outside of the firehouse remained busy. I kept at my studies for the upcoming lieutenant's exam, and Deb and I were enjoying life. We easily accepted each other's kids, which totaled six, and did our best to form a family circle, providing them not only with material things, but the attention, structure and love they needed. I admired Deb's knack for knowing what was best for them and following through. We did our level best to treat them fairly, and not only as a family, but as individuals. It didn't dawn on me then that they could lose sight of that, especially later in life when they formed relationships and raised kids. But, for now, all the kids got along. People called us "the Brady Bunch." Somehow, in her small house, Deb accommodated all the kids, even making the sleeping arrangements work. Family outings, even a trip to St. Louis, were fun-packed, memorable events. It was heart warming to see how my kids, Jeff, Joanna, Joe and Jason, warmed to Deb. She opened her arms to them, while deftly walking the tightrope of being a step-parent, being sure to remind my kids that they had a mother whom they should respect. I treated Deb's two kids, Andy and Chris, likewise.

Getting the fire folks used to the idea was quite another story. I felt from the beginning of our relationship that we shouldn't remain reticent to avoid the inevitable persecution; we would face rumors outwardly and squash them, rob the gossip hounds of

The author and wife Debra. Debra's career as a Milwaukee Fire Department paramedic ended after she suffered injuries during a horrendous accident in 1990 that involved her paramedic vehicle and a stolen car being chased by police (courtesy Francy Paquette, Allied Digital Photo).

their fun. I never felt that I owed anyone an explanation for my divorce, and especially not an apology, nevertheless, we told friends and co-workers to feel free to ask what it was they needed to know so badly. And we attended department-related family functions, such as campouts and fire-police baseball games, as just that — a family. Even with our relationship being an open book, it didn't stop one of my supposed friends from saying — when I wasn't around, of course — that my mind had snapped. I never had much use for cowardly backstabbers, and it changed how I viewed friends. My circle of true friends got smaller.

Since Deb and I wore the same uniform, we became sounding boards for each other. Some mornings after getting off shift were spent decompressing, comparing notes. Sometimes we stumbled because we didn't give the other enough ear, or one of us was wound too tightly or was simply too tired. But we were fortunate to have in each other that one person we could trust with our feelings, our thoughts and dreams. At work, I could hear on the radio when her med unit went out and sometimes what they were getting into. It was the same for her. We kept excess worry in check, because we knew how the other performed. Once, Dick Kaiser, who was on our partner engine, came back from a run with Deb's med unit to tell me she had been attacked by the patient and scratched. Dick was a good man and I was glad he had been there. Deb was at busy Med 5, where one of her worst duty shifts didn't get into full swing until after dark, not an unusual occurrence at the busiest firehouse in the city. Within a short span of four hours, Med 5's crew handled half a dozen shootings. The last, the worst of the bunch, happened in the wee hours. Somewhere on a dark street, gunfire shattered the quiet, the sensible-ness — a drive-by, a dispute, who knows. One of the wild slugs went through the window of a home where a little girl, no more than six or seven years old, lay sleeping. The bullet slammed into her skull and she died despite the best efforts of Med 5's skilled trio. Darkness was giving way to daylight by the time Deb finally could lie down and rest. But the fire guys, true to their mischievous characters, would have none of it and lobbed pillows and books at her, effectively ending any chance of alleviating the stress that had accumulated during the long night. It would have been interesting to find out what our stress management team thought about that.

Milwaukee recorded 95 homicides that year; Deb likely had gotten in on many of them. As a safeguard against storing emotional baggage, she didn't remember victim's names. That little girl's name she remembers.

Deb also found it difficult to shake an early morning run where a coworker had been severely injured in an accident driving to the firehouse. Most bothersome, she admits, were the details about the firefighter's condition repeated at the kitchen table.

I still have a drawer full of notes, cards, trinkets and gifts Deb and I hid in each other's bags. They made me smile and flush with gratitude for this woman who had captured my heart, and to whom I was willing to dedicate my life. Oh, yes, we became an issue on the job, an item, as they say, but not a very secret one.

Since I was into the job, one of my pet projects was designing patches. When I toyed with the idea of designing one for Ladder 9, Pepie suggested adding the slogan, "Rats, cats, and bats." His idea had foundation for there seemed to be a stretch when the majority of our runs were animal related. We often encountered rats bailing out of a building that we were running into, and sometimes we got the creeps seeing them launch through smoke chugging from under roof eaves. We had broken open walls to free rats or squirrels when occupants complained of the noise, we had rid houses of bats, and we had fished unwanted newborn puppies and kittens from sewers. I've never taken the proverbial cat out of a tree, but on one occasion, we nearly had a riot on our hands when we decided not to rescue a cat that had gotten onto a roof.

Things went badly from the start. The towering two-and-a-half-story house was next to a sloped alley, which was the only place we could position our longest extension ladder. The alley was ice-covered, ruling out the possibility of sending someone up to retrieve the feline, which now seemed amused watching the commotion far below.

People standing around insisted that we do our job and go for the cat. They didn't like our explanation that it was too dangerous and that when the cat got cold or hungry, it would find its way back in, the same way it got out. We reminded them that *we* didn't create the opening in the roof from which it had escaped. The bystanders got louder and more hostile, which, predictably, drew more onlookers to give the contention more steam. We simply wouldn't risk life and limb to retrieve a cat that wasn't injured or in danger. In a clipped tone, Pepie suggested that the cat's owner go into the attic and coax it in through the opening. We knew that no one would, or could, claim the cat, which likely was one of a horde on the premises. But winning the argument was more important to the people than the cat's future.

Knowing that a swelling mob only gains collective strength, before things really got out of hand, on cue we walked together to our rig and left, leaving behind a cat that had to have enjoyed all the attention, and a chorus of rants and a few names I was sure I hadn't heard before. On a run a short time later, we cruised by the house. The crowd — and the cat — were gone.

One of our animal runs had us meeting a woman at her front door complaining that a bat was loose in her house. With arms bouncing off of her beefy sides and slippers flopping on worn wooden floors, she shuffled through the big flat with us in tow. We reached an attic room, where, there on the wall, perched the still creature. This seemed well within our capabilities, and we were in a giddy mood. Maybe we were just happy to be on a lighter call that didn't smack of death and despair. *Well, step aside ma'am, we're Ladder 9. If she had only known.*

Brooms were the weapon of choice, and our rig had enough of them. So, after shooing the woman out of the room, we closed the door and someone took a whack at the bat. Missed. It only pissed him off, and he darted and fluttered over our heads. Another swing. "Ow!" Pepie got it in the head while the bat drove on. Another wild swing and a lamp went down, a helmet sailed and clattered on the floor. Swinging and laughing like school children, and at the poor woman's expense, we heard her screeching outside the door. "What the hell ya'll doin' in there? Don't ya'll be wreckin' my house!" Finally, thwack! A broom found its mark, sending our winged nemesis to the floor with a barely audible thud. We were the Red Baron. "Crashed and burned," someone lamented. Pepie saluted the lifeless form.

We slowly creaked open the door, emerging with me holding the small furry body by its wingtip. Hands on stout hips, the woman glared past us to survey the damage, then at us. Not amused, she stretched a flabby arm with finger pointed to the steps. "Out!"

I would later learn that a bat was best dispatched with the freezing blast of a carbon dioxide fire extinguisher, which did less damage and kept us on friendlier terms with our customers.

Someone did finally design a patch for Ladder 9, which features a caricature of a rat.

Since the exams for the position of lieutenant were getting closer, I altered my study patterns, focusing on the points I was certain would be most important, and then focusing on none of them. I was confident about getting promoted, which would mean a transfer. As much as I enjoyed being at Ladder 9 and was grateful for the experience, I was ready for change.

Other events signaled change, although I didn't realize the impact it would have down the road. On an especially busy day when we had been exposed to a lot of smoke, we had a smoky house fire. I went in to search for a man someone said was still in the building. For us it was fairly routine, not a big house, a first floor search, probably a snotty mattress fire. I came up empty, staggered outside and fell to my knees. I couldn't get air and I couldn't get up. *What the hell is this about?* No one saw me, so I didn't say anything. Climbing up into my tiller seat felt like climbing a steep hill. One of our two department physicians, whom I admired and respected, Dr. Robert Adlam, would later explain that smothering carbon dioxide and lethal carbon monoxide accumulated during each fire, and my heart had more difficulty pumping

The author, assigned to Ladder Company 9, was at center helping to ventilate a stubborn basement fire in January 1988 (courtesy *Milwaukee Journal Sentinel* © 2012 Journal Sentinel, Inc., reproduced with permission).

clean, oxygenated blood throughout my body. Extreme exertion and underlying stress energized my heart, enough only to deliver minimal bits of oxygen. He understood that I was dizzy and disoriented, adding that if I hadn't gotten out of there when I did and gotten oxygen, I would've been unconscious. That seemed a stock explanation for what we did on a normal basis, so I wasn't alarmed. He showed a genuine interest in monitoring me and agreed to provide a fast-acting, broncho-dilating inhaler, but it came with his stern warnings and my promise that I be more careful. Doc Adlam was right, so I tucked it in a bit.

8

An Officer
and a Gentleman

I had always held that anything I chose to do would be done to the best of my ability, and with conviction. Since that especially held true with the fire service, it was natural that I would aspire to climb the ranks. I had made the climb before; in the Boy Scouts, in the Civil Air Patrol, and in the army. As much as I became a part of the fire department, it became a part of me. It was, after all, a lifestyle, and an identity, which called for carefully balancing career and family.

I was, and remain, a voracious reader and researcher, my mind having become a virtual sponge for anything related to the fire service. As a firefighter, I was on a fast track of development. I had established core values and honed my sense of responsibility, all while trying to keep my morals right. My dedication was unquestionable. My pride ran deep. Yet, my rebel self was alive and well, not only shaping my character but also playing a part in my quest to become an officer.

I was driven to become an officer. I viewed climbing the ranks of this great organization as a means of achieving my purpose and making a difference. I remembered the aplomb of the lieutenants who ruled the Gas House Gang, and of those in dress blue uniforms who walked among us 2,000 applicants at South Division High School as we took the written test to become firefighters. If I never became more than a lieutenant, I would be content. My quest was to lead people, call the shots, and guide and train a crew I called my own. Seven years of service as a firefighter was required for eligibility to take the lieutenant exams. Once I had set my sights, I became immersed in the process. As I neared the five-year mark I embarked on a self-imposed two-year study program. I crammed for eight to ten hours per day. Seldom did a day go by without some form of mental preparation, yet I was mindful of my need and desire to spend precious time with family. I could quote the fire resistive ratings of every type of door; I could quote the flammability ratings of volatile liquids. Department rules and procedures, along with fire tactics, were etched into my brain. Discipline and repetition became close friends. I researched study methods. Acronyms, which I had always enjoyed toying with to remember things, now became an important study tool. The more ludicrous and unsavory they were, the easier they were to remember. And there was the valuable on-the-job training — learning the job in the streets.

Nearly 200 firefighters and MPOs crowded into a meeting hall for the written fire lieutenant exam. When I had finished, noticing that everyone's heads were still buried in their papers, a panicky chill ran through me. Had I missed something? Had I done something terribly wrong? No, all the pages were there, and all the boxes filled.

Then came the day of the oral interview, the key segment of the exam process; the wobbly-knee, sweat-trickling-down-the-middle-of-your-back, knuckle-biter that flirted with humankind's greatest fear — the unknown. The same questions burned in everyone's mind: *What will they ask me and how will I respond?* This was where the rubber met the road, and those who hadn't prepared, or who were intimidated by interviews, would veer, skid, or even crash. Those who were simply going through the motions were grabbing the wheel with sweaty palms. The humor would drain from lewd jokes about "doin' the oral."

On the big day, I got into my car and found on the seat next to me an inspirational card from Deb. Next to the card was a rose. Spirits soared like eagles. Determination hardened to iron.

Milling about in the hall of the Fire Academy were the prospective lieutenants, all wearing the standard black or dark blue suits. I knew them all. And some, I knew, would become fine officers. *But none will outdo me today!* A couple of them commented about my appearance. *That's right. Here I am in a gray suit, pink shirt, and cowboy boots.* Deb had done well. *Ah, dare to be different!* One even chided, "C'mon Wayne, you've got to be kidding — a pink shirt?" My knowing grin seemed to make him nervous.

When my name was called, I was ready. I had forbidden myself to rehearse. I was relaxed. A key element, I believed, in preparing for exams was to cease study one or two days prior to the event. No additional knowledge could be gained, I reasoned, it being more important to allow the brain to relax, to recharge. Confidence surged. Intimidation and nervousness did not exist. *This job is mine and I'm here to take it.*

I was convinced that the three interviewers I faced, all chiefs of different departments, were no different than me. Respect and poise came naturally. *Look 'em in the eye. Show 'em what you're made of.* After introductions, they asked me to be seated. "Thank you." One of them explained the first scenario: I was to imagine that they were recruits who had just completed training, and they had been assigned to a fire company; my company, of which I was the officer. They'd come to the firehouse for their orientation. "Tell us," they said, "how you would make us feel comfortable and show us the ropes." *Tell you? I'll show you!* My "Yes, sir" came with a broad grin, followed by standing abruptly, almost knocking over my chair. Standing with my hand outstretched, still beaming, I left them no choice but to rise for my welcome. *You did say comfortable.* Their surprised looks melted into smiles as they rose to shake my hand. It was my turn to ask them to be seated. A collective "thank you." *Hell, this could even be fun.* I played the role they wanted me to play, telling them that they were in the best fire company in the world. More smiles. I talked about teamwork, expectations (theirs and mine), pitfalls, and dangers, yet emphasized their brilliant choice of career, the satisfaction and rewards. I provided insight to the culture of the profession and "our" firehouse, leaving room for questions and making sure they understood that my door was always open. *The ropes, gentlemen, was what you asked for.*

Introducing the second segment of the interview, they seemed as relaxed as I was. "A female firefighter," they continued, "is working in your firehouse. Someone has posted on the refrigerator a sexist cartoon, which, the woman tells you, offends her. How do you handle that?" Periodically making the requisite notes on papers in front of them, their nods told me that they were satisfied with my response to the situation. First outlining the logical sequence of my actions, I went on, with firmness, vowing to remove the cartoon, find and reprimand the offender privately, suggesting a heartfelt apology, and then explain to the entire company the seriousness and consequences of sex discrimination, and the need for fairness and respect. But my actual dialogue with the moronic offender teletyped across the back of my mind: *Did you leave your brain on the kitchen table this morning? Get with the times, man. There's no room on the job for this shit. You want respect. Well, that's a two-way street. Would you put this mindless crap on your mother's refrigerator?* All in my soft voice, of course.

By the time I had finished explaining how I would handle two firefighters — one black and the other white — who were engaged in a verbal tussle in public, the interview had taken an interesting turn. No longer were heads dipping to take notes. In fact, they laid down their pencils and sat back, obviously relaxed. Our meeting became conversational, with the trio asking questions about fire department matters obviously not part of the exam. I enjoyed their curiosity and sincerity during the interesting exchange.

When I finally walked out, other candidates pacing the hall threw me puzzled looks. Frowning, they griped that I had been in there longer than anyone else, and that I was the only one who had come out smiling. "What did you say to them?" one demanded. "What did they ask you?" A sassy retort reached the end of my tongue: "*When you have 'em by the balls, their hearts and minds will follow.*" But my lips remained sealed.

I'm on top. How much on top was confirmed days later. The phone's shrill ring shattered the blissful dimension in which I basked. On the other end was the exuberant voice of friend and deputy chief Jerry Frank: "Mutz, you made number one. Congratulations!" I rolled over and kissed the woman who had nudged me on my climb up the ladder. Life couldn't get any sweeter.

During my time as a firefighter in busy stations, Dennis Michalowski introduced me as "the best firefighter in the Fifth Battalion." "An ivy league firefighter," he would add. It reminded me that Dennis put a lot of stock in formal education, so it's likely that his glowing accolade was based on my hunger to learn. It's true that I'm big on life's lessons. I hope I'm able to learn something on my last day on earth. I not only strove to be a top-notch firefighter and worked in acting positions that groomed me for promotion, but also collected lessons, observations, and techniques, which went into my cranial filing cabinet. In my passion to become an expert at firefighting, I discovered that some techniques could be improved to optimize efficiency, and to save time — and lives. But change did not come easily since the fire service, not unlike the military, was steeped in tradition. Many of the old-timers were resistive to change. I grew tired of hearing "We've always done it that way" and "Why upset the apple cart?" Apathy seemed pervasive. "Just put in your 24 hours and go home."

I clung to a few basic principles: think positive, keep your thinking flexible, and think ahead of a situation. *What's the worst that can happen?* Another element of my approach to the profession was a theoretical understanding of tactics. Putting theory into play was quite another thing. *What's really happening, and what am I going to do about it? What are my goals and how do I get everyone to get involved? What techniques will work best?* These grass-roots questions lead to the development of strategies. And the best leaders play the answers as the best conductors play an orchestra, blending many distinct sounds into one magnificent piece. Especially vital to the profession, I believed, was to have a sense of a situation, called situational awareness in some circles. Such sensing is where the fire service most closely parallels the military. Like soldiers in battle, rescue workers cue in on sights and sounds, and respond accordingly. Such sensing, I believed, came only from experience. Alarms, whether fire or EMS, at first were a wild mix of sights, sounds, and emotions. Although I came on the job with some street smarts, I found it difficult to anticipate a person's next move, whether that person was a coworker or a civilian. It seemed impossible to determine a fire's spread. But I learned. Oh, how I learned.

After Deb pinned one shiny silver lieutenant's bar on my collar at the

A happy day in February 1988: promotion to fire lieutenant at headquarters, better known as "the third floor." Deb pinned on one of the silver bars; Dick Kovatch pinned on the other (courtesy Dale Mutza).

ceremony, and Dick Kovatch the other, it was official. I was an officer; the gentleman part was open to debate. "I can't even spell lieutenant, and now I are one," went the phrase. Another held that when you made lieutenant, you lost some friends. When you made captain, you lost some more. And when you made chief, you got them all back.

I harbored no doubt about my ability to lead people. I was comfortable with who I was. I was sure I could be known as someone who could get the job done. I had learned that leaders lead by example, that they didn't expect anyone to do what they themselves would not, or could not, do. Good leaders worked alongside their people. And I knew that both panic and calmness were contagious, so it was up to leaders to decide which one they showed their followers. Although the recipe for leadership is vague and elusive, its ingredients include instinct, self awareness, and emotional intelligence. Being smart or tough pays dividends, but it has more to do with creating and maintaining a positive environment, and being passionate, one of my favorites. I suppose the authoritative voice and that look I was told I had couldn't hurt.

My position at the top of the list spared me from a roving assignment, filling vacant company officer slots within a battalion. In February 1988 I was assigned to Ladder Company 18 on the eastern edge of Milwaukee's central city. I would have an old ladder truck in an old firehouse in an old part of the city. It was perfect. The old, worn Brewer's Hill district comprised enough of the inner city, the east side, and downtown to provide a variety of work, and lots of it. Immediately north of the blighted area that yuppies struggled to revitalize was Milwaukee's original black community. Tiny but neat lawns and gardens surrounded by cyclone fences marked where the old-timers survived the times. Shuttered in at night, they would hunker down to the frequent pop, pop, pop of gunfire, and they would wonder what had gone wrong with the world.

Ladder 18 was quartered with busy Engine Company 21, commanded by Captain Jim Martins. Jim was fair and even tempered, a fine leader who not only would climb the ranks but would become chief of nearby Franklin Fire Department.

My first fire as an officer actually happened before I hung my hat at Ladder 18. While working an overtime shift at Ladder 12, the city's busiest truck company, we were driving down the street when I happened to look past driver Leo Harper into some yards. In their midst I spotted the silhouette of someone hanging out of a second-floor window with dark smoke behind him. "Turn it around, Leo, guy's hangin' out of a window!" I called it in and yelled to the guys in back, "We got a worker down the block." My ace crew made quick work of getting a ladder up to the guy and crawling inside to pinpoint the fire's origin, while we waited for the first-in engine.

It turned out that our boarder and his friend, while occupying a vacant house, or "squatting," had argued, so his friend waited for him to fall asleep to set the place ablaze. Lucky for the guy, his friend was an amateur fire bug and he woke up before things got worse. Since I had become an avid student and practitioner of investigating causes of fires, I worked with the police arson squad to determine how this fire had been set. Arson was easily determined and the hunt was on for the guy's jilted boyfriend.

This was just one of many examples of why we made interior attacks on fires in vacant buildings; often they weren't vacant. Squatters holed up in them, often starting small fires to keep out winter's chill; kids played in them; druggies used them as "shooting galleries"; and scrappers went in to strip them of whatever materials were drawing a good price. Sometimes, vacants hid crime victims, whose murderers often lit the place to destroy evidence. So we fought fires in vacants with the assumption that someone could be inside. Sometimes firefighters suffered injuries at vacant building fires before life hazard could be ruled out. Often we took flak for that, but there was this pride thing.

One can't help but undergo a shift in perspective after being promoted to company officer. When it comes to tactics, there simply are too many variables at each fire to rely upon a fixed pattern. Thankfully, experience provides an expansive inventory of indicators that allows you to quickly process them and come up with a decision. I felt comfortable applying this to fireground management, but dealing with personnel problems proved to be another story. I was blessed with a dedicated, hard working truck crew: Mark Holdmann drove and operated the rig, Rich "Rev" Rewolinski was my senior firefighter, next was Bob Norton, and my cub was Jim Mueller. I found Jim a joy to have aboard as he was conscientious and a real eager beaver. Jim had already planted his feet in the fire service, having come from the Sheboygan Fire Department, and he would rise to an officer position.

We worked hard and we played hard. The makeup of my crew, our character and our abilities determined the level of harmony in the house and how well we performed in the streets. Sometimes, on a hot summer night, when humidity covered the city like a damp blanket, I'd announce into the house microphone, "Ladder 18, let's take a ride." They didn't question it, they simply mounted up. I radioed the dispatcher that we were going to another firehouse for supplies. I'd direct Mark to an ice cream parlor, load up on monstrous cones, and then tell him to park on the Holton Street bridge. "Shut the rig down, Mark. I'll have my portable radio on." And there we'd sit atop the rig, hoist up some of the neighborhood kids so they'd have a better view of distant fireworks, and marvel at city lights while ice cream dripped down our hands. And livin' was good. I may have bent the rules a bit, but such times were priceless.

It wasn't long before I began to feel the weight of that shiny silver bar. A chief was told that he'd filled the ranks of his battalion with the cream of the crop for long enough, and now he would have to take one of the less desirables. And since he didn't want the guy in his house, he said he was passing him off to me. Labeled by other bosses as unmanageable and a discipline problem, the guy was assigned to our house for Captain Martins and me to deal with. When the guy showed up, I had a heart-to-heart with him, explaining that his reputation meant nothing to me, only how he performed from that day forward. I explained how we did things, and made sure to tell him that he could come to me with anything; questions, complaints, problems, anything. Treat everyone the same, that's how I played. I wondered what I did differently than his previous bosses.

The guy toed the line, and word around the campfire was that he had shaped up, or that I had done something special. I hadn't. The only change I made was curbing jaunts out of our area in case he ever needed leverage in a scrap. When his performance lagged at fires, I called him on it. His claim that he was too weak prompted my suggestion that he begin a workout program to build strength and endurance. I could have been blunt and told him simply, "You're in the wrong line of work." I knew I wouldn't tolerate much more of his whining about working too hard. He must have sensed it, because he preferred charges against me for working him too hard at a fire. I was both angered and amused by his claim. Although the chiefs felt the charges didn't hold water in view of his reputation, and mine, I had the two firefighters he worked alongside at the fire write explanations of what I had had them do. Both claimed that I had the trio open a roof peak that had caught fire when an adjacent house exploded from a gas leak. The female firefighter went so far as to say that the amount of work was nowhere near that required for a standard roof opening; "We never broke a sweat," she wrote. She added that I never worked my people beyond their limits or treated them unfairly. So much for his avowed attempt at garnering support from another minority group. The shallowness of that sickened me; I found it a slap to the woman, who pulled her own weight.

After a chief read the charges, he called to ask if I had the situation handled. "All handled, Chief," I answered. The charges were dismissed, and I had a heart-to-heart with my whiny firefighter. That didn't satisfy the chief and it only highlighted the penchant of some leaders for micro-managing. I was seeing a side of leadership I hadn't known, and it only got worse.

Not long afterward, a chief came to the firehouse to tell me that one of the HEOs in the battalion was undergoing treatment for drug abuse. Not only was I to keep that confidential, but I was to allow him to continue to drive the rig and allow him to leave whenever he wanted to go for his methadone treatment. I couldn't believe what I was hearing. This chief, who had forged an image of a dedicated professional, was ordering me to do things that violated an untold number of policies, things that I believed he would never do.

I was livid. "Am I to understand," I began, and then verified that he wanted me to allow this admitted drug user to drive a 12-ton rig with five souls aboard, with lights and siren, and be responsible for either getting water to hose crews or raising an aerial to save people. Plus, I should let him off duty whenever he dictates, no questions asked.

"That's right, Lieutenant, you'll do as ordered," he answered.

"Like hell I will!" I snapped back. I asked him who was going to back me up. Him? The city? I'd had enough of him and his contemptuous attitude toward me. I was now a steamroller. I went on that maybe one day this guy would roll my rig, someone would get killed, and they would check my driver's blood, and then the family, the city, everyone who's anyone, would point at me and ask if I knew he was under treatment for drug abuse. And when I answered truthfully, they would ask why I allowed him to drive this big rig with lights and sirens with five souls aboard.

His answer was what I should have expected, but didn't. He said that if I didn't let the guy work, he'd have me on charges.

"Well," I piped back, "you do what you have to, and I'll do what I have to." Simmering, I vowed to lay the guy up as soon as he walked through that door. I'd have a deputy chief take him for a blood test and when it came back positive, I'd sing like a canary about this whole stinking mess.

They were careful never to assign the guy to my shift because they knew I'd keep my word. Another chief confided in me that two of our three deputy chiefs said something on the order of "Good. Put this guy with Mutza and maybe we can bring this crap to a head. We're tired of having it shoved down our throats." It made me wonder how many other cases there were of people under treatment for substance abuse, people exercising their rights while stepping on the rights of others, people who held the lives of coworkers and citizens in their hands.

Ladder 18 was proving a crucible in personnel problems, and there was more to come. It quickly became obvious that a male and a female assigned to the engine were at odds. Although it was more Jim Martins' problem, discord between the two affected the entire house. Their dislike for each other went beyond the revered pecking order, the firehouse banter quickly giving way to fanged confrontation. It seemed that the male initiated the bouts, which were laced with sexist remarks. Proof of the department's apathy toward sexism lay in the official rule book, which contained one sentence vaguely defining discrimination, with no mention of sex discrimination, much less directives about how to deal with it. The department preferred to sidestep formal charges and official review, reverting instead to its customary practice of putting distance between warring parties; "transferring the problem," some of us called it. After a vicious shouting match between the two, whom I had to physically get between, one of them was transferred.

The problem would hit much closer to home when Deb tangled with a male firefighter. While in a supervisory position, Deb asked the guy to turn the volume down on the TV, a reasonable request, considering the TV was to be off during morning housework hours. The offender not only refused but told Deb, "Get in the kitchen where you belong." He then followed her upstairs, where he crowded her. When he didn't back off, she warned him that he was in her personal space and that she would call for help. Luckily, a paramedic arrived and told Mister Testosterone he was out of line and led him toward the stairs. Adding insult to injury was the way in which the guy's officer, who was also ranking officer of the house, handled the situation. He not only heard only the male's side of the incident, but did so in front of his crew. Since this was both a male-female and a black-white issue, he opted to stick with the boys on this one. For Deb, the handwriting was on the wall.

Since then, department heads have stepped into the daylight, establishing not only policies defining sex discrimination, but procedures for dealing with it.

When personnel problems seemed to mount, and on the home front the emotional roller coaster ride of divorce seemed unending, the streets were a welcome diversion. There, at least, issues seemed more tangible, simpler. The worst that happened to my crew at Ladder 18 was ending up in the middle of a gang fight when we were called to a report of someone injured in an alley. Often, calls in which only vague information was given our dispatchers were a sign of trouble. Citizens — and I use the term loosely in this case — wanted only ambulance attendants there to patch someone up; they didn't want the police. Even if it took using coded terms on the radio in front of hostiles, we got the police there. We knew when a situation, such as the gang fight, was out of our league, so we backed off and let the police handle it. It was our job to pick up the pieces when the area was secure.

Never did we feel more out of our league than when we were sent on a report of a woman injured. The young woman, alone in her shabby home, had been sexually assaulted. Sitting outside, wearing the marks of having been roughed up, she sat quietly, eyes wet. After basic EMS care, there was nothing left to do but wait for an ambulance and the police. Seeing the window screen slit and pulled outward infuriated me. Despite my crew's sensitive and compassionate approach, we were fish out of water; five men standing there not knowing what to say. My feeble attempt at comforting words had little effect and only made our presence seem more awkward. I didn't blame her for deny-ing any help we offered. Never did waiting for the police seem so long. Later we admitted feeling a jumble of emotions, including anger, pity and maybe even guilt for our gender.

Only once at Ladder 18 do I recall facing personal danger; that was at the tip of our aerial ladder, which I had climbed to check the effectiveness of large streams lobbed onto a massive blaze at a wastepaper company. As I bal-anced 100 feet up, Captain Dick Forecki in an excited tone radioed for me to get down immediately. When I radioed back, "What?" he said that the rig's outriggers were sinking into the asphalt and the rig was tipping. Instantly realizing I was the load at the end of the lever tipping the entire truck, I spun around and bounded down the rungs, before I was tossed into the smoking heaps. Worse, I jokingly thought later, might have been surviving and having to explain how I wrecked a ladder truck. Although our stabilizers had plates under them to enlarge their footprint, a temperature pushing 100 degrees under a July sun had softened the asphalt parking lot on which we had set up. Another lesson learned, and a tip of the helmet to Dick Forecki and a nod to my angels.

Rumblings about eliminating fire companies emanated from city hall and from our headquarters. The talk was nothing new; in fact, one year earlier, companies were temporarily shut down due to manpower shortages. When Ladder 18's house was targeted for closure as part of department reorganiza-tion, residents and the local Harambee Association vowed to stage a sit-in. They held marches and a Harambee board member said, "If you try to move it out, the ladder truck will have to run over people." But now, in mid–1988, the focus was on pulling two ladder trucks from service permanently: Ladders 8 and 18 — my Ladder 18, my first company-as-an-officer Ladder 18 — I tried not to take it personally.

Despite our chief's admission that closing Ladder 18 would jeopardize safety, and despite the rallying efforts of local citizens, Ladder Company 18 fell to the budget axe in October. I happened to be working its last day in service, so at shift's end at 8 A.M., I went on the radio net to officially announce the end of Ladder 18's 40 years of proud service to the community. Doing that stirred in me a mix of emotions: pride in paying final tribute to those who served with Ladder 18, and disgust at a political system that somehow could have, and should have, found a way to maintain the safety margin that citizens deserved.

I put it behind me and focused on my next assignment, Engine Company 6, on fashionable, zany, and historic Brady Street.

9

Brady Street

Milwaukee's east side is not only one of Beertown's earliest communities, it is unquestionably the most colorful. Its rich history dates back to Civil War times when construction boomed in the area and immigrants thronged to work the factories and tanneries. Street names remain as testimony to the movers and shakers who rose to prominence on the city's slates. Italian accents had joined those of the Polish, German and Irish by the time motorized vehicles began replacing the clop-clop of horses' hooves.

At the heart of the walk-around lower east side is Brady Street. More than just a named street in Milwaukee, Brady Street evolved into a lifestyle, an identity. As a teeming thoroughfare lined shoulder-to-shoulder with trendy shops, restaurants and nightlife hangouts, Brady Street's colorful and curious blend of cultures clinched its status as the crossroads of Milwaukee. And keeping alive its reputation as the hub of the counter-cultural hippie era of the turbulent 1960s, the trendy area retains its pull on young people who display their independence.

You could get anything you wanted on Brady Street, and sometimes, that caused problems. Nevertheless, the prospect of immersing myself in the neighborhood's history and its unique flavor excited me. That bubble would soon burst.

My welcome to Engine 6 was anything but warm. The morning I walked into the place, the house captain, hands on hips and a simmering look on his doughy face, greeted me with, "Well, I know how you got here!" Automatically clicking to defensive mode, incensed at his inference that I was shown favor, I shot back, "I drove here." He droned on that my arrival meant that his good friend, whom I had replaced, now had to go to a busy ladder company, an assignment he had yet to experience. Stunned by the ludicrous pity he showed for his pal, I said, "Maybe he's in the wrong line of work." I'd already had enough and leaned into him, my eyes boring into his. I told him I hadn't unpacked my shit yet, so he could call downtown and keep his boy there at his beloved Engine 6. I didn't give a damn where I went. He stormed off but it wouldn't be the last of our heated confrontations.

Our first-in area was expansive, from the lakefront inland to the fringes of the ghetto. It bumped up against downtown's northern cityscape, stretching to the more affluent upper east side. I was ecstatic about indulging the love affair I had had with the lakefront since childhood, and I vowed to spend as much time there as possible. The makeup of Engine 6's area offered a wide variety of work, from tired 100-year-old shacks to high-rises, from major industry to commercial buildings, every kind of business, heavy traffic flow, and people from every walk of life.

A well-known drawback was the area's population density, which caused us — well, some of us — to worry about not having a ladder company nearby. The elimination of Ladder 18 made the wait even longer. At fires in buildings that were heavily occupied, we would be alone for too long and spread too thin. It was dangerous for everyone.

Shortly after my arrival, my MPO, Tom Wagner, cornered me in the office. "Hey boss, got a minute?"

"Sure, Tom. What's up?" Creasing his brow, which hooded his brown eyes, he explained that his urging the bosses to obtain an extra-long pike pole for him to break windows had fallen on deaf ears. Not only did I appreciate Tom's sincerity, I understood the importance of ventilating a fire-charged building so we could get in with a line. And it bought time for trapped occupants. Tom added, "And we only have two axes." There should be one for every firefighter.

I liked Tom's professionalism and his sense of what was right. I knew his reputation and I was happy to have him as my MPO. Plus, his quick smile and jovial manner made him a joy to be around.

Sidestepping Tom, I swung open the heavy wooden door of the tiny office and boomed through the firehouse, "Let's go for a ride!" An hour later we returned with an extra-long pike pole and an axe we had specially requisitioned at the shop. Tom's satisfied grin and the respect my crew showed me more than compensated for the heat I expected from the captain for doing what he should have done long ago. How many unnecessary beatings from heat and smoke, I wondered, had the guys taken because the MPO had no means of ventilating the building? Worse, I wondered, had anyone been injured or killed because the crew couldn't get to them quicker?

During the inevitable nose-to-nose, the captain demanded to know how I had gotten the tools, threatening to saw the pike pole in two. I asserted that no one was going to die on my watch because we had to wait on a ladder truck, because my MPO couldn't find bricks to lob through the windows so we could get in.

I couldn't take the captain seriously anymore, so I laughed, remembering that this really was a comedy. And I laughed even more remembering the story I had been told about how he caused his marriage to go belly-up. That was his problem, but it seemed to affect how he played in the sandbox. As the tension subsided, and especially after the captain was transferred, living on the fashionable east side became easy. Being assigned to a small, single house had merit. Firehouse life was subdued, and any house without a chief held promise. Besides the volume and the variety of calls that made life at Engine 6 interesting, there was plenty of activity on the street. Fair weather hosted festivals and bazaars. Such events weren't lost on enterprising, testosterone-laden firefighters, who displayed the remnants of their attics on the firehouse stoop to lure the ladies.

True to its jumbled, yet titillating character, Brady Street provided some of my most memorable experiences. For example: heading the "I can't believe that happened" category was a summons to a traffic accident just down the street. Accidents were a dime a dozen on the crowded streets of the lower east side, especially when winter's white made the streets even smaller. But you keep an open mind because you don't know what you're truly facing until you pull up. We had already factored in that a light snow had fallen, making roads slippery, and it was late in the evening, meaning revelers had logged ample time atop bar stools.

Nearing the scene, what I saw in the middle of the street didn't register as typical for a vehicle accident. A car appeared to be sunk in the street, wedged between two high walls. Tom pulled straight in to light, as well as to protect, the scene. Quickly eyeing what we faced, a chill ran through me. I muttered, "Oh, man, I don't believe this."

A large square hole, its sides shored up with high, heavy timbers, had been dug in the center of the street. The ends of the hole that faced traffic flow had been barricaded. Straddling the hole was a mid-size car, its front and rear bumpers perching precariously on the hole's asphalt edges. The driver had driven straight in, smashing through the barricade, between the timber walls, with just the right amount of inertia to plant the car balancing precisely over the hole. This defied, in the most abhorrent sense, the laws of probability. It shouldn't have happened. But it had, and now we were faced with a challenge. We could wonder about it later.

A quick assessment with my hand light revealed three things that could only make this worse. I could make out three or four young people in the car — thankfully, they weren't moving. Close examination showed that the car's bumpers were bent upward, with only a couple of inches of their metal resting on the hole's edges. Shining my light down into the hole made my heart skip a beat. It was about 25 feet deep and at the bottom, the reason for the dig, was a large gas main, no less than six inches in diameter. *If those kids inside get rambunctious, or the asphalt gives, it's all over.* I tried not to picture the car and its young cargo plunging to the bottom, rupturing the main and being incinerated.

It was decision-making time. My crew quickly tied off the car to our rig, although I doubted the rope's ability to handle the car's weight if it slipped off the edge. I radioed the dispatcher for a ladder company, as I wanted their saws to cut through the timber shoring to get the victims out. Things were too unstable to crawl atop the car and bring them out through the windshield. I also called for the battalion chief in case this went bad, a rescue squad and an ambulance, and then I told the dispatcher I needed the gas company and two tow trucks. He questioned the two but I knew he would comply when I said, "Trust me on this and I need them fast."

A comment from one of my guys reminded me that we were far from turning the corner on this: "Boss, they're moving." Sure enough, the kids were stirring, despite being drunk or stoned, but the front seat passenger remained unconscious; the windshield in front of him was cracked and I could make out a red blotch on his forehead. Their every movement transmitted through the teetering car and my priority now was to convince them to remain calm and not move. *Damn this long wait for a ladder company.* The driver got antsy so I gave it to them straight, telling them that they were balancing over a deep hole in the street with a gas main at the bottom. "If you make one tiny move, the car falls and you will die violently." I could hear the two girls in the back seat sobbing. We kept up the dialogue with questions that ranged from their injuries, which seemed minor, to where they hung out, went to school — waiting, waiting for that ladder truck. As more cops arrived, they expressed concern about the gas main, even discussing evacuating the area. Every way we looked at this thing, there was no more we could do to stabilize that car. I was considering trying sections of fire hose when, finally, the ladder truck's siren broke through the distance.

I quickly explained to the truck boss that we needed more ropes on the car and that I wanted the towering timber walls cut down so we could bridge the hole to the car to remove the passengers. As they made quick work of the timber, I had one of my guys tie a bowline knot on me. He was the "weak sister" of my crew so I felt it important to give him responsibility and show trust. We would have one kid slowly open a door (thankfully, it was a four-door), then we would slide a plank across and I would ease over to take them out. I didn't expect anyone on my crew to be over that hole if the car plunged and blew the gas main. Those terrified kids hung on my every word and didn't move a muscle until I reached in and got a grip on them, gingerly sliding them across to outstretched arms. The kid who had been unconscious, and was now stirring, proved the most difficult to slide across. When I was back on solid ground, I looked down at the rope around my waist. It hung loosely, the knot having come undone. Tom saw it and broke into his engaging laugh. When I raised my arms and did the hula-hoop, the rope plopped onto the ground, sending us into hysterics.

Although he knew I had requested him in case things took a bad turn, the battalion chief asked why I had wanted him there. "You handled it," he said. Nodding toward the planted car, I replied, "Oh, just thought you'd get a kick out of seeing this."

I enjoyed the bewildered looks on the faces of the tow truck drivers when they eyed the car's upward-bent bumpers. The skilled pair each hooked up to an end and, in what seemed a bizarre mechanical tug of war, in perfect synch, suspended the car in the air. With one creeping forward and the other holding cable tension, they eased the car solidly onto Brady Street. I assumed the gas company would re-examine how they barricaded holes in the street. And since I couldn't fall asleep that night, I wondered if the kid rendered unconscious would believe his buds about what had happened. A recurring thought about carrying a small camera popped into my head.

Despite everything the job had shown me during the past 13 years, nothing could compare to the immense variety, the sheer zaniness, of life at Franklin and Brady streets. And it would last during my three years at the old firehouse. No other firehouse, I was convinced, was as much a part of its neighborhood. I was equally convinced that no other street in the city served as so conspicuous a stage for an endless cast of characters. Through the old wooden-sash windows we watched the timeless parade: the elderly — the real deed owners of this corner of Milwaukee — the young, the simply weird and bizarre, the down-and-outers, the fashion plates, business types and students, in all sizes and colors. Some moved purposely, briskly, head down, while the curious took in the sights. Some moved aimlessly, open to whatever came their way. For some who popped in — like old George, laden with gear for perch fishing — there was always a pot of coffee going. Cops were regular visitors, whether friends, such as Tom's detective pal, or Jim Oliva, whom I had known for years, or our resident beat cops. Eddie was our regular bluecoat, his small stature belying a tough, no-nonsense, yet fair, demeanor. Eddie always had his finger on the pulse of Brady Street, which helped us put red flags on danger spots. I felt for him when he reappeared after an absence because he had been dragged by a deranged driver whose keys he had tried to yank from the ignition.

Strollers often walked in to pass the time of day, or ask questions. It was public relations at its best. Panhandlers were quickly shown the door, along with the usual rabble that were down on their luck, or who simply had chosen to chuck any sense of normalcy. Pierre, our loud and boisterous Otis of Mayberry, usually got a pass, probably because he bellowed that he loved us, and often we saw him carrying groceries for his mother. But even he could quickly become overbearing. Pierre often wore fresh marks on his face, not because he was violent but because he defended ownership of the bottle in the rumpled brown bag he clutched.

Summer Sundays were my favorite day to watch the parade, hang over the metal porch railing and play ambassador to the masses attending St. Hedwig across the street, and all who came to marvel at the uniqueness that was Brady Street. Usually on Sundays we saw then-mayor John O. Norquist meander by, his bride Ms. Mudd in tow. Hizzoner pretended he didn't see one of his firehouses, which was fine by us because he was unpopular among city workers. When he made good on his goal to redefine the term "disabilities" as it applied to eligibility for housing in government high-rises, we said he was as useless as tits on a bull. The imprudent move earned him names such as "Nork the Dork" and "Johnnie-O." We would see the results of the changes he sanctioned in most of the two dozen complexes dotting the city and run by the Housing Authority. Fourteen were high-rises, with the one we served, Arlington Court, just around the corner. With 230 units occupied mainly by elderly and the remainder by passive, disabled persons, we went there daily. Usual runs to Arlington Court had us assisting elderly, doing CPR, or going through the motions of investigating and resetting the fickle alarm system. Periodically, the incinerator chute became clogged, making for a snotty but small, controllable fire.

When Johnnie-O, backed up by newly established HUD guidelines, declared that alcoholics and drug addicts too were disabled — as though it were a revelation — it all went bad. True, they were afflicted with disabilities under new federal definitions, but to the mayor it didn't seem unwise to move them in with elderly. Nor did it seem to dawn on him that most were young and violent. As expected, the elderly became afraid to come out of their units. They told us of the awful noises they heard through the walls, of being afraid to answer the knock on the door in the middle of the night. They no longer congregated in the lobby, especially after we responded to a couple of stabbings there. We saw the urine puddles in the stairwells and even in elevators. I ended up in a nose-to-nose session with a wild-eyed maniac who admitted he had pulled the alarm system for kicks. I found it odd that the cops on scene were wearing latex gloves, a rarity then, and were not overly anxious to close with the guy. When I too found out the man had AIDS, I couldn't shake the memory that he insidiously sprayed spittle as he raved. It was time to reevaluate how I did things. I was afraid for the old folks and I wrote letters about the nonsensical housing guidelines, citing run statistics and details. I haven't heard anything yet, but hopefully it's safer to live out your twilight years at Arlington Court. *Way to go, Johnnie-O.* After admitting to a long affair and being regularly engaged in battle with other city leaders, Johnnie-O did go, stepping down before his final term was up.

Prominent in the Brady Street area were luminaries of Italian descent with whom we pleasantly brushed shoulders. Many ran the time-honored businesses that gave the neighborhood its rich ethnic flavor. Walking into Glorioso's was a step back in time; there's something about the give of an old, worn wooden floor that creaks when you walk. Not only did the shop's Italian trappings and heady aromas bring a smile to your face, but one of the family behind the old butcher counter was sure to give firefighters a deal on meat. To the firehouse cook, Felix Glorioso, in full white apron behind the bulky counter, might chime, "Hey, how's it goin'? What are ya gonna make for the crew today?"

"I'm thinkin' lasagna, maybe," the cook might say, his head swimming in the aroma of the array of hanging sausages and pungent oils that coated heaps of colorful pasta behind thick, cold glass.

"Tell ya what," Felix would answer, wiping his hands on his pink-stained apron front, "I'll give you a deal on bulk Italian sausage and some nice sliced mozzarella."

"Sounds good. Thanks."

Sciortino's Bakery, which occupied the opposite corner of our block, offered its own blend of aromas. At the beginning of every shift, Tom, the cook or I made the short walk to buy their signature rolls. If we felt like spending a couple of extra bucks, we threw in some crullers or Italian cookies, and we were kings.

Periodically, we stopped at Busalacchi's on Van Buren so Tom could feed his addiction to their fresh nuts. Also loyal to the red, white and green in the area is Pitch's, with its retro appeal, on the corner of Humboldt and Hamilton, having stayed in the hands of the Picciurro family since World War Two. Stalwart turn-of-the-century architecture draws regulars to the Regano family's Roman Coin bar occupying the corner of Brady and Astor. The Fazzari family of restaurants, now Calderone, placed stakes on the lower east side, becoming top contenders in pleasing the palate. And we could do no wrong in the eyes of Mimma Megna, owner of Mimma's Cafe, after we took care of her husband Joe when he suffered a heart attack.

Then there was the element of Italian culture that wasn't talked about openly, yet whose blackhand was the stuff of folklore and popularized in film. With the roundup of Frank Balistreri — along with other organized crime bosses of major cities — during the 1980s, the feds felt confident that they were capping Mafia activities in Milwaukee. Some crime figures, however, remained in the sights of federal authorities and Milwaukee Police Department detectives into the late eighties. Among them was Maximillian Adonnis, a high profile, yet low-on-the-totem-pole Mafia wannabe. Max was a sawed-off, stout, one-armed scrapper who came with a long rap sheet, quick to threaten violence and make a show of being connected, a fancy only he believed. His convictions included extortion when he was maitre d' at Sally's Steak House, a renowned lower east side establishment owned by Sally Papia, who, according to authorities, had connections to organized crime. Sally's happened to be Deb and my favorite spot, five-star, nothing less. Max lived just five short blocks west of Engine 6 on Brady and Van Buren streets. Kitty-corner from his house was Giovanni's Restaurant, where Max worked as manager and maitre d.' He would be the main character one quiet Sunday morning in March 1989 when I, along with a makeup crew on Engine 6, was in the thick of this dark side.

Foreshadowing the event less than three weeks earlier was a drive past Max's house as we returned from a run at the break of dawn. Tom spotted it first. Cruising slowly past Max's car, he looked down out of his window, pointed, and said, "Hey, boss, see that?" Leaning over, I caught a glimpse of what I knew were holes made by shotgun slugs in the door of Max's big black Lincoln. "Ah, shit," I muttered, "better go around and see if he's in there. Looks like someone either finally got Max or they're sending him a message." We went back, got out, and looked inside the shot-gunned cruiser, and I radioed the dispatcher to have the police meet us. *Those five 12-gauge holes in the driver's door would make anyone get out of town.* It was no secret on the street that Max had a bull's-eye on his back. Five years earlier he had survived an attack by a nemesis who plunged an ice pick into his chest. He made enemies and friends with equal intensity, and the FBI was investigating him for large-scale narcotics involvement. Climbing back into our rig, I said to no one, "Some day we're going to *have* him."

On March 18th, having received a call for "unknown trouble" in the parking lot of Giovanni's, we hit the street under a silvery sky, quickly covering the short distance. After pulling into the lot, the seeming calm of an older couple milling about their car quickly dissipated. In my report, on the standard EMS forms we used, I provided these details:

> We were met by a woman who stated, "We need an ambulance." She directed us to auto in lot where I found female lying in back seat in obvious distress, her torso covered with blood, a puncture wound to front of neck. I requested a Med unit and directed company to administer aid to victim. I asked witness to tell me what happened and she stated that victim stumbled towards them from restaurant's north door. She further stated victim mentioned "two black guys." Witness told me that two black men just walked past her in parking lot from restaurant towards Van Buren Street, walking south. Witness also stated victim told her that someone, or people, were still in building. Considering the possibility of perpetrators, or victims, still in building, plus the proximity of suspects, I requested a 10–54 for a robbery in progress.

While tending to victim, firefighters Mueller and Savagian heard her state two or three times, "Max's friends." Victim also stated, "Bang, bang," prompting firefighter Mueller to ask her if she was shot twice, to which she replied, "Yes." During this time, the two firefighters noted a puncture wound to her left mid-neck region, in addition to the frontal wound.

During this quick interview and assessment, when the woman pointed in the direction the two men had headed, I followed her outstretched arm and glimpsed a pair of black men dressed in dark clothing, just turning the corner and disappearing. They were walking, playing it cool. *These guys play for keeps, and if we had gotten here any sooner, this could have gone devil bad.*

I found the main door of the restaurant locked, but the north door that the shooters, and later the victim, had come through was unlocked. I knew I couldn't go in there. Just then, a police car pulled in, just one, with one cop. In a quick conference, we presumed the shooters had left and we decided to go in to search for possible victims. Our bloody victim did say someone was still inside.

The cop pulled out his gun. I had my hand light but left it off, not wanting to make us a beacon. There was just enough light for us to make our way down the dark hall. We moved slowly, quietly, our backs brushing the wall. Edging along, we nodded to each other, both pointing at the heavy blood trail, stopping to take in large, glistening blood smears on the pale wall. *Man, this is some scary shit.* Then a thought hit me. I stopped and whispered in his ear, "I was just thinking, since you have the gun, why don't you go first?" He pondered it for a moment and then whispered back, "Good idea." It was comical, really. I chuckled as he gingerly slid around me, gun at the ready.

As we neared the bar and front reception area, I nudged him, pointing to a pair of legs on the floor, the remainder of the body hidden by a hostess stand. I turned on my light, sweeping the room, and shined it on the one-armed body lying in fetal position. My official report reads:

> Close examination with light revealed a puncture wound to left temple above ear with significant blood pool, from apparent exit wound, on floor at right side of head.
>
> I requested a second Med unit and pulled victim's jacket away from head to palpate carotid pulse, finding none, although skin was still warm. When Med 7 entered premises, I informed Paramedic Officer James Radtke of my findings and we rolled victim onto his back. Meds found victim to be asystole [flat-line] and P.O. Radtke made the decision not to initiate ACLS [Advanced Cardiac Life Support]. I noticed that both victim's eyes were swollen and purple and with lighting turned on, found nothing in close proximity disturbed other than approximately six business-type cards on floor near victim's feet.

The cards lay fanned like a hand of cards. Max had died in the image to which he so fervently aspired.

When I stepped outside, the lot was crammed with police vehicles and more were arriving. Detectives said they were going to question me so thoroughly that I would be on scene for a while, so I told the dispatcher we were out of service at their request. After repeating my details to countless investigators, they swore me to secrecy, advising that I pass that along to my crew. I would never know if the badly injured woman lived, but what a key witness she was. The couple who had pulled into Giovanni's lot, it turned out, were out-of-towners looking for breakfast. Had the man not needed food since he was diabetic, the injured woman might never have gotten help. Funny, the twists of fate. The phone rang all day at the engine house, but there was little I could say, until I talked to Deb.

Of particular interest to me is that this not only presented a study in varying perspectives of witnesses but also spotlights discrepancies in reporting. My reports, although done in the clipped official tone familiar to uniformed reporting, recorded the two events — Max's shot-gunned car and his murder — within hours after they occurred. Books, articles and newspapers published since then said the car was white; it was black. They said our bloodied victim was a cleaning woman; she was dressed too impeccably for that, detectives agreeing she likely was Max's girlfriend. The list goes on.

The mystery only deepened when two years later the bodies of two black men who fit a loose description of Max's killers were unearthed from beneath concrete in a basement on Chicago's south side. Both had been shot. The informant said that they were Max's killers, but authorities aver there is no connection and the case has run cold, with the solving of Max's murder left to the history of Brady Street.

At the beginning of our next shift, 48 hours later, the Adonnis murder, for me, at least, had become old news, although my regular crew now ribbed me about getting the big news story when they were off. I consoled, "Maybe we'll get a revenge killing today. A lot can happen in 24 hours." It was a new day and I was open to whatever it might bring. Few days at Engine 6 were typical, but we preferred it that way. A day that might be labeled typical began with "taking down" the off-going boss, check my mask, and give the rig a once-over. Then I connected with him for an exchange of gossip and pertinent information. Heavy on his mind today was the problem drinker on his shift. He was not sure how to handle it and asked if I'd be willing to talk to him. He added that the guy had made some trades and would be working on my shift in the near future. "I'll do what I have to do," I asserted. And I remembered what I had said to the boozer when I needed him at a south side apartment fire, where his only contribution was dropping a pile of hose on the ground. I had mixed feelings about my counterpart's request because he wore a lieutenant's bar just as I did, and he should have been capable of handling his own personnel problems. I decided not to talk to his guy unless he posed a problem for me.

After breezing through department notices left on the desk, I went off to the kitchen where the aroma of hot coffee and fresh rolls added to its inviting warmth. Mario's excited voice dominated the conversational buzz as he described an especially gruesome run they had the day before. Two young men were moving out of their second-floor apartment and decided the easiest way to get their refrigerator out was by lowering it with ropes from the rear porch. As they struggled to get the bulky thing over the railing, one guy's sweater snagged on the coils and he went over with it. The fridge landed on the hapless renter's head. Clapping his hands together, Mario described in detail the separation of the poor guy's brain from his skull. His face glowed with fascination even as he told how the scene made the boss retch. "Like a grape," he finished in wonderment. *Better them than us.*

The off-going shift drifted out the door, leaving me and my crew to go over business. Often I would ask if anyone needed to go anywhere that day. They knew that I appreciated their professionalism and hard work, and they knew that I believed in rewards, even if it meant bending the rules a bit. No one had to go to a store, a bank, or any other place so I told them we'll take a ride later to let the cub get some time behind the wheel. It is customary to train our greenhorns in all aspects of everyone's job not only so they become well-rounded, but also so they can step into any slot in a pinch. The morning paper was shuffled about the table, and John "Heino" Heinowski held high a full pot of coffee: "Anyone?"

Tom answered his usual, "I'll have some if you're buying."

"If it's Catholic coffee, I'll have some," I added.

Steam rose from bulky, worn mugs, and talk drifted from fishing and hunting to sports, to shop talk, to women, and back to fishing and hunting. A "skirt" sauntered by the windows and the fire guys stumbled to get the conversation back on track. One of them ran to the windowed front office for a longer view. When he returned, he got razzed about falling in love and being dumped all within two minutes. "I'm too good for her, anyway," he fired back. Two cups of mud for me and I went to my tiny office. Heino, who I was blessed to have on my crew, was cooking so he made his shopping list while rummaging through the cabinets. So measured was John that even his moves seemed to have consciousness. He wore his years well, despite a thick mane of salt and pepper hair that accentuated his light blue eyes. Not only was he an excellent EMT, having years of experience on a rescue squad, he was my senior man and a splendid individual. Someone said in a film about firefighters, "The thing about firemen is they're always firemen." Only recently did I discover how much that described John, when he opened up about saving a three-year-old boy from a burning apartment in 1980. On an off day, John was at Wilson Park when smoke billowed from a nearby building. A woman who dashed out the door clutching a baby told John a little boy was still up there. Up John went, crawling in thick smoke toward the child's cries. After John brought him out, looking up to see the fire blowing out the windows, he saw an elderly couple, one of whom was wheelchair-bound, on a second-floor porch. He climbed up and was helping them down ladders when the troops arrived. The chief later told John he should not have been able to crawl through the vicious blaze. John said blandly, "Saint Christopher was with me."

My MPO, Tom, along with firefighters Ralph Kornburger and my cub, Paul Singer, who were my other stars, began house work. As the promoted person on the floor, Tom was the straw boss. The odor of Jansolv cleaning solution wafted into the office, blending pleasantly with the smell of wet, smoky hose and a stiff Lake Michigan breeze. If there was lots of hose from a fire the previous night, I would give them a hand in keeping with my reputation as a working boss

We were two hours into our 24-hour shift when five rings came in for a fire. The dispatcher called us off first, meaning we were first due. That, in itself, quickened the pulse. "We have reports of smoke in the area, east Brady and Cambridge Streets." We knew that was a few blocks east. And he said "reports," plural, a sure thing. We were out the door and on Brady Street in 30 seconds, all of us donning turnout gear. My mask was recessed into my seat so I had only to slip my arms through the straps, which I cinched tightly. I wore it snugly so it became a part of me. Squinting into the sun, we immediately saw heavy black smoke boiling above the sea of vehicles. It was slow going in this press of traffic, but Tom expertly wove through the congestion, swearing so loudly at a couple of lumber-headed drivers that I was sure they heard him. I had the radio mike in hand in case I had to lean on it, in case they were tap dancin' on the window sills, as Paul Collova used to say. But this smoke was too black, too concentrated, and moving in a boiling fashion, unlike that from a building on fire.

We were close enough for me to make out a roofer's tar wagon in the street, fully aflame. Tar, sure, that made sense; dense, boiling black smoke. I radioed it in, keeping only the first ladder truck coming, and added that we needed police for traffic control. "Grab a hydrant, Tom. This could take a while." "Gotcha," he answered as he zeroed in on one close by. I factored in that the wagon was large and had a correspondingly large liquefied petroleum (LP) tank to fire its burners. So catastrophic are they when they explode, their fireballs can spread havoc hundreds of feet. I warned the people mesmerized by the drama that were too close. I admired the respect they showed by responding, as I do drivers who do their utmost to clear a path for our mammoth rig. The guys quickly laid a line, keeping their distance, knowing too the LP tank must be cooled. "200 pounds," I yelled to Tom, meaning the psi that would produce a safe high-pressure spray. Then I looked Ralph in the eye. "Spray only!" A straight stream boring into the boiling, flaming goo would violently erupt. Tom worked his magic at the pump panel, water came quickly, and my gang made quick work of the spectacle, leaving it a sizzling, steaming hulk. I liked the tar smell, which reminded me of my days in road construction, and how grateful I was to be where I was. Now to talk to the roofers who owned this thing.

Back at the barn, Tom left the rig on the ramp and our dirty hose was dragged to the back of the apparatus floor. Clean, dry coils were yanked off of the rack, unrolled and added to the neatly packed hose bed. This seemingly mundane procedure too is timeless and smacks of tradition. If it's large diameter hose, the MPO, later HEO, climbs up into the hose bed, pulling in the flat, cotton-jacketed hose. At the back of the rig, another ensures the end folds are tight and even, forming what we call accordion folds. Those at floor level feed the hose up, usually from the coil lying atop a homemade turntable

The author in a light moment in the office of Engine Company 6 on Milwaukee's trendy east side. No assignment could match the variety of work at Engine 6, thanks to the character of Brady Street (courtesy Debra Mutza).

on a pedestal. When the end of the 50-foot section comes off the spinning disc, a person holds the male-threaded coupling, while the next person in line checks for a gasket and then screws on the swivel female coupling. If he fumbles with it, he's sure to hear, "Put some hair around it." As they pass it upward, they shout "Knuckle," warning those on top a coupling is coming. Rows of tightly packed, folded ends form a neat symmetrical wall, a matter of pride to engine companies.

I retreated to the office to do paperwork. Heino yelled, "Goin' shopping, boss," and I heard the rig humming out on the ramp as Tom put the powerful 1,500-gallon-per-minute pump through its paces. Above the din I heard playful shouts and I grinned, knowing the cub was getting an unwanted shower. A rap on the window startled me. It was Fred Thiel, waving vigorously. "Hey Fred!" I yelled through the glass. He lived nearby and his son was on the job. A few minutes later another rap. It was two cuties, laughing and waving, in their early twenties, I'd guess. "Hi girls!" It would be hard not to like this place.

Soon, everyone was back in the kitchen, the hub. Neil Diamond's "Red, Red Wine" is pushing through the speakers of the old radio on the window ledge and I turned up the volume, singing along. The cub was helping Heino empty grocery bags. I noticed Paul's soaked shirt and asked, "Paul, is it raining?"

"Got caught in a cloudburst, Lieutenant," he grinned at the others.

A coffee cake was plopped onto the table. Large, dark red chunks of beef went into a huge cast iron skillet for browning and soon sizzled loudly, smelling oh so good. Heino removed the meat trimmings, including fat, from the pan and put them in a bowl, which he set before us. The hot beefy morsels tantalized us and made us look forward to the sauerbraten he was preparing for the noon meal. Simmering onions and boiling pickling spices added to the fervor of the senses.

Cooking adds to the complexity of firefighters. Who would think the central chore owned by our mothers would characterize firefighters? Imagine macho smoke-eaters who serve in the bastions of altruism, alien to any sense of savoir faire, delicately balancing sauces and spices to create the sacred meal. You will hear that someone on the job is a good cook before you will hear that the person is a good firefighter. Some are excellent cooks. The meal is often devoured with a sense of urgency, everyone knowing the bells can halt the fork's blissful arc from plate to palate.

Out on the apparatus floor, the cub yelled, "Chief in quarters!" Our battalion chief walked in, making his daily rounds. We exchanged small talk and he asked about the tar wagon. "My boys nailed it," I said proudly. As we exchanged mail pouches, he half informed, half admonished that "the third floor" said too many rigs were cruising Lake Drive. "So stay off of Lake Drive." I asserted that that was in our first-in area so we did spend a lot of time there, not only inspecting but training. "In fact, I said, "we'll be down there this afternoon." The scowl on his face said he didn't like my response, but he knew I was within my operating parameters, and he was not at all surprised I stood my ground. *Save those chicken-shit rules for someone else.* I hated control tussles. I'm sure he also remembered that shortly after my arrival at Engine 6, I pre-fire planned the entire McKinley Marina, noting hydrant locations and pressures, firefighting stations on piers, underground fuel storage for boats, and other hazards. I then drew up three charts: for us, for his car and for the deputy chief's car. Along similar lines, we visited the city engineer's office to obtain a large street map of our area, which Tom and I highlighted and mounted on the wall for quick reference. Fill-in drivers and bosses found navigating the maze-like east side challenging, especially since there are no numbered streets. And if driving around in circles, lost, lit up like a Christmas tree and with siren wailing wasn't embarrassing, I don't know what was.

The chief ambled out of the kitchen with, "Don't call me unless it's through the roof." Kiddingly, I got away with, "Yeah, yeah, don't let the door hit you in the ass on the way out." His comment harked back to my days at Ladder 9 when he was our chief and often commented that at workers he could stay in the car because we made him look like a star. He said to just let him know when it was under control and he'd call it in.

At precisely noon Heino yelled throughout the house, "Soup's on!" Oh, yeah. No need to look under our plates for change today. Heino had done well. We feasted on a fresh garden salad, savory chunks of steaming sauerbraten accompanied by mashed potatoes and gravy nestled on our plates next to buttery carrots frosted with brown sugar. And there is fresh bread and cold milk. Kings, that's what we are. "My compliments to the chef," I said, and we dug in. I said a silent prayer: *Thank you, Lord, for this thy bounty, now please keep those bells silent and I promise I'll straighten up.*

We barely had gotten through the meal when five rings came in. We were going alone to "meet a citizen with unknown problem." That could be anything under the sun. Outside of an apartment building we were met by a panicky man who explained that he had just purchased the building and had been trying the various electrical switches to see what they controlled. Before he got to the point, someone bolted through the door behind him, coughing, and I saw a smoke-filled hall. I told the guys, "Mask up and lay out!" and radioed for a full assignment, adding that I had smoke in an apartment building. Moving quickly, we found fire involving a room at the far end of the hall. Trading vision for a snoot-full of smoke, I didn't strap on my face-piece, leaving it dangling from the strap around my neck; but the biting brown smoke had killed any remnant of that wonderful meal. Although we quickly knocked the fire down, I kept the full assignment coming since the place held a lot of people and I had no idea of the fire's extent. I was anxious to get the first arriving company above that room since this had begun as a slow-moving, unchecked fire. We emptied the room of damaged material and began opening the heavy wooden ceiling and walls. *Why wood?* It made sense when we discovered the room had been converted to a sauna and then used as storage. The electrical circuit for the heating elements had simply been turned off and not disconnected. When the new owner flipped the unmarked switch to on, he didn't realize he had energized the sauna system in the enclosed room now packed with combustibles. Shame that he paid the price for the previous owner's carelessness.

Despite the unusual circumstances of the fire, it doesn't qualify for most unusual. That title was claimed by an inferno in a high-rise apartment, an intense blaze from which we never saw a flicker of flame. When we finally reached the floor the fire was on, we smelled smoke and fully expected to be engaged in fierce battle once we forced the hot door. After hooking up to and charging the building's standpipe system, and with all of us combatants in position, masks on, lines charged, we hunkered down while a truck crew took in the door. Nothing. Light smoke and heat wafted through the doorway. We slowly peered in, and then moved in, carefully, crouching, nozzle ready. The place was an oven. Our lights revealed that the entire apartment had been destroyed by fire, a charred tomb. It was eerie. The blaze had to have burned a long time, undetected, smoke venting unseen, consuming every single item, but never extending beyond those walls, and when it had completed its destructive sweep, having no fuel left and little oxygen, it burned out, died. Had we come knocking earlier, we likely would have faced a backdraft. Horrific if unsuspecting occupants had opened that door and given the smoldering beast air. In 18 years, I saw this phenomenon only once.

After we completed hose and mask work back at quarters, I told my crew, "Let's take a ride." I hopped in back so Paul could drive, with Tom in my seat to instruct him. "To the lake, James," I told Paul through the window between the cab sections. "All right!" Ralph beamed. Tom radioed, "Dispatcher, Engine 6 is on the air practice-driving." I pictured the chief's broad face frowning when he heard that. We three in the back chewed the rag, taking in the warm lake air. I felt good about the sunshine, the busyness of Brady Street, and how well my crew — my friends performed. And life was good.

Paul wheeled our monstrous diesel-powered Pierce past the tennis courts where an exceptional pair of toned, tan legs grabbed our attention, past the beautifully ornate North Point water tower, and onto Lincoln Memorial Drive.

I loved this panoramic view and gazed up at the high-rises, dreaming about some day living up there. Some strollers and joggers waved. A little girl pumped her arm and Paul obliged with a blast of the air horn. We ended up at the old Coast Guard station at the water's edge, well distant from the busy roadway. Tom, Paul and Ralph prepared to connect to a hydrant on the grounds to learn the pump, and Heino drifted off to talk with fishermen on a nearby footbridge. I planned to join him later, but first I wanted to check out the old building. It being long vacant and boarded up, we could easily end up here for a fire some night, and I didn't like surprises. The imposing, all-white two-story structure featured a five-story watch tower and boat launch doors on its shore side. I grabbed my hand light, put the long strap of my walkie-talkie over my shoulder, turned up the volume and headed for a hole made by vagrants who camped in the old place. "Fire department," I shouted through the hole, making sure not to surprise anyone who might think I was an intruder. *What a ludicrous thought. Like they're not.* Once inside, I heard only the water slapping the stones outside of the launch doors. I felt a brush of chill, not from the mustiness trapped inside, but at the thought of hearty watchmen swinging wide these heavy wooden doors, slipping heaving lifeboats into icy waters on frigid nights to risk it all for the sake of humanity. *Sounds familiar.* My sweeping light fell on a stone corner smudged black where someone had stared into firelight, out of the cold wind. *Maybe this winter, they'll reclaim the spot.* Back outside, I joined Heino and the old-timers on the bridge to hear if *they were biting,* our pumper humming away in the background.

The guys got in a good training session, and no sooner had we stowed the bulky suction hose and capped the hydrant when the radio beckoned, "Engine 6." We were sent to one of the nearby marina's parking lots where we found a big guy on the asphalt. He had dumped his Harley trying to make a tight turn. The lower part of one leg went in different directions and the jagged end of a broken bone protruding through his jeans glistened white in the sunlight. He arched his back and hyperextended his head backward as he howled in pain. There was little blood. Since his vital signs were good and there was no head injury, I called for a private ambulance, per our EMS protocol. We immobilized him, tried to calm him, and checked his mangled machine for leaking gasoline. *Bummer summer for him.*

It was 5 P.M., supper time, the lighter of two meals, and Heino shone again, serving us whopping cheeseburgers and fries. Dessert was an ice cream malt mix with pineapple he had made earlier. I let mine melt in the bowl just a bit to take off its icy edge. "Nice job, John." *Nice job, indeed.*

As the day got longer, we drifted, some guys watching TV, while others hung out on the front porch. I called Deb, who was working on a med unit on the opposite side of the city. On a warm night like that, chances were they were out on a run. It was a thrill for me when she was at a med unit close by and we ran into each other, or if it was med 7, our closest, and they stopped by for a visit. As night fell, Brady Street took on a new face, usually a meaner face. The old folks and tourists disappeared from the streets to be replaced by younger crowds, some of whom over-imbibed on "liquid asshole" and went into their Jekyll and Hyde act. Of all the violent characters we encountered, the most memorable never made a move, yet he proved the most disconcerting. He was a big guy, late twenties maybe, who people in the area said had assaulted his friend. When we pulled up, he sat hunched over, at the bottom of a staircase, not moving, his head in his hands. His friend said he had mental problems and was on medication. *Great.* We kept our distance. Squatting a few feet from him, I told him who we were, asked him a few questions. No answer. He didn't move. I expected him to come alive any second and my heavy hand-light would have to suffice. I hated the uncertainty, the kinetic potential, of runs like these. I checked on our police help but they were delayed, as they often were on a warm night. I wanted to leave but that was abandonment, especially if our boy went berserk and someone got hurt. I heard him call his friend's name and when the guy squatted to listen, I heard him say quietly, "I'm gonna off that motherfucker." That was me, and I knew he meant it. I now steeled myself for whatever came next. Absolutely nothing happened during the 20 long minutes we kept gawkers away from him. He never moved. Finally the police rolled in. When they stood him up, he loomed even larger than I originally had guessed. He didn't resist, he just stared. I am afraid of no man but this guy gave me the willies.

As night wore on, we got called to the Up and Under Lounge, which was within view down the street. It was a fun, popular place, hosting good bands, but often soccer or rugby players ended up there and mixed it up after a few belts. It didn't matter to them where they drew blood, on or off the field. We offered to patch up anyone who cared, but they declined. Since everyone was standing, I was able to convince their leader I wouldn't call the police if they simply shook hands and took their celebrating elsewhere. Being good sports and friendly, they complied, limping off with their wounded.

It was getting late and although there was every chance we would face a busy night, I decided to get some shut-eye. Sleep often comes in segments, between runs. It's only half-sleep anyway, with an ear cocked for the bells, so I usually go home tired even if we get a night in the rack. We ran the window air conditioner hoping the white noise would mask the street tempo, but a thumping music beat from Franklin Place next door reverberated through the walls. Bar closing time in the wee hours is a sure bet for trouble, usually an auto accident or a pissing contest that escalates and spills out into the street. The high-rises filled with elderly that line Farwell and Prospect avenues, along with a few nursing homes in our area, are good for an EMS run or two. Our average seems to be eight to ten runs per day, enough to keep us honest.

Traffic noise overwhelming the hum of the air conditioner meant the erratic night, finally, had given way to daybreak. John and Tom were early risers, so when I finally shuffled out of the small, stuffy dorm, the din of the kitchen downstairs drifted up through a pole hole along with the aroma of strong coffee. Shafts of sunlight poked through front windows and I looked forward to the day. A self promise to crawl back in the sack when I got home vaporized. The sun was out and it was too good a day to waste on sleep.

As I scanned the headlines, my relief walked into the kitchen and chirped, "You're down," signaling that my 24 was over. We went over a few notes, shop talk, I gulped down the last of my coffee and washed the heavy mug. After dashing to the corner for Sciortino's rolls, I jockeyed out of our lot. Parking space was a precious commodity on the lower east side and our cramped lot was no exception. I headed west to Deb's busy firehouse so she could end her day. We usually drove to work together, unless she was working at a distant house. It was common for her med unit to be out on a run when I got there, so I went inside if I knew this bunch, or waited in the car. When she emerged, seldom did her face reflect her past 24 hours. She was usually high energy, smiling, and given to affection. The ride home, or to a diner for breakfast, would be laced with animated conversation, sometimes just listening, unwinding, or de-stressing; whatever it took.

Whatever Deb and I did that day would probably involve the kids. We made sure of that. We had great times sharing our lives with all the kids. As much as we provided for them, and as much as we valued those times, it didn't occur to us then that it could be lost on them as they grew older and formed their own relationships. Little did we know that the "step" element of our put-together family would harbor unresolved issues that would never go away. Our lives changed constantly. We rolled with it, the good and bad, and tried to make the best of it. I don't believe all of our kids picked up on that. Maybe it's generational; maybe it's a mystery of life. Nevertheless, Deb and I learned, and we grew, our lives ever in a state of flux. Having accepted that, and each other, we decided to tie the knot.

On October 14, 1989, a brisk, fall day sparkling with sunshine, we exchanged our vows in the cozy Rathskeller of the John Ernst Café in Milwaukee's East Town. We tailored the ceremony so that it was meaningful, which meant including our six kids. It was a happy, wonderful day shared with 50 friends and family members. And off we went, kids in tow, down the road into our future, where change would prove to be the law of life.

When Deb decided she should sell her house on the southernmost edge of the city so that we could better accommodate our Brady Bunch, we bought a bigger home in a south side area referred to as Municipal Meadows, a fitting description given the area's saturation of municipal workers. Ever on a bent to make things better, Deb and I gave the place a new look inside and out. Besides being blessed with wonderful neighbors, we were happy in our work, we pulled out all the stops to provide for our kids, who seemed content, and life was good. My mother lived on the south side, as did Deb's folks, not far away, in fact. It was difficult for our parents, much less anyone, to grasp completely the nature of our work, but they were proud of their fire department son and daughter. And wasn't that all that really mattered? Deb's parents, Tony and Wanda Tomasino, were no strangers to the job since Deb's older brother, David, already had a dozen years under his belt as a Milwaukee firefighter/paramedic. Tony and Wanda's fire-police scanner created constant background noise in their kitchen, and when they recognized our company numbers over the airwaves, we could be sure that questions about the run were forthcoming.

It seemed easier for our kids to accept our marriage than for the fire department community. Deb and I didn't pioneer the concept of relationships on the fire department, but we were the first active duty members to marry. We were a novelty, although the conscientious Fourth Battalion chief didn't find us amusing the day that scheduling had us both assigned to the same firehouse, his firehouse. We heard that he wouldn't have it, but when I called him to allay his concerns and tell him he should worry more about couples that weren't married, he relented. That didn't stop others assigned there from playfully pushing our beds together in the dorm, or placing flowers at our place at the table. Nice touches, really, but we played it cool, with me grabbing the watch bed in the office.

Deb fought her own battles, and when someone who was trying to get her dander up said, "Sure, you'll just run to your husband who has lots of pull," she replied blandly, "No, but you won't want to crawl into a hot attic with him."

It seemed that to some of the boys I had crossed the line taking up with one of those female paramedics, identifying with them. I found such narrow mindedness amusing, and reminded myself that we all have a little Archie Bunker in us. Deb had such abiding respect for the job, for rank, and for me that in front of others, on duty, she often referred to me as "Lieutenant." When people asked why she called me by rank, she answered, "Because he earned it." When the novelty of us wore so thin that we no longer were good rumor fodder, even to a couple of hardcore busybodies, life returned to normal, or as normal as could be.

Speaking of tangling with someone in an attic fire, an incident comes to mind that, like most, in the end, made us laugh.

At a fire on the fringe of the lower east side, my company ended up on the upper floor, which was a combination second floor and attic. On the same floor was Ladder 5's Lieutenant Dean Thomas and his gang. There was one hose line between us, and he and I found fire extending from the first floor and breaking through the walls. Simultaneously, Dean and I ordered our crews to grab the line to attack the spreading flames. His pipeman had used it and dropped it, something one just didn't do in our game. Since a relinquished line is fair game, I pointed to it and my guy jumped on it like a fumbled football in a Bears-Packers game.

That pissed Dean off and he yelled, "Pass the line back!"

"I have fire over here!" I shot back. That didn't sway him because, of course, we both thought our company was better than the other's. Clearly, I had exploited the age-old tradition of stealing another company's line, but, in the same vein, there was enough fire for everyone, and the line lay there, up for grabs. Pride ran deep.

Dean and I went toe-to-toe in the smoke, while our able crews, unruffled, fought the blaze around us because that's what they did. Hearing the commotion, Chief Kovatch came up the steps, bellowing, "What the hell are you two doing? Get this thing under control and I'll talk with you two later!"

Later, out on the street, as I pulled off my mask, Dean stomped over and put his face next to mine. Again, we became locked into a shouting match fueled by high blood pressure and carbon monoxide and adrenaline-laced post-fire highs. Sure, Kovatch got a piece of us, but the next day our crews saw Dean and me exchange apologies, shake hands, and we got to laugh at ourselves, fully understanding that tempers come with the territory and can't be taken too seriously.

I laughed again when my MPO, Tom, told me that people were afraid to get between Dean and me because we were Vietnam vets. *Ooh, yeah, scary, boys and girls, watch out for us.* Dean was top-shelf and I was intensely proud of him when a photo ran on the front page of the newspaper, showing him giving mouth-to-mouth resuscitation to a baby he had rescued from a burning building.

Now and then came subtle reminders that I was a Vietnam vet; I didn't advertise it, but neither did I deny it when asked. Once, my crew and I even exposed it.

We were hunkered down with some cops behind cover outside a house where a disturbed man was holed up, threatening to torch the place with five gallons of gasoline. When one of the cops asked what five gallons would do, one of my crew quipped, "Well, one gallon would do the trick, but five will give you a hell of a fire to watch. You'll get a nice sunburn even from here."

For reasons that are obvious, this photograph of Dean Thomas made the front page on June 16, 1988. After rescuing the baby from a burning home, Dean performed CPR until paramedics took over (courtesy *Milwaukee Sentinel/*Patrick Murphy-Racey, © 2012 Journal Sentinel, Inc., reproduced with permission).

Another cop mumbled something to the effect that it had to be one of those damn Vietnam vets. "Crazy motherfuckers."

One of my guys shot me a sideways glance that said he wanted to have a little fun, to call the cop out. I slowly dropped my eyelids in apathetic assent. He turned his gaze back to the cop and asked, "Really? Why d'ya think so?"

"Cuz they're all fuckin' crazy," he scowled, finally turning his eyes from the house, and then darting them back as though not wanting to miss the big fire.

"Must be a story there," my guy persisted, his tone more serious.

Now he turned his head, thinking he had our interest. "See this?" he complained, lifting his pant leg to reveal a scattering of long, purple scars on his lower leg. "One of them vets did this, with a knife," he said, his eyes round and white. "Took nearly a hunert stitches!"

My firefighter came back with, "You really believe they're all off kilter?"

"Sure they are!" he asserted, pouting his thin lips. He squinted, which carved deep furrows in a squat brow under short blondish-red hair. "Fuckin' nuts."

Peering intently and nodding at the house, the firefighter turned on the sarcasm, saying that if this guy was a vet, and he could find a match and did what he said, it'd be one less to worry about. And the world would be a safer place.

"Got that right," the cop shot back defiantly, his red, pudgy cheeks quivering.

A cop kneeling nearby, who had heard the exchange, looked at us sorrowfully, and hung his head, slowly shaking it. He brought his head up and stared intently at the house, but his thoughts were elsewhere. Slowly lowering his chin to rest on the stock of his shotgun wedged atop our rig's bumper, he said through compressed lips, through the quiet, through the waiting, "Ten bucks says he's not a vet."

Officer Gruff spun his head toward his peer and snapped, "Bullshit!"

My guy apologized loud enough for all to hear, adding that he guessed I didn't care to hear this.

"Don't mean nuthin," I spat, resurrecting the dusty term from 20-year old "Nam-speak." The shotgun-armed copper flashed a smile that must have taken three days to wipe off.

Only once did I see violence on the wrong side of the law. Often we ran in with cops assigned to the district, some of whom we got to know quite well. Only one did I keep at arm's length — a small, nervous wiry guy with thinning black hair that topped a pinched, stern face set with black-framed glasses. I called him the little-prick cop. Whenever we saw him, it was obvious he had a big chip on his shoulder and was out to prove something. He made a show of shooting his mouth off and dominating a scene with his rough manner. He liked to put his hands on people.

The call was for an overdose on the second level of a small east side apartment. Near the top of the stairs a woman in her late thirties lay on a couch moaning, her two young kids standing silently nearby. She wasn't in a bad way, having taken a few too many pills that couldn't possibly cause her harm. She obviously had mental issues, and this was a call for attention, a dicey position, I thought, to put her kids in.

Cops always came in on ODs. It was routine for them to question the drugs involved, not bothering with the patient unless the person was violent. Up the steps behind us trudged the little-prick lawman. I didn't want him around so I played it low-key by saying something like, "No big deal, woman's upset, only fouled up her prescription stuff, nothing that's going to hurt her. We'll probably get an ambulance and there's someone downstairs to watch the kids."

Quickly shifting his glance from me, he smirked and stood over the woman, hands on hips. That was one piece of body language I tried to avoid, but it was part of his act. It didn't take long for his accusing line of questioning to piss the woman off. She became agitated and kicked a leg into the air. It wasn't aimed at anyone, but done in frustration. But it was all the excuse Officer Nasty needed to prove his manhood. In one swift motion, he grabbed her, rolled her onto the floor face-down with a solid thump and cuffed her, hands in the small of her back.

"Hey-hey, what's this?" I barked. "Not necessary. Maybe you're jumping the gun here!"

He didn't answer but lifted her painfully up by her cuffed hands, edged her on tiptoes over to the stairwell, and leaned her out over the top stair, daring her through gritted teeth to give him a hard time. Her eyes went wide and she gasped. I'd had enough. I pressed against him, my lips almost touching his ear. "You do it," I hissed, "and I'll not only have you on charges, I'll have your badge. I promise. I'll take this all the way. Now back down."

He glared sideways at me as though he could put a bullet in me. But he pulled her backwards. A huge cop appeared around the stair landing and when he got up to us, I told him we had a problem, that the woman hadn't done anything. When I said he could be a witness, he lowered his eyes. He knew. Little-prick cop mumbled and disappeared down the stairs. I looked at the big blonde cop, nodded toward the steps and said that his little guy with the Napoleon complex needed to work on his people skills.

"Yeah, I know," was all he said, looking down at his notebook.

The cub on our crew that day was a liberal sort, and I guessed by his stares afterward that he had seen something in me he hadn't expected. My other two firefighters would have backed me as well, but they knew I wouldn't expect them to.

Sometimes we didn't have to look far to find characters; they were right under our noses. The day came when the alcoholic worked on my shift. As I expected, he volunteered to take all-night watch. I nixed that, knowing he'd be loaded by daybreak. As the day wore on, he seemed to be getting sloshed, so, with a witness, I went through his locker but didn't turn up his hootch. I watched him more closely and it became clear why he made frequent trips to the parking lot. When I called him on it, he admitted the booze was in his vehicle. He called a close friend on the job who came to the firehouse so we could discuss his problem. I veered from the personal angle, vowing to his high-ranking friend that I would enforce the rules if I worked with him again. "We're not flipping burgers here," I finished; "we're dealing with life and death."

10

More Characters on Brady Street

Sometimes I felt like a chameleon, constantly changing to adapt to whatever environment I happened to be in, or whatever self-imposed project kept the wheels turning. I was comfortable switching gears, actually. I was comfortable too at work on Brady Street, but I felt the tug of responsibility when a nagging vexation became problematic. In reference to the problem, I joked that there were more full moons on the east side, since studies pointed not only to increases in 911 calls on nights of a full moon, but also to more of a bizarre nature. The most logical explanation held that the moon had a gravitational pull on cerebral fluid, thereby affecting behavior patterns. Full moon or no moon, our contact with the lower east side's down-and-outers remained steady, accounting for more and more of our runs. We found them wherever their mind-altering cravings told them to sleep — in vacant buildings, in doorways, under bushes, in fields, even on porches to scare the crap out of residents. Our intervention, sometimes requiring gentle prodding or our air horn alarm clock, consisted of simple, to-the-point dialogue to get to a shelter or find a better hiding spot — to stay off of private property or next time they'd be talking to the police who wouldn't be as easy-going.

Some were our regulars, mostly Anglo and Native American, all male except for Colleen, late thirties and older. We knew most by name and we came to know their habits, their hangouts, their poison, and most importantly, their propensity for violence. Pierre, of course, we saw the most and he palled with them, but he was in our corner. Colleen's poison was heroin and when we got the call for her, she was usually in a bad way, barely responsive. She did confide in me once that she wanted to get off the stuff and off the street, but the chillingly euphoric powder held a firmer grip than anyone's offer of help. It saddened me to see what probably was once a cared-for complexion etched by despair, the energy gone from her light blue eyes, now sunken and framed by shorn, straw-colored locks. It was difficult to guess her age since the streets had aged her beyond her years. She never fought us.

Kelly, on the other hand, was fierce when he drank. He claimed that he had been very successful in business, had a palatial home in the affluent North Shore, and a beautiful wife and daughter. He once produced from his shredded wallet tattered photos of them in front of a stately mansion. Giving credence to his story was the obvious attention he had once paid to his physical state. Kelly never said what turned him, why he caved in to the 80-proof that dulled his toned muscle, his ambition, his will. A paunch hung on his muscular frame, and we knew those perfect, gleaming teeth we admired would soon begin to deteriorate. Remnants of a deep, cared-for tan also indicated his newness to the streets. Maybe that's why he was so full of fire. Maybe he hadn't completely given in. Maybe there was hope of averting this train wreck, and maybe that's why I gave him leeway.

But Kelly forced my hand, literally. The call was for a person with trouble breathing. We found Kelly, his back to the wall of a store at the foot of Brady Street. Nothing new, just Kelly again. Appearing more in distress than usual, he complained of chest pain, adding that someone had jumped him. The rescue squad crew that responded with us didn't want to give Kelly the time of day. He was just another street bum and they were all for calling a private ambulance. Since Kelly's gasping seemed genuine, I insisted they take his vitals again. I didn't make any friends that day but I wasn't about to make a bad call, violent street person or not, and we could hear wheezing even without a stethoscope. It was hard to get past Kelly's belligerence but I got him to lift his shirt and there, on the center of his chest, was a distinct footprint, taking on a red and purple hue. That was enough for me so I called a med unit.

The paramedic crew that showed up wouldn't have been my choice to win Med Crew of the Year Award. In fact, I felt they might add to the problems in dealing with Kelly. When I relayed our findings to them, I added quietly, "Careful, he's one of our most violent." When their crew leader plopped a medical kit in front of Kelly and sat on it, head buried in his clipboard to begin asking questions and filling out forms, I knew my warning had fallen on deaf ears. Alcoholic or not, Kelly was smart and he picked up on their lax approach. I saw his nostrils flare and his eyes narrow. To the med boss I offered to give him Kelly's background since he agreed Kelly had chest trauma. "So let's just get him in your rig." He quickly agreed, I sensed, because he was known to have a drinking problem and maybe he could relate.

Lying on the stretcher in the med unit, Kelly had had enough of their ho-hum attitude, and the overriding importance of completing their paperwork. I knelt behind him, out of his sight. When the paramedic sitting beside Kelly made a smart-ass remark about Kelly's agitated state, Kelly began kicking at him. The paramedic, a large hairy man I called Sasquatch, screamed, "Lieu-tenant, Lieutenant, he's kicking me. Do something!" My first impulse was to laugh, but they hadn't strapped our boy down, allowing him to rear up and lunge at the big guy, so I swung my arm from behind, "clothes-lining" him. Pinning Kelly to the stretcher, I barked at them to strap him in, but Sasquatch bailed out of the rear doors and no one would go near Kelly. So I hissed at him, "Goddammit, Kelly, you wanted our help, now knock it off!" I admon-ished that it was up to him to ride to the hospital in this thing or in a paddy wagon. "And you know I'll call 'em," I warned. When I felt him uncoil, I said, "Now let them strap you in for your safety, and please behave." The meds had called for police assistance so a cop rode in the back to keep Kelly in line.

Then there was Burt, whose loud claim of entitlement was his supposed veteran status. Although he claimed to have served in the Korean War, his age would have made him a 12- or 13-year-old combatant. As with all of our regulars, there was a routine with Burt. He'd get soused on the streets and then have someone make the 911 call for his supposed chest pain. He knew the drill: we'd show up, call an ambulance to cover our asses, and he'd go to the hospital where he'd get attention from nurses, clean sheets, something to eat, and, if he played his cards right, a warm bed for the night. And if we didn't play along, his galling rant went something like this: "I'm a vet, I served, you have to help me, blah, blah, blah." The only thing I despised more than vets crying in their beer about what was owed them was fakes posing as vets.

I was at the brink. The cops in the area gave my plan the green light. The next time we had Burt, I feigned agreeing that we would take care of him. "After all, Burt, you're a vet and you deserve the best treatment. Hell, you served, so why not?" I made a radio call and enjoyed watching his smile vanish when our police wagon pulled up.

"Ride's here, Burt."

He sputtered, "Wait a minute. I need an ambulance. I ain't going in that thing. I have chest pain."

"Your vital signs are better than mine. Free ride's over, Burt." I explained that this was the way it was going to be, that he should spread the word. No ambulance, no warm food, no clean sheets, and no nurses. I told him that if he really was a vet, he was a disgrace to all of us other vets, and especially to those who couldn't be there to look at him in disgust.

The cops, having agreed we needed to clean up Brady Street, laid it on: cuffs, frisking, explaining charges. We followed through with others, and word spread fast. So successful was the strategy that we got feedback from grateful residents and business owners in the area. Seldom did we see our reg-ulars anymore.

Months later, a friend stationed on the south side called to tell me he had heard of our efforts to clean up Brady Street. He kiddingly added, "Thanks, asshole, they're all down here now." I laughed because that's what you do at a comedy. But he wasn't kidding. I'd heard from others that street people on the south side complained about "those firemen and cops up there, on Brady Street."

On two other occasions, both while at Engine 6, I manhandled violent people. A young woman wearing a blood-stained yellow T-shirt ran out of a house when we pulled up. I thought she was our patient, but no dice. That would have been easier. In hysterics, she blurted that her boyfriend had been "doing mesc," the hallucinogen peyote, and now he was upstairs crushing glasses with his bare hands. She said that he wanted to fly out the window but she had stopped him. Looking up at the height of the old house, I coldly thought, *Well, then he'd have been easier to deal with.*

I had her stay with us by the rig and got Milwaukee's finest on the way. A cop showed up quickly and when I explained what the wannabe Superman was up to, he called for more cops. When a substantial police presence was on scene, in they went. I found it interesting how they surrounded the place and moved in, hand guns and shotguns at the ready, all business.

We expected to hear shots, but a few minutes later, a shotgun-armed cop waved us to the back door. "Get him?" I asked. "Yep," he replied, and asked that we take a look at his hands. "They're like hamburger." Just as we got upstairs, the guy got a second wind, and it took all of the cops to subdue the flailing maniac and get him down the stairs. Outside, they sat him down on a picnic table, and he agreed to settle down so we could wrap his shredded hands. It looked like a slaughter. There was blood everywhere, including on most of the cops. He reared up again and since I happened to be behind him, I repeated my Kelly move, arm-collaring him and planting him back down on the table. They'd had enough, cuffed him, and dragged him kicking and yelling into an ambulance.

The third episode occurred on a call for a woman with trouble breathing. A nervous, wide-eyed young woman led us to a small bedroom where her girlfriend lay on the floor in a narrow space between a wall and a bed. The patient, who was in mild respiratory distress, wasn't a problem; her girlfriend was. Despite our pleas to let us examine her friend, the woman didn't just hover over her supine lover, she lay on her, kissing her, straddling her, smothering her, constantly promising that she would protect her and not let harm come to her. It was a sure bet that these extreme dramatics had led to her friend's stress- and anxiety-induced problem. *I mean, who doesn't like affection, but there are limits.* I tried to convince the emotionally overwrought woman that we could help her friend, but that we needed to get into that small space to examine and talk to her. She only became more agitated, and when we tried to move her friend, she became physical, shoving us while straddling her friend, fire in her eyes.

Screw this, I thought. This was fast becoming a police matter so I made the call. The standoff went on and, like every EMS run, had run its time limit. Something had to change. The cops and the ambulance were delayed. The patient wasn't in dire straits, so we couldn't justify restraining her belligerent lover.

My temper was rising as the woman and I stood face-to-face in the narrow space, my back to the bed, hers to the wall. My crew stayed quiet but near as I bellowed at her to back down and leave the room if she wanted us to help her friend. I told her she hadn't broken any laws with us, but if she persisted, I'd have her arrested.

I never saw it coming. I was flying backward but when I hit the bed in a sitting position, I sprang back up as though on a trampoline, my hand cupped and aimed for her throat. The move must have looked comical. Pinning her to the wall, my nose touching hers and seeing only the wide whites of her eyes, through clenched teeth I hissed at her to shut the hell up and behave or I'd have her taken out of there hog-tied. She seemed shocked that our role as patsy had ended abruptly, and she just stood there, slouching, spent.

When the police finally arrived, I decided not to file a complaint or even have her arrested. Seemed she had enough problems. I just wanted to end that run. *Let her girlfriend deal with the psycho bitch.* I did make a mental note that if we were sent there again, I'd hold the door for the cops.

On another run that was all too common, I didn't have to touch the troublemaker, because he had pissed off enough other people. Just around the corner from our firehouse, on Humboldt Avenue, we found the young, scruffy guy, holding a bag of groceries and rip-roaring drunk, staggering about in the street, cars jockeying around him. We approached cautiously and talked him to the curb, but he became belligerent. Alcoholics touched a nerve with John, and he stepped in to take over. Since I liked and trusted John, I obliged. When the guy spouted off, John put his hands on Mister Mouth's shoulders, planting him firmly on the ground, sitting against a tree. Keeping restraint, but simmering, John enlightened our friend about the ills of drinking. I was reminded that he once had slammed a booze bottle on a table in front of a drunk who whined that he *had* to drink. Another time he probed under the seat cushion of our wheelchair-bound "pickle" and produced the bottle, which he smashed.

When this sot tried to get up, John again pushed down on his shoulders. When the guy spit at us and called us names, John picked up and dropped the grocery bag. I thought that would send our drunk over the edge, but he just stared at something leaking through the bag's soggy bottom.

The young drunk reminded us that we couldn't release him because he'd get hit by a car and we'd be responsible. He was right. Since our mayor now classified his ilk as disabled, I called for an ambulance — a $300 ride, thank you, taxpayers — and the police. The ambulance arrived first. Since its arrival distracted us, our boy came up swinging. One of the ambulance crew, to my surprise, got to him first, charging into him, head down, his tackle ending with one violent drunk pinned against a chain-link fence with the wind knocked out of him. *Whoa! That was impressive!* After we pinned the guy down, I told him his ambulance ride had just turned into a paddy wagon.

The police finally arrived and one of them asked, "Do you know who you've got here?" never taking his eyes off of the drunk.

Snidely, I answered, "I can hardly wait to hear. No, let me guess. A thoracic surgeon? The CEO of Briggs? Aw hell, I give up."

His halfhearted chuckle barely made the corners of his mouth move, and his face again turned icy, his gaze locked on our boy as he said through tight lips, "The Marquette arsonist-murderer." The cop knew this guy all right, and his tone and that stone stare told me he had been close to the case.

I knew exactly what he was talking about. At a Marquette University frat-house party, this uninvited loser had blocked the doors with furniture to prevent escape and then set the place ablaze, killing a student and injuring others. Tragedy followed tragedy when the case unraveled because there was insufficient evidence to convict. Regret about our earlier efforts to prevent him from staggering into traffic washed over me.

A call early one evening took us to the other side of the block, on Humboldt Avenue, where a couple of young people were in hysterics, looking down at a body in the middle of the street. A quick glance with the sweep of my light showed a young man with massive head trauma, likely dead. I stood quickly, grabbed a young girl's arm and begged, "Talk to me now. What happened?" In her traumatized state, she could only sob that a guy came up and hit him with a two-by-four "for no reason."

We were continuing CPR when paramedics arrived, followed by the police. A teenager — a juvenile in legal parlance — had indeed walked up to the young man and swung at his head with a piece of lumber. One swing. For no reason. The dead guy was a musician who lived on the trendy east side, like lots of other kids unfolding their wings. The paramedic officer and I testified in court at the murder trial. I heard medical testimony describing trauma to the skull so severe that the dead kid had an "eggshell fracture." The visual came easy. Since this was the juvenile offender's first offense, he would serve no jail time. Oh, he was assigned various forms of retribution, such as community service, but no jail time, because this was the first time he had hit someone so hard with a board that it shattered his skull, like an eggshell, for no reason.

We would get a stark reminder — no, an insane reminder — that murder had descended from being the crime of desperate men to mere curiosity, a gang initiation, dark adventure, or simply a means to an end.

"You have someone in the water off Government Pier," the dispatcher said. The pier is a Milwaukee landmark near McKinley Marina, a concrete pier jutting hundreds of feet out from shore, less than 20 feet wide, with a short concrete wall down its center. Since this could be anything, Tom was heavy on the gas pedal. Our last run to the pier had us fishing an 81-year-old woman out of the water, still alive, after she had slipped in to commit suicide. Her life went on, to what purpose I could only wonder.

I wanted more information so I radioed the dispatcher. "All we have is 'someone in the water,' Engine 6. Police are on the way." *Dammit, that's not much. I don't like the unknown.* It was easy to conjure up images of everything from a boat crashing against the pier to someone taking a late swim. It was a good night for that, warm and humid, with a gentle breeze. *All right, we'll hit this one cold,* I thought, *no preparation, and my guys know to bring ropes, tools, medical kit, and lights.*

Briskly walking down the pier, all seemed normal until out of the darkness some distance down the pier emerged three young men. Seeing the anxious look on their faces when I put my light on them and their hurried walk, I was certain they were part of whatever had happened. I pointed back toward shore and told them those flashing lights were sheriffs and to keep walking until they met up with them. They were black, and when further down the pier I bumped into three young white people who were in a panicked state, the premise of a racial incident hung heavy in the damp air. There had been a young man with them, they exclaimed, who had jumped into the lake trying to escape repeated blows from the trio. We listened and searched the black water with lights, but came up empty. Meanwhile, the trio had jumped off the pier onto shore and escaped. We concentrated our search in the area where water that had splashed onto the concrete pointed to where our victim had jumped in. One of my crew tended to two of the victims who also had been beaten, while we searched, frustratingly, shining hand lights beneath the surface. Nothing. Every minute that passed brought us closer to the realization that the guy wasn't coming up.

Jim Piech arrived in good time with his dive team, which got quickly into the murky water. Despite their efforts, the young man's body wasn't found until the next day, in 12 feet of water. Although the 21-year-old had drowned, the death was ruled a homicide due to blunt force trauma to his head. One of the homicide detectives assigned to the case later explained that the wheels of justice had ground to a halt. Although the assailants, aged between 18 and 21, admitted the unprovoked attack, even stating it was racially motivated, the three were charged with aggravated battery, with the ringleader serving one year in jail. The detectives had requested that a hate crime charge be added to what they were certain would be homicide charges. But the district attorney's office had made the call and made it known to the homicide squad that the decision was final. "Mind your own business," one of the DAs told the detectives.

But evil begets evil, and for some, it becomes habitual. Three years later, one of the three killers slit his girlfriend's throat, and then choked and stabbed her daughter to death. He then poured gasoline on his girlfriend's body and added arson to his rap sheet. Three residents upstairs barely escaped the burning building.

By now your thoughts may be echoing what we often heard: "But I thought you only fought fires." Remember, more than 70 percent of our work involved EMS, every aspect of it, and much of it crime related. And for that reason the time had come to turn up the heat on a project I had kept simmering on a back burner.

Since my days at Engine 5, and especially while at Ladder 9, I had taken a passive-turned-active interest in addressing the violent side of our work. Other than department directives concerning calls for police assistance, we were on our own to deal with street violence. No policies were in place, no standards established, no training provided, and no one to turn to for advice or guidance.

A paramedic had been shot with a pellet gun. We often faced guns and were threatened. Two paramedics I knew admitted they hid weapons in medical kits. Spotlighting the problem, although facetiously, was a photograph of Engine 5's crew armed with an array of military machine guns and automatic rifles. Two officers I knew admitted having cold-cocked someone who attacked them. Shamefully, one officer I knew was so anchored in his belief that he should only fight fires that he divorced himself from squad runs to the extent that he sat in the rig while his crew went in to face the unknown. He should have been harshly disciplined, I thought.

I saw the frustration on the face of the captain of busy Engine 13 when he described an incident where he and his crew were pinned down behind their rig during an actual firefight. He said that even the cops were pinned down, that it was Vietnam all over again. The only thing missing was the helicopters overhead. That should have grabbed top story on the evening news and front page in the papers. It didn't. The city fathers made sure of that. Admitting that such violence occurred in the city would make Johnnie-O and his cohorts look bad.

The captain, along with countless others, was enthusiastic about my intent to do something. I just wasn't sure what. Many offered support. People who knew I had a plan brewing called me for help. The story was usually the same: Their boss had ordered them into a building where a violent crime had been committed, and they didn't know if the attackers were still around. The police hadn't shown up yet. They knew what could happen if they went in, but what would happen if they didn't? Pointedly, I'd answer that they could be disciplined for disobeying an order, but then they'd be alive to dispute it. I reminded them of a department notice stating it was the company officer's responsibility to determine if a scene was safe. Additionally, I made sure they knew about a rule on the books that said officers were responsible for the results of their decisions.

Thankfully, our union, Local 215, stayed on top of the problem. In some of its shining moments, union leaders urged the chief to take action to ensure our safety during responses to violent situations.

In October 1990 I sent Chief Erdmann a letter asking that he consider implementation of a safety training program. "Officer training," I wrote, "would provide the insight necessary to recognize and manage dangerous situations." Emphasis would be placed on self control, threat assessment, and techniques for diffusing a sudden or impending violent situation. I felt it important to note that safety training for emergency care providers that respond to violent situations was required by national agencies, including the National Fire Protection Agency, OSHA, and the Department of Transportation.

In the meantime I began work on a safety awareness program geared for emergency workers. I obtained every document I could find, I contacted fire departments across the country, I gathered statistics, and I talked with countless people, including our police department's gang squad and training cadre. I came up with an impactful program, which I presented at a statewide paramedic conference and at a Milwaukee area paramedic training seminar. Feedback from these presentations was positively overwhelming, and departments across the state began asking about it. Sadly, an ad hoc safety committee formed under union auspices dissolved after one of our members decided to grandstand with the results of our efforts, even going to the TV media without our knowledge. But my safety awareness training program held momentum.

I received calls from both the chief and the union president saying that the program was a go. Both expressed that this was necessary and that they had heard good things about it. I would be assigned to the academy for about three weeks to run everyone in the firefighting division through the in-service course. It felt good knowing there was something I could do to give our people an edge, to broaden the protective curtain.

Less than one week later, the academy chief called me into his office to tell me that my safety awareness training program had been shot down.

"What?" I said, braced into a rigid stance. "What are you talking about?"

Hands folded on the desk in front of him and looking up at me, he went on to explain that this came right from the top. Supposedly, when the mayor heard about it, he said, "Definitely no," and that such training by the fire department indicated that we had a violence problem in the city.

I was temporarily at a loss for words, which didn't often happen when my blood boiled. "You gotta be shittin' me!" I managed to roll from my throat.

"Sorry," was all he could say.

"That's it? Just like that?" I demanded with hands on hips. He pursed his lips and dropped his gaze to papers in front of him, as though we were done and addressing those was next, as though I were dismissed.

My pointing finger came up, jabbing the air over his desk imploring that he and I and the whole world knew there was a violence problem in the city. "You're all burying your heads in the sand," I protested. I went on to promise that if one of our people was attacked and injured, or worse, got slapped in the head with a two-by-four and became a vegetable, or died, I'd go to their family and tell them and the media everything that was going to be done, that should be done. I'd help them file the lawsuit. He answered with an upward, sorrowful glance that said *Don't shoot the messenger.* I had been shown the back door of politics. *Johnnie-O again. Johnnie-O could fuck up a wet dream.*

People in the department from all ranks shared my dismay with the news. One battalion chief asked to borrow my material so that he could run a training session for his people, and the Madison Fire Department contacted me about setting something up, as did the hospital at Oconomowoc, which trained EMTs. But it wasn't going to happen in Milwaukee; damn the federal requirements and crime statistics and the safety of our people. Despite what they say about fighting city hall, I could have gone on, alone, but the whole thing sickened me so. The chief, possibly pushed into a corner to do *something,* issued a notice allowing our crews to wait down the street, or out of sight until police arrived. At least then we couldn't be accused of neglect or abandonment. Nevertheless, it was a shitty feeling keeping the rig out of sight and peering around the corner, wondering if the perpetrator had fled and someone was dying. I tried to expound on the chief's notice by pushing for a radio frequency that had commonality with police, but no dice. It wasn't that I had bigger fish to fry, but other issues vied for attention.

Semi-automatic defibrillators were coming on line, which increased the odds of cheating death, especially since CPR wasn't living up to its reputation as a lifesaver. Since their placement was determined by the number of PNBs to which an engine company responded, and by distance from a paramedic unit, Engine 6 easily qualified to receive the first unit. Besides training with the defibrillator, I was a CPR instructor for the department, and I had become immersed in teaching and practicing arson investigation. I had learned a great deal from picking the brains of Noble "Red" Heller and Brian Wachowiak, our resident experts in the field. The establishment of a department arson team was an on-again, off-again affair. I felt it was my niche and kept a hand in it should rumors about resurrecting the team become reality.

I loved arson investigation more than anything I did on the job, even teaching and fighting fires. For me, there was something about kneeling in fire ruins, having the signs speak to me, challenging me to turn back the clock and accurately replay the sinister, destructive event, even get into the mind of the "torch." Few understood that I found it a form of reverse creativity, and fewer understood when I said that fire doesn't destroy evidence, it creates it. It wasn't unusual for chiefs to ask that I have a look at a scene and try to figure out cause and origin, even motive, albeit in an unofficial capacity. Tricky cases involved fires set by professional torches, while some eluded explanation, despite their simplicity — such as when a bird picked up a lit cigarette butt to add to its nest-building project under the eave of a house, or when a fishbowl caught sun rays and focus-fixed them like a magnifying glass to a combustible. Then there were mice playing with matches ... just kidding. Arsonists — torches, fire bugs, fire-for-hire experts, pyromaniacs, whatever you want to call them — often set fires near electrical outlets or appliances to take advantage of the firefighter's commonly stated cause of many fires — "electrical." At least then they could say they had found a cause — that not only kept their egos intact, it let them avoid logging "unknown" or "suspicious origin," which too often spelled incompetence or complacency.

If there was one aspect of Engine 6 on which we could rely, it was variety. We were never disappointed. It was often said that one could write a book about the variety of work that came to Engine 6 in spades. *Now there's a novel idea.* On the extreme end was a massive blaze one month after Deb and I married.

We didn't get pulled in till about the third or fourth alarm, so by the time we arrived on the far north side, the fire in a chemical complex was well underway. This was a made-for-TV fire, complete with streets clogged with fire apparatus filling the night with a dazzling array of lights, and a multitude of hazards that included exploding chemical drums, falling walls, multiple exposures, and even a nearby hospital threatened with evacuation due to toxic smoke. So choking and toxic was the smoke from a silica-based product that it shut down the diesel engines of rigs parked downwind. Just moments after I backed my crew away from a loading dock stacked three-high with barrels, the thing blew, sending a couple of barrels skyrocketing into the darkness. It was impressive, really. Heavy smoke pouring from an exposure building filled with chemicals suddenly drew inward, meaning something big was about to happen. Just before the flashover chased out a hose crew inside, the sudden air reversal sucked the helmet off of the crew's boss.

A couple of other bosses and I got into a huddle to discuss strategy, with all of us agreeing it was best to let this thing free-burn. Since smoke is the product of incomplete combustion, by fighting this fire we were only delaying the inevitable while creating clouds of smoke that made this corner of the city a health hazard. But the cameras were there, and letting something burn defied our intrinsic reactivity, what we were conditioned and expected to do. The chiefs would have no part of letting the fire run its natural course. I went to the Fire Bell Club's canteen for coffee and watched the pyrotechnics show.

Within days, the expected injury reports listing pulmonary complications began arriving on the third floor.

Smaller, residential fires often did not make the news. They were common, so if no one was injured or killed, they served as news fillers only. It also seemed to depend on whether the media had film coverage, or if anyone of political importance happened to be on scene. One house fire became a news sensation not only because we rescued people, but, I suspect, more because a group of city officials including the chief, mayor, and fire and police commissioners were spectators. We surmised that they had been gathered at a meeting, or had had lunch nearby.

We found four victims on the smoke-filled second floor. I found a young woman unconscious on a bed and another guy and I got her outside. She was nude, and I felt horrible about laying her on the front lawn. There was no one around to answer my shout for a blanket so I tried to shield her with my body as I breathed into her mouth. Thankfully, someone eventually brought a blanket, and Gene, a lieutenant, knelt near me with a bag mask to continue CPR. I was grateful Gene was there. I didn't mind the woman's sooty mouth and face, but my forced breathing was stirring vomit, which I tasted and knew would soon surface. When Gene popped open the stubborn plastic case, I saw in slow motion the various parts of the bag, tubes and valves catapult and tumble in the air, like a juggler's act gone bad. Gene's eyes went wide and his mouth opened in surprise, and then closed to form the "f" of the first word that came to him. It wasn't his fault, but I hoped that the flying parts weren't captured on film. While he fumbled to assemble the parts, I went back to CPR, thinking that now the audience would be treated to a firefighter and victim sharing vomit.

All of the victims survived, and the news clips were complimentary. We were grateful for that and put it away, but the big wheels turned and set in motion recognition for the saves. When Chief Dan Gengler called to say that I, along with others, was being put in for an award, I respectfully declined. "It was a nothing fire, Dan," I begged, "I'm just glad everyone survived." After tossing the issue back and forth, I agreed to a team award recognizing Gene's crew of Engine 21, my crew, and Ladder 5, led by Dean Thomas.

A lot of flame lived and died between my days as a looper and Brady Street. Especially memorable among the countless fires was a ferocious blaze in a school. No one died, there were no saves; I don't even recall if anyone was hurt. There was no daring-do other than an engine crew's push into a particularly nasty fire that threatened to overwhelm all efforts and take down several buildings. The fire on that cool night exemplified the age-old battle between warrior and destructive force.

Ken Glisch, who I thought an excellent firefighter and officer, had just pulled in with his gang from Engine 27. After I jumped out of the rig, he yelled, "Looks like it's in the basement, Wayne. We're trying to find a way in." We knew by the amount of smoke pushing from the building and yellow flames shooting laterally from basement windows that this fire had plenty of fuel and had a good head start. An aggressive interior attack would have to be mounted quickly to stop it, or this would become an all-night surround-and-drown.

One crucial aspect of size-up was forming a mental picture of what the inside looked like based on what I saw outside. Once we got inside, we would be blinded, and I'd have to retain that image and my sense of distance and direction. The critical importance of size-up was emphasized by the certainty that the school basement was a maze and we could easily get lost, or worse, trapped.

My experience now paid dividends. I was able to look past the excitement and slip into assessment mode, and in a dash around the building, calmly but quickly take in all factors, such as building size, construction, and the fire's size and movement, relative to wind. I didn't have to worry about occupancy this time of night; I knew my MPO was getting us all the water we'd need and that other companies weren't delayed. Taking stock of my crew, I knew that they were short on experience and not particularly aggressive. One of my three firefighters was my cub, Paul Singer, who I figured would outshine the others. Responsibility never weighed heavier.

After that dash around the building, a couple of key factors determined a plan. I pointed to the doors I was sure would ultimately lead to all points of the basement and the fire, and yelled to Ken that that's where we were going in.

"Gotcha," he shouted back, "we'll bring another line." Ken's presence was reassuring. I couldn't ask for better company right then.

While a truck company worked on the heavy doors, we snaked out plenty of line for our stretch in and masked up. Our line snapped to life, becoming rock hard with pressure. The battalion chief squatted next to me, placing a hand on my shoulder. "Easy does it, Mutz. She's a nasty one." He advised backing out when we couldn't go any farther. "Kenny's comin' with another line," he cautioned.

"Piece of cake, Chief." *Piece of cake, my ass.*

As black-gray smoke rolled over our heads between the sprung doors, I smiled widely through my face-piece at my bulky trio. "Ready?" Exaggerated nods all around, and I pointed into the blackness and said, "School's in session. Keep body contact."

Next to my pipeman, with two in tow, our world instantly disappeared. Having gone through a double entrance door, I was sure that steps to the basement were close. They were. I had taught them not to walk in such blindness, but to slide a lead foot, keeping weight on the rear foot. You needed only one frightful, painful misstep to drive the lesson home. Movement was always in a crouch and usually on our butts going down stairs. We had about 15 minutes of air; 15 minutes to find the fire and kill it. I knew that we had to keep moving toward the rear of the school and bear left. Every step we took into the hot blackness felt like putting the tangible, sensible world a thousand feet behind us. I didn't like to tie up the radio, answering only when the chief checked our progress. He too knew to keep the airwaves open when a company was deep in the bowels of a fire.

Creeping as a unit along the walls of passageways in coal blackness, we heard only the mechanical clicking of our face-piece valves from Darth Vader–like breathing, and the subtle thumping of the line we dragged. Now and then I asked, "Everyone OK?" I mentally logged an estimate of distance, and a left turn, then a right, and another left. Finally, we were met by a wall of heat, driving us to our knees, and a faint glow, the devil's welcome mat.

"We've got the fire," I radioed.

"Ten-four, Engine 6," came back.

With my hand on my pipeman's shoulder, I urged, "Okay, move in, closer, stay low." We approached until our ears, our built-in thermometers, stung. "Now work it, work it." The powerful stream punching the searing wall of yellow sounded good, satisfying. We put just enough water on it to knock it down and let the scalding steam push over us, sending our faces to the floor. Heads back up, we moved in again. On the radio, I could make out companies above talking to each other, reporting the fire's spread and what they were doing. The blaze devoured everything around us, hungrily eating its way through vertical openings, pipe chases, and wall spaces, angrily reaching through walls.

I let my pipeman work a while, hoping to hear from above that we were hitting it, that they were seeing changes such as flame giving way to smoke and then lightening, but word didn't come.

"Shut it down!" That must have surprised my crew, but it was time to rotate. All three were going to get pipe time on this bad mother. This was their fire. I wanted them to claim it, to have the victory.

"Next. Take the pipe. Move in. Work it. Get mad at it. Kill it!"

I recognized Deputy Chief Koleas' voice on the walkie-talkie. *Christ, they must have leaned on it for him to be here.* "Engine 6, how you doing?"

"We're on it, Chief," trying to intone that we were "making the fire." Truth be told, it was a stubborn standoff and we were sucking precious air from the steel cylinders on our backs. We needed more time, another line, or we needed to be even more aggressive and push into the fire.

I stayed on the pipeman: "Beat it down. Nice. Nice."

Over the roar of the blaze, I kept a trained ear for other sounds, structural sounds. But I didn't sweat it, knowing how solidly these old buildings were constructed. Schools seemed to be some of the toughest buildings to overhaul, as though the old craftsmen were mindful of their importance.

Koleas gave me more time. Seasoned beyond description, he pictured what we were doing down there. And he knew me and that I would want to use every minute I had to avoid defeat. He read my thoughts when I heard radio reports of the fire's extension upward through the first floor. *Do what you have to up there,* I thought, *it's not going any farther down here.* Until the last wisp of steam drifted from soggy, charred wood, Koleas owned this building.

Ken's crew had made their way into a tunnel connecting the school and church, and they too had all the work they could handle.

"Shut it down. Singer up!" It was time to put my cub on the pipe to "bust his cherry," we said. The fire seemed to diminish somewhat, offering a glimmer of hope that we could beat it and would not have to back out. "Work it hard now, all around. Stay with it." The heat was punishing. It became difficult to squat, my knees no longer able to tolerate kneeling in hot embers and debris. We were operating on adrenaline, our muscles having checked out long ago.

I knew that Koleas was monitoring the time we were below. Finally, his easy voice pushed through my radio. "Wayne, how's it going? Not much time left before you have to back out of there." When I asked how it looked on top, he said they were chasing it and it was lightening up in the basement. That was all I needed to hear. We had to have stopped the fire's possession of the basement. We saw less flame now. Although I couldn't see it on my hip, I pictured the needle of my air regulator gauge edging into the red.

A couple of minutes passed and Koleas radioed, "Engine 6, you're going to have to get out of there."

"One more minute, Chief. Give us one more minute and we've got it." I was foolish to think he didn't hear the warning bells on our masks blaring.

Given his reputation, one didn't refute Casey Koleas, the "Greek fire god," but he knew I wanted this, that we could beat this. I pictured him grinning, eyes sparkling, or shaking his head. "You have one minute, Engine 6."

Paul never slowed on the line. He was like a programmed machine. He didn't even shut down the pipe when I slapped his shoulder. At long last, we saw little flame, and the smoke not only lightened from black to gray, but openings and shapes, another dimension, began to appear. And through the radio blared, "Engine 6, Engine 6, you've got it! Man, you've nailed it!" On hands and knees, head down with helmet dipped into hot, filthy black water, came relief, supreme satisfaction. I lifted my head, peeled away my face-piece and told my crew they had done a hell of a job. "Let's take a breather."

A backup crew helped us to our feet and we retraced our path, staggering out of "our" basement. Outside in the dizzying lights, bent over, we sucked in cool air as helping hands changed our air bottles. I felt slaps on the back and familiar voices saying, "Hell of a job, sixes," and "Nice work, sixes." There was no greater compliment to a firefighter than to hear that from your peers.

Back in the basement we went to overhaul. After all, we weren't done, and this was "our" fire. It was our line laying down there in the charred debris and

The legendary Gustave "Casey" Koleas, respectfully nicknamed "the Greek fire god," overseeing a four-alarm fire on the city's south side in January 1981.

water. I noted with interest in the faint light our long path to the fire. Now we could see where we had knelt, where we had drawn the line and fought to the last minute. The fire's destruction was vast, but it didn't go beyond where we had held the line. Slipping into arson investigation mode, I surmised that gasoline had been poured through a basement window into a huge storage area packed with Boy Scout equipment being readied for an outing. That the school-church complex was a historic landmark of the upper east side only seasoned the taste of victory. I especially appreciated accolades from Ken on our stop. There would be ribbing that we stole his fire, but Ken didn't see it that way. His crew worked hard and he had my respect.

Totally unexpected but lastingly memorable was when Chief Koleas walked over, joined by a fire and police commission member and other officials. He set his jaw, tilted his head slightly and said, "Lieutenant Mutza, that's the best stop I've ever seen." Those with him said things about saving the historic buildings and other nice things, but only Koleas' words rang in my head. For those words to come from this resolute, uncompromising man, who did not mince words, who did not hand out compliments, who made firefighting his life, was mind boggling.

"We did it, Chief. We."

By the time the age-old order was given to "pick up," euphoria had dulled to exhaustion, but the feeling of accomplishment remained as deeply embedded as the exhaustion that racked our bodies.

I could never be sure if the lower east side was conducive to the variety of runs, or if it was simply the hand we were dealt. But the variety, the weirdness, continued. One day the supporting structure of the North Avenue Bridge was intentionally set ablaze. The timbers were so deeply charred that the bridge's structural integrity came into question. So although North Avenue is a major thoroughfare connecting the east side with western districts, I had the bridge closed, which really set off some politicians. "What is this?" I could imagine being asked over hot phone lines. "One of your company officers orders the damn bridge closed?" Despite the bitching, I wouldn't allow it to be reopened until city engineers inspected everything and gave the OK. My chiefs had no problem with it.

Another call for fire had us on upper floors of the University of Wisconsin Milwaukee (UWM) lab building, where we found smoke-filled hallways. This wasn't run-of-the-mill smoke so masks were imperative, along with a quick evacuation of the building. Light gray, noxious smoke that puffed through the vents of a locked door rose and crept along the hall ceiling. No one could tell us what chemicals were involved. To make matters worse, the steel-jambed door was nearly impossible to take in, and the standpipe in the stairwell was jammed. Our pumpers had the system charged with water, but we couldn't open the valve to supply the hoses we had humped upstairs. The smoke kept coming and things got tense. Finally, one of our guys craftily opened the valve without snapping it off and a truck company forced the door. Lab officials who later wandered in awe through the charred mess said the room contained so many chemicals that they could never identify them all. It only made us shake our heads at the cumulative damage surely being done to our lungs and hearts, despite our breathing equipment. The overhaul process, when face-pieces are removed because the fire is out and air is depleted, is one of the most toxic stages of a fire.

As if unusual fires didn't keep life at Engine 6 interesting enough, the weirdness existed in the realm of EMS. Topping the list was a call to the wooded surrounds of the Milwaukee River, where we were led to an old stone wall partially hidden by brush. The haggard street person couldn't explain what was wrong with his drinking buddy, so he just pointed behind the wall. Expecting to see a down-and-outer passed out, we were greeted instead by an incredibly odd sight.

On the ground in a sitting position, knees drawn up, arms tangled in brush and leaning backward, as though in an invisible reclining seat, was a disheveled man. It didn't immediately register why he was sitting that way or what held him up until I focused on a thick steel cable entering his mouth and protruding out the left side of his face. I don't remember what I muttered, but it must have been original. His buddy broke the pregnant pause by waving his hands, pointing to the top of the high wall, and calmly said something like, "We was just sittin' up there havin' a swig 'n' he fell backward. Kin ya help 'im? He's been sittin' there like that fer a while."

"We'll help your pal," I reassured, kneeling close to inspect his predicament. The man's eyes were wide as he tried to look sideways at me, the pleading look you give the dentist when your mouth is propped open and he or she is about to go in with the drill. I felt pity for the man. I wrapped my hand around his arm, put my face in front of him and said, "We're going to get you out of this." He slowly blinked in acknowledgement, or was it, *Really? Good luck, pal.*

The multiple-strand steel cable, about five-eighths of an inch in diameter, was the upward-jutting trailing end of a cable supporting a utility pole. Protruding about 10 inches beyond his upper cheek, just below his eye, it actually supported him. One of my crew quickly got behind him to take his weight. My first action was to request a paramedic unit. In major impalements, standard procedure had a truck company cutting the object with a power saw and transporting the patient to the hospital with the piece in place and supported. I held off on the ladder company because I felt the saw would violently vibrate the cable in its sensitive location. Thankfully, there was little blood. When I checked on the med unit, they expected a quick arrival, so I thought best to consult with them.

We passed the few minutes by clearing brush and reassuring our patient, asking only a couple of key questions he answered by blinking. He remained calm and didn't budge. I wondered if this would make him reconsider his life on the street, viewing the world through the bottom of a bottle.

After the meds pulled in, I gave them a moment to let the impact of the gruesome sight pass and then got down to business. They were a trio of newly trained meds led by an old head, Fritz Ambroch, who was one of the first paramedics in Milwaukee County. With those four, our crew of five, plus cops, our patient glanced around wide-eyed at all the attention he was receiving. Kneeling by him, we had a quick conference with Fritz, agreeing a power saw was too risky. He called paramedic base and, per protocol, a doctor was on the other end. After Fritz described in detail the entrance of the cable and how far it protruded from the man's face, the doctor said they'd have to administer such-and-such drugs and cut their patient's face to free the cable. Seasoned Fritz answered calmly, "Ten-four." I heard one of his students blow out air and whisper, "Fuck."

Fritz spun around to face us in his kneeling position and asked, "Who wants to do this?" I broke the silence. "I'll do it." I'm sure he was more interested in having one of his meds do it, so he countered, "No, I'll do it." And after his white-coated charges started an IV in our leaning friend, slice with a scalpel he did, each slice deeper, expertly, deeper than I had imagined necessary for the thick cable to finally appear through the bloody crevice. Our patient closed his eyes and we eased him to a supine position, the meds hovering, dressing his wound. With the liquor in his system and the sedative, he sleepily gave me his name for my report. I said, "Now you'll have quite a story to go with that scar." I was warmed by his grin, his bony fingers patting my forearm. We got him onto a stretcher, loaded him and cleaned up the area as though we did this every day. I made a mental note to call the power company to secure the dangerous cable. The man was lucky, actually, considering how close to his eye the cable had been. I turned to his drinking buddy and said, "And stay off of that damn wall," not quite understanding how they had gotten up there in the first place.

That summer we were summoned to the same area for "someone in the river." Two teen boys had ventured out onto the dam for some adventure swimming. One of them dove, not realizing how thinly the water rushed over the concrete curvature at the bottom. Luckily, his friend was a strong swimmer and got the unconscious boy to shore, an incredible feat, undoubtedly accomplished with sheer adrenaline. The teen had suffered massive chest injuries. He was in respiratory distress and turning dangerously purple. We struggled to carry the large lad in a litter, while bagging him, up the slippery hill to the waiting med unit. Very sad. I never found out if he made it.

Death came calling often, more often than we cared for, and in its most hideous forms. Most repulsive was a call to an apartment building, the type that dominated the east side. The call came in as "neighbor not seen for two weeks." This is not what we wanted to hear in the summer's heat, but it reminded me that this was what we did. It was the unglamorous side of our work, when those who were anxious to take our place took a step backwards. Although the man lived on an upper floor, when we entered the building it was obvious we had been called not because the man hadn't been seen, but because they could no longer tolerate the odor coming from his apartment. There is no mistaking the odor of death. *I'm surprised they waited this long.*

After forcing the door, we were assaulted by the stench. On the bed in the confines of the apartment was a body, face up, hugely boated and black — although we would discover later this was a white man. A couple of my guys only glanced, not wanting to take in the details, wisely scurrying for the windows to get them open. This was one of the rare occasions when I didn't expect them to get involved, but they hung in there and helped John and me look around for anything that yielded the man's name or anything else about him. I had already called for the police and the medical examiner, or ME. Over time — over all this time that no one in the building had thought that something might be amiss — the man's fluids had drained into the mattress. John pointed out the crevice that was his neck, now teeming with maggots. So intense was the odor that it made your head hurt and your eyes water. It forced you to swallow to keep in check the rise from your stomach. It made you believe that you could never wash it completely from your clothes, or from your body or your mind. I had to remind myself that somewhere in the past this monstrous, grotesque form had been a living, breathing human being, complete with ambitions and a range of emotions. Maybe he had family and was productive. Maybe he liked to laugh. I wanted to sanitize all that was his life into something other than this total absence of dignity.

I went to the door to make sure no curious neighbors were loitering. A cop appeared at the end of the hall, holding a handkerchief over his mouth and nose. He wouldn't come any farther. During our exchange of information at this distance, he said he trusted that I had ruled out foul play, although I was not qualified to make that call. I could tell from afar that he was feeling the effects of the odor that had been released out into the hall. He was satisfied in knowing the ME had been notified and made a hasty retreat down the stairs.

There was no more we could do so we filed out. I looked back at the swollen form, made the sign of the cross and thought, *I hope death came quick for you*. I closed the door and told the cop downstairs that he'd have to secure the apartment.

On the solemn ride back to quarters, I recalled a run we had months earlier to the affluent upper east side, a run that contrasted sharply with this one. Crossing the threshold of the stately mansion, I was reminded of tales from North Shore firefighters who told me they took their boots off when crossing such porticos. *Sorry, no such thing here. We are who we are and you called us, heavy soot-stained boots and all.*

We were met by a kindly old woman who explained that her husband had expired, a completely expected event due to his age and terminal condition. She did not expect us to do CPR; our presence was merely part of the process of officiating death in the home. I told her that since we had been called, we needed to see the body. She obligingly led us upstairs to a massive, opulent suite where her husband was in death's repose, seemingly at rest, a quilt up to his neck. When the woman told us she had said her goodbyes, we offered our condolences. I explained that the next step would involve the arrival of a private ambulance and the police, all as a matter of necessity, of course. Her polite understanding told us she had been briefed. The information she provided that I needed for my report confirmed my belief that the deceased was a renowned TV personality.

Back at quarters, when I was writing my report, I received a call from the attending physician at the hospital where the man's body was taken. He sternly informed me that he was concerned that the man's body still harbored warmth and that we hadn't performed CPR. I immediately took umbrage at his implication that we hadn't done our job. I explained further that this was all cut and dried and that the body was warm because the woman kept the bedroom very warm and she had covered him with a heavy quilt. "He was terminal and the wife said no CPR," I informed him. He insisted that he still didn't like it.

I finally told him I didn't give a dead rat's ass what he liked and to cut the bullshit and admit that we both knew who this man is, or was, and that's why he was pushing this. I asked him what he was afraid of. "I did my job," I fumed. "Take this as far as you want," I went on to tell him that he'd end up with the egg on his face. "We don't treat a *name* any differently than we treat a street person." And never another word was heard.

More disconcerting than repugnancy and indignation were suicides, which we seemed to get in streaks. I approached suicide with a curiosity unlike that of any other cause of death. My curiosity focused more on the victim's preemptive thought process than the method chosen. We found it difficult to understand, and we didn't readily accept the willfulness of the act as we did death by accident, medical malady, old age or even violence. Regardless of the motive that brought one to the precipice, we found a particular sadness in someone deciding their fate. *She was so young. He had so much to live for. What drove them to it? He did it on Mother's Day, in front of everyone. Christ, what was in his head?*

For all the gallows humor we hid behind, I couldn't apply it to suicides. I was certain it was based on our resentment of the victim for having to deal with the aftermath. I didn't buy into the belief of some that only the weak and the stupid die young. And I couldn't dismiss the existence of an emotional abyss that drove people to pull the circuit breaker on their future and sentence loved ones to eternal pain.

Why did we end up at suicides? Because we were sent to check on the welfare of a neighbor, or family member, or because we could medically treat someone who attempted suicide. If we ended up as the voice intervening with someone in desperation, we were unqualified to deal with such psychological convolution, so we were left to wonder how much of ourselves we saw in the victim and go from there. As for the moral implications of suicide, I'm on the fence. There were times I felt someone was justified in finding peace the only way they knew. I could relate, albeit in a more transitory sense, to the Vietnam War, where suicide as an option for combatants was more common than most realize. I vowed that if capture was imminent, I would save one bullet in my .38 revolver. Pacts between comrades assuring the other would not be taken captive also were common. Forlornness, I thought, was the saddest of circumstances that led to the final option.

The call was to one of the high-rises we frequented, a high-rise tailored for elderly who formed a community within its walls. The old woman said she hadn't seen the man for a couple of days. *She knows. I can see it in her eyes.* We set the spreader bar we always take into high-rises against the door jambs and worked the ratchet handle until the jambs bowed enough for us to get through the lock.

The familiar odor that hit us when we pushed open the door told us we didn't have to announce, "Fire Department." We politely shooed away the woman, who was trying to peer in over our shoulders. "Thank you, ma'am, for your concern. We'll talk to you in a few minutes."

Not far inside was the body of an elderly man slumped in a kitchen chair. Over his head was a gray plastic garbage bag, a rubber band around the neck. We didn't remove the bag, we didn't touch him. Rigor mortis had long set in. I brought the radio up near my mouth and keyed the mike: "Dispatcher, Engine 6 requests a 10–53 [police] for a DOA." His "10–4" sounded pitying. *Or did he lose a bet with another dispatcher when we radioed in a DOA.*

The man's body faced a counter where family photographs were set in a row, his final view, his final thoughts. While we waited, our conversation centered on wonderment at what went through a person's mind as air diminished. How did one get past the panic of suffocation? It would be so easy to tear the bag off. It was only thin plastic. *What were your last thoughts?*

A note stated simply: "I don't want to live like this any more." *Like what? I'll bet the people in those photos know.*

A similar situation, similar setting. We forced the door and found in the small kitchen area an old man in a chair, a small, worn .38 on the floor. His head was back, mouth open, arms limp at his sides, empty eyes staring at the ceiling. Surrounded by blood dried black was a hole at the top of his head. A neat hole in the ceiling marked the trajectory of the bullet. A perfectly circular blood-spatter pattern surrounded the hole. In death, bodily functions release; bowels, bladder; blood pools in the lowest parts of the body, which presents as reddish-purple swelling; we call it morbid lividity. We believed that we were conditioned to ignore such smells and sights.

His body faced a table on which there was a note. His too was simply stated: "I can't live like this any more." But he had added, "My kids don't care about me." I hated reading suicide notes.

I ended up working an overtime shift at the busiest house in the city, Engine 13, so I looked forward to a change of pace, more firefighting, and a break from the streak of suicides. No dice. One of our many runs had us cautiously searching a dark basement where we found a young man hanging from pipes, his body rock hard, an electrical cord around his neck. I was suspicious because there was white powder on the table next to a makeshift bed and the knots around his neck were elaborately tied, not a slipknot and far too intricate to have been done by the young man in his death throes. And there was nothing nearby from which he could have taken his final step.

Qualifying for most unusual suicide attempt was a call for a shooting in Engine 21's territory. During a spat with his girlfriend, a 21-year-old had put a .22 to his head and pulled the trigger. We arrived with a med unit led by my brother-in-law, Dave, whom I was content to have apply his expertise. The young man had been sitting on a couch with a bullet hole in the side of his head but he bolted out the door and down the stairs when it dawned on him the cops were coming. I looked out a window and saw him dash across a vacant lot and disappear. Dave and I exchanged blank looks and shrugged. We agreed that the guy must have tilted the gun, which deflected the bullet off his skull. "Oh well," Dave said, "let the police deal with him."

Insight into my time at Engine 6 would not be complete without mentioning one of our most memorable characters. Heather was about 20 years old, a pretty girl with curves in all the right places. Curly, ash blonde hair cascading past her shoulders accented her cheekbones, which sloped back to puzzling gray eyes. Heather had medical or psychological problems that were controlled by medication, but she didn't control the medication. So lax was Heather about regulating her meds that, for a time, Engine 6 was seeing her every day.

Heather wasn't a problem patient in the sense that she became unruly or resisted us; quite the opposite, in fact. When we got the call, often we found her in different locales, and in a perpetual state of seductiveness. I was never able to ascertain if her amorousness was by design — a call for attention — or a result of medication foul-up, or a combination of both. Regardless, her persistent calling was excessive, but she wouldn't accept the medical attention we insisted upon. Heather was getting all the attention she wanted from the fire guys, thinking, perhaps, that none of us would think to put an end to her siren role.

Once, Heather answered the door, head tilted coyly, sleepily blinking those big gray eyes, wearing only a cut-off T-shirt emblazoned with huge letters that read, "I Like Dick." *Maybe we should find Dick and talk to him.* She didn't say much; she didn't have to. I said, "Let's go inside and talk, Heather." When she turned and bounced off, her milky white globes below the small of her back rocking like a rowboat on a wake made me bite my lip to stifle what some would consider impure thoughts. Staggering back into professional mode, I said "Heather, get something on." My three firefighters shot me a look like a kid whose new toy had just been taken away.

Another EMS call had us going to Heather's apartment where we found her nude, sprawled on a bed moaning and slowly gliding her hands over her suppleness. One of my firefighters, Tom, froze, instantly mesmerized, stepping completely out of work demeanor. I looked him in the eye and tapped his arm. "Tom, snap out of it, and Heather, you knock it off!" No response, from either of them. "Tom!" I snapped. He broke his trance, looking at me sheepishly. I looked at Heather, still self-luxuriating. Regardless of whether her erotic state was real or feigned, I threw a quilt over her, scolding, "Heather. Knock it off! My guys can't do their job here!" She stilled and lowered her eyes to look at me over the quilt. Again, we went through the motions of treating her, and again I gave her my speech about abusing her medication and getting help.

I told Heather that we couldn't keep coming because she was going off track with her meds. There was nothing more we could do for her except call an ambulance, and this was not an emergency. She needed to talk with someone about this. "Besides," I asked her, "do you want us to miss a fire where someone might be trapped?"

Maybe my appeal to her compassion and sense of responsibility worked because we, and the other two shifts, didn't hear from her for a while. Until one day, we were sent to a sub sandwich shop for someone having medical problems. We were led to the cooking area, where we found Heather on the floor in a state of delirium. This seemed serious, and I knew she wasn't faking. We got oxygen on her, calmed her down, and called an ambulance. Through tears and, finally, with sincerity in those pretty gray eyes, she explained that she had been making sincere efforts to control her medication. She had become more responsible, even getting the job at the sub shop. I was sure I was seeing the real Heather. Feeling somehow responsible for her, I told her I was proud of her and that we'd help any way we could.

When we helped load her into the ambulance, she called me over to whisper that she'd try real hard to straighten up, but now she was worried this could cause her to lose her job. I held her hand and reassured her that an employer couldn't fire someone for medical problems alone. I promised her that I'd talk with her boss, whom she said was "kinda pricky."

I went back inside and asked him about Heather's work performance. He said she was a hard worker but he was concerned that her health problems could cause lost work time and he might have to let her go. I briefly explained the effort Heather was making to get her life on track, despite medical problems, and gently reminded him of worker's rights. I broke eye contact and made a show of looking around his place, especially at the grills and the grease-coated vent systems above them. "You know," I said, "I don't recall doing a fire inspection here." I pretended to shake the thought, looked back into his eyes, which seemed more intent now, and pleaded, "Heather will be just fine, please just give her a chance." His eyes seemed to relax and he said he would. "I believe you if you say she's a good girl," he finished.

Tom stuck his head around the counter into the kitchen. "Boss, they're calling." I turned up the volume on my walkie-talkie and heard, "Dispatcher to Engine 6."

11

The Beginning of the End

The beginning of the end of Deb's fire department career preceded mine. Two years into my stint at Engine 6, Deb's fire service ambitions crashed.

Drifting in half-sleep, I heard the department phone ring. *Probably the chief with a manpower change for tomorrow; the watchman will write me a note.* Someone was at my bedside: "Lieutenant, important phone call for you." *Damn, this can't be good.* A slight tremor rolled through my gut. The conversation went something like:

"Wayne, it's Pat Austin. I'm at County Hospital. Deb was brought in here. She was in a bad accident. Her med unit got hit and she was hurt. She said to tell you she's doing okay, and not to worry."

The tremor rumbled into a quake. A thousand pins pricked my temples. I quickly tried to absorb and process what Pat said, while waiting for the flush of dread to pass.

"How bad, Pat? What are her injuries?"

"Looks like a concussion and broken nose," she answered. "Neck injuries too. Not sure what else."

"Jesus Christ," I murmured.

We talked more and she offered to keep me posted. No sooner had I eased into a chair to think things through when Chief Fehr was in the locker room.

"I'll drive you to County," he stated flatly.

His words spoke volumes about his concern and they reminded me of how we took care of our own. I politely declined, explaining that I'd like to take my own car so I could be more flexible. He understood, asking, "You have someone who can act?"

"Yeah, Heinowski can jump in the seat."

It seemed that pandemonium reigned in the emergency room at County Hospital. All of our five med units were there. Deb was on a bed in a curtained space, disheveled, with head and facial injuries, spattered liberally with blood from the patient they were transporting, and wearing a cervical collar. She hadn't been attended to since they brought her in. And when I saw on the floor near her bed a puddle of urine from the dreg on the cot next door, I saw red. I bellowed throughout the ER arena, "Why aren't these paramedics being treated? Is this how you take care of your own?" It got everyone's attention, but more importantly, it got Deb the attention she needed.

Deb's two partners, and a cop who had been aboard, also waited. Despite a nasty jaw injury, Paramedic Officer Jacque Kelsey seemed to be in good spirits, and I especially wanted to talk to the paramedic driver, since he had a reputation for erratic behavior. Unsurprisingly, his statements about the collision didn't add up.

Med 7 had been rushing to County Hospital a man who had been struck by a car and appeared near death. Deb and Jacque were in the back of the modular unit, along with the cop, working on the severely injured man. Cops regularly rode along if a patient was violent, or to get a "dying statement." At the instant of impact, Deb recalls being flung about in the "box," crashing into a wall of cabinets.

"I heard my neck crack in multiple places. I fell backwards and when our patient ended up on top of me, his feet by my face, I said to myself, 'You're gonna die, because I can't get up.' I felt blood running down my face so when Bill Ingram crawled into the med unit, I asked him how my face looked. He said it was fine but I didn't believe him, knowing the sarcasm of firemen."

The impact shoved the med unit up onto a lawn near a house, reducing the life-saving vehicle to junk. Despite the chaotic scene, replete with fire trucks, ambulances, police units, and even the Flight for Life helicopter, which flew her patient to the hospital, Deb recalled little of the events following the crash.

To this day not only do some of the details of the incident remain unclear, but the reasons they were suppressed remain muddied. What is certain — and was reported by the media — is that Med 7 was struck by a 14-year-old driving a stolen car. Police and fire department officials sidestepped mentioning that the boy was drunk and that he was being chased by the police. For some time, police chases, especially those that had proven fatal to innocents, had been a sore spot with the public and the media, and officials may have felt that this one would really put the cops in the hot seat. To add insult to injury, in the most literal sense, the paramedic driver of the med unit was going the wrong way, headed in a direction opposite the hospital. His erratic disposition aside — he admitted that often he shut himself in for his two off days and drank — earlier in the shift a supervisor had considered replacing him as the driver, establishing doubt in his ability to drive.

My astonishment quickly turned to anger when I discovered that the paramedic driver wasn't given a blood test. A 14-year-old drunk kid driving a stolen car being chased by the police versus a paramedic unit with lights and siren driven by someone doing his civic duty — why test the paramedic? Because, for one, he was headed the wrong way, despite being in a familiar area and on the way to a hospital he had driven to countless times.

It got worse. The fire department was required to convene an investigation panel in such matters. It never happened. And when I pressed the people who would have comprised the panel — including the deputy chief, a union representative, and the motor vehicle operator instructor — I was the proverbial gnat they tried to shoo away. I remained the burr in the saddle of many, but that didn't stop the department from sitting on its laurels. The investigation never took place and it only reminded me that this job had more standards than any I had ever seen.

Deb was placed on the injury list and while convalescing at home, it was difficult for me to see her with raccoon eyes and multiple scars, and straining to move her head. After the scarring healed, the neck damage remained pronounced and led to tests and treatment by numerous doctors and therapists. Deb's long road to recovery stretched for miles and really saw no end; part of her treatment involved returning to work, but the neck pain persisted and Dr. McCabe, an orthopedic surgeon and one of the department physicians, placed her on duty disability pension. McCabe's reputation was one of not handing out "duties" so when he sanctioned someone's disability, it wasn't questioned. With her fire service career ended, and knowing how much change was a part of our lives, Deb re-invented herself many times over, amassing educational certificates and even establishing her own business as an aesthetician. To this day, not only is she reluctant to get behind the wheel, but she says when it's going to rain she can tell by how her neck feels.

Deb heard that the patient they had that fateful night, amazingly, lived. With permanent jaw damage, Jacque Kelsey too left the job. The fate of the ride-along cop is unknown. The errant paramedic driver? He not only remained on the job, he cut yet another notch in his belt by firing a pellet gun in a firehouse, striking a coworker in the eye, causing injury serious enough for the department to place him on disability pension. I thought: *In wartime, we'd be sending him to the other side.*

As much as I was into my profession, it became difficult to maintain perspective in view of how the department handled, or didn't handle, the crash of Med 7. It had a snowball-rolling-downhill effect. My partiality to Deb and my belief in what was right fostered bitterness. I withdrew to a more subdued level of social interaction on the job. Regardless, I was confident in my ability to perform at peak proficiency, as the job demanded. I not only missed Deb on the job but also was saddened that her chosen profession had ended. She had been on the eligibility list for paramedic officer, a position I knew would have fit her well. And I was concerned about prolonged effects of her neck injury and what her future held; but her blend of moxie and profound work ethic would put those concerns to rest.

My three-year anniversary — the rotational period then considered normal — at Engine 6 was approaching. Being at the 15-year mark, I had seen much of what the job entailed, internally and on the streets. Nothing surprised me. I was skilled at reading people and, as a result, my circle of friends became smaller. At social functions I was most comfortable with those who Myron Hooks called the "old scouts," a dated but revered term for those who had seen and done much. We didn't mince words and we looked each other in the eye when we spoke.

Our social functions, of which there were many, seldom were tame events. And they usually made for great buzz at the firehouse kitchen table for days to come. Sometimes a few of our guys and gals got a little crazy, but I figured it was par for the course we played. We knew that the public generally accepted the work hard, play hard balance, but sometimes the god of political correctness was fed sacrificial lambs wearing fire department uniforms: *We'll expect you to lay your life on the line, suffer injuries and heartache, and question your moral rectitude after you deal with every form of violence and human indignity, but don't you expect acknowledgment.*

As much as I had likened Brady Street to a stage rife with characters, however superficial the analogy, there was no denying that they were real people with real problems and real needs: Heather, whom I never saw again; a street person with a scar on his face that some guys would be proud to have; Kelly, who I hoped had finally settled down and found his way in life; Pierre, who probably still tromps down Brady Street bellowing how much he loves the firemen, and countless others, many of whom have since bid their problems a final farewell. And there were the people I worked with at Engine 6, mostly stars and some whose star did not shine so brightly.

Next to my name on the transfer list was written "Engine Co. 31." I'd be going back to one of my south side haunts, but as an officer this time. With little fanfare I bid Brady Street farewell.

12

Later Lessons

Except for a more modern rig, little had changed at Engine 31. The area had fallen more into decline and the number of runs had increased as a result. Again, I was fortunate to have a good crew, which included the venerable John Heinowski and Dick Kaiser. I saw Dick earn his stripes as the cub of busy Engine 32, which was housed with Ladder 9 during my days as a truck man. Unsurprisingly, Dick would serve out his days on the job wearing the gold badge of a battalion chief—and what do you do for someone who had laid his life on the line to save yours?

Fires were infrequent and usually of malicious origin, which meant that I was often kneeling in ash trying to ascertain if the blaze was set by human hands. This was good hands-on experience for me since I had become an instructor in Milwaukee Area Technical College's fire science program. Arson investigation was my favorite subject to teach, with tactics and strategy a close second. During my two-year tenure with the college, I would also conduct National Fire Academy arson investigation seminars, the students of which included not only fire service personnel but also building inspectors, and insurance and law enforcement investigators. With Milwaukee's arson investigation in the hands of the police department, four men assigned to the unit were hard-pressed to handle the workload of the burgeoning crime. That prompted a resurgence of interest in forming a combination fire-police arson unit. Since a couple of people like me were waiting in the wings to join, staffing wouldn't pose a problem, but budget constraints, as usual, put the study on the back burner.

There was a profound psychological dimension of arson that dealt with motive, which I found intriguing. Some of the reasons why people burned things were murder, crime concealment, revenge, financial gain, vandalism, attention-seeking and pyromania. The latter proved a category all its own, as did juvenile fire-setting. For the novice, the pyromaniac was difficult to spot. But at a fire theirs was not the typical face of awe at fire's fury. Theirs was one of satisfaction. So you scanned the crowd. Our torch might not look

Firefighters of Ladder Company 10 had just scrambled down their aerial ladder before it was caught in this flashover. The fire went to a third alarm and involved seven buildings before its spread was stopped. Amid a storm of controversy, in 2009 Ladder Company 10 fell victim to budget constraints and was eliminated after 106 years in service (courtesy Dale Mutza).

deranged, but he might be the guy with his hands in his pockets, fondling himself in self gratification at the monster he brought to life. At a suspicious fire where we recognized a torch, detectives pulled him into a secluded doorway and had him drop his pants, which revealed the fresh stains and brought a quick confession. The common belief that arson is the most difficult crime to prove tempts the most stalwart of characters to light the match, or find and pay someone who will.

Branching out from each motive are tentacles that wrap around fascinating details of individual cases. Like detectives who deal with heinous crimes on a regular basis, one has to be prepared for the bizarre circumstances and the gruesome results of arson. Sad yet disturbing was the case of a young fire buff who frequented fires so often that firefighters across the city took a liking to him. With a camera hanging from his neck and wearing a blue construction helmet to access fire lines, he was easily recognized. Sometimes after riding his bike great distances in bad weather to be at major blazes and watch the firefighters he so admired, he was given a bunk at a nearby engine house and was welcomed at the table. The young man had physical deficiencies that not only prevented him from passing the rigorous firefighter exam but also translated to deficits in normal social interaction. But the altruistic firefighters looked beyond that, and the buff seemed content with his association with his firefighting pals.

But his voracious cravings went unnoticed, except by a few skeptics who thought better to steer clear. One summer day when the temperature simmered in the 90s, flames erupted in the bowels of a large building in the heart of the city. The fire spread and the battle quickly was lost, the smoke from the greater alarm fire visible for miles. The intensity and vastness of the fire made it difficult to pinpoint the cause and the origin, but eventually investigators pieced it together. The enthusiast that firefighters had befriended had been seen at the building about the time the fire started. Hours later he was discovered at his place of work a short distance away, having hanged himself with a method today called auto-erotic asphyxiation.

The most troublesome blaze I recall at Engine 31 occurred in a riverfront warehouse in which pleasure boats were overhauled and stored. A gasoline-fed fire spread from a boat to the building, which featured a high metal ceiling with tar-coated roof. Well into the blaze my crew and I were deep inside the building when it felt as though it had begun raining. Black dots began appearing on our yellow turnout coats. "Don't look up," I warned; "it's raining tar." No one had to tell us twice to bolt for the door, but by the time we got outside, we had been rained on with a liberal spattering of hot tar. We were never able to completely remove the pesky black dots since flammable cleaning solvents compromised the fire resistance of Nomex.

Since training was a byword on the department, despite our EMT experience we were required to attend EMT refresher courses. Not only did it get me out of the place for a few hours, I was learning new trends in emergency medicine. Leo Harper, who had been one of my recruits, picked me up for the long drive to the academy; Leo was my class partner and great company. He came from the police department, which was their loss and our gain, and he would retire, deservedly, as a "white shirt."

Engine 31's old house was nestled into a rather sleepy neighborhood, which came alive at night, thanks mainly to a preponderance of bars. The local gin mills guaranteed a run or three, even on a slow night. Most were the outcome of pissing contests that had turned violent. Often, we walked on floors covered with blood, beer and broken glass. We were especially cautious entering such a place, even if the police were on scene. More and more women were joining the ranks of the police department, and we had front row seats to their debut on the streets, where the bars made good testing grounds. Only once did I see evidence of grumblings by male cops that more female cops on the street meant more calls for assistance. Seeing the police car parked outside a noisy bar, we went inside to find a melee, with the officer cowering behind a door, clutching her radio and calling for help. In stark contrast, at a similar scene, a lone female officer, vowing to end the racket, unstrapped the gun on her hip and stomped into a noisy bar where patrons were mixing it up. I looked at my crew, shrugged, and said, "Follow her." Physically, she was overpowered, but I admired the confidence and guts she used instead to end the fisticuffs. Since bars often were dark sanctums, crowded, and reverberating with loud music, their tempo ran high. While watching for agitators, our goal was to reduce the tempo by connecting with an owner or manager to lower the music, turn on lights, and calm and thin out the crowd. It would have helped to have eyes in the back of our heads to watch angry patrons who didn't like our crashing the party.

Responses to tavern incidents had their lighter moments. One afternoon we ended up with a basement fire in a tavern on busy Lincoln Avenue. Through drifting smoke, a couple of die-hard patrons spilled through the front door clutching glasses, trying not to spill their contents. As though proud of his insightfulness, one of them waved his glass toward the smoke and slurred, "Goddamn place ish on fire."

"Nothing gets by you, does it?" I laughed.

Even funnier was the big, well-dressed, middle-age guy planted on his stool at the middle of the haze-filled bar, hunched over his drink as though protecting it. As we scurried past, lugging equipment, we all took turns yelling at him to get out. He would only glance sideways as though confused about the commotion. The next time I passed through the bar, he was still there, now only partially visible in the smoke, occasionally casting an eye toward the activity behind him. I found it hilarious. Everyone took a turn admonishing him, but the big surly guy only snarled back so we gave up, more in awe of his conviction than caring about the headache he was sure to have later. Besides, the fire was under control and we had begun ventilation and overhaul. His obliviousness triggered the age-old banter of firefighters:

I heard, "Tell him to throw his clothes on the truck."

"Hey, Lieutenant, he looks like you on payday," someone quipped. That was followed by someone suggesting we take him back with us so he could be on the pipe at the next worker.

I wondered if he was going to walk into a home where his stench of smoke would be questioned. Lincoln Avenue, I often thought, was much like Brady Street in having its own cast of characters. In fact, I expected to see some of the familiar faces from the east side.

Sometimes, we seemed to have enough characters among our own numbers to contend with. There were times when I felt everyone should have been made more accountable for their actions. That would have had a more pronounced effect at higher levels of leadership. An alternative form of accountability aimed at superiors was mandated in a letter from the chief. I felt it missed the mark because it stripped away self-accountability. Now, if the cub's mask malfunctioned, it was the boss's fault; if an HEO cracked up a rig, the boss in the right seat was held accountable. The latter was especially disquieting because assigned to our company was the HEO said to hold the record for number of accidents and damaged rigs. He had great fun giddily telling the crew how he had made me flinch when he bolted into traffic, causing a driver to screech to a halt just short of ramming us. This warranted my stepping outside of my own rules, telling him in front of everyone that if he drove recklessly again, I'd hang him. He never spoke to me again, and I slept fine afterward. The chief's mandate didn't produce the desired effect of forcing bosses to make their people more conscientious; it only manifested dissent. Like most rules, it fell into disuse and was occasionally dug out of the dusty rule book for leverage in a particular case, or to prove a point.

I had made a point of knowing the rules, and I professed that if you knew the rules, no one could trip you up. I sometimes used the rules to full advantage and found it humorous when someone searched for the thin black book to substantiate or refute something I had said or done. I wasn't the only officer to monitor those rules. My favorite example is a captain of an engine company who had had enough of his crew's shenanigans. The young bucks pushed until the seasoned captain felt it was time to remind them who was in charge. So one day he announced that they were going to change every section of hose on the engine. It would take the better part of the day. So that they would not be caught without hose on the rig, one by one the compartments were stripped, and every section of hose was cleaned and then hung in the hose tower to dry. The number of each 50-foot section was recorded and then clean, dry hose was neatly packed into the beds. His boys were appalled, convinced that they were being unduly mistreated. The captain simply grinned when he informed them that the rule book required that all hose on an engine be changed every six months, and they were well past that mark. He easily regained his grip on the reins. I loved it!

Conversely, another officer I knew was so intimidated by his feisty crew that he relented, pleading with his challengers that if they gave him half of the day, the other half of the day was theirs to do what they wanted. I thought making deals was bad policy, and when I heard his arrangement, I said, "Bullshit! You're the boss. You call how the day goes." You can balance work with rewards.

A firefighter at Engine 31 zeroed in on a rule that he exploited. I was in favor of the department's involvement with sports, which promoted health, teamwork, competitive spirit and social interaction; and it was good PR. But I didn't care for a rule on the books that allowed members to sell tickets to the annual fire-police baseball game while on duty. The firefighter took it the distance by showing up for 8 A.M. roll call, informing me he was going out selling tickets and not returning for the remaining 23 hours of the shift. The ludicrous rule basically gave a person a paid day off, and there was no minimum number of tickets that had to be sold. I took it up with the chief, telling him that I wouldn't run with a reduced crew because sports, and that rule, took precedence over our very purpose. I suggested he give me another firefighter to fill out my crew or I would call for another engine or ladder company for manpower every time we rolled out the door. The media, seemingly always eager to watchdog city services, picked up on it and let the public in on how some of their tax dollars were being spent. The exposé, and my forcing leadership's hand, only reduced the hours that our people went selling tickets. Some of the guys bragged that most of those hours were spent on bar stools. One firefighter, in fact, got loaded at an inner city gin mill, spouted a racial remark or two and was severely beaten.

Had he sought medical treatment, I wondered, how would the city's legal and benefits system view the incident? Was it an on-duty injury that warranted coverage of medical costs? A cook going shopping with his or her private vehicle, was considered to be on duty. If the cook was injured in an accident, what was the city's liability? The ramifications of disability and death in such cases were far reaching. The myriad questions and scenarios that played out in my mind drew the same conclusion, spelled C-Y-A, for "Cover Your Ass." It was the reason I was big on documenting everything in the daily journal.

The fire department had scores of good people, of all ranks, and I felt blessed to have worked with many of them. Some were at their best wearing a black helmet, the color signifying firefighters (company officers wore red and chiefs wore white). As with any organization, some slipped between the cracks and were promoted beyond their capabilities. Neither the ten-dollar words they learned nor their pompous demeanor could mask their true abilities when the heat was on. The experience and character qualities that were the stuff of good leaders couldn't be measured, or even legally included, in exam processes. The system had flaws. And multiple standards manifested gross inequities. It was the reason I sometimes said: "If we were a private corporation, we'd be out of business."

Being at Engine 31 didn't change my perspective, but pushing two decades on the job did. It didn't help that our union president at that time ran for political office, ignorant of the skeletons in his closet. Hearing in the ranks the support for his campaign, despite his reputation, reminded me how much I had changed, how different from them I had become. I was perplexed at the union's rallying call for rebirth, a return to the '60s. *And to what part of that era should we regress? Let's resurrect the social and moral disorder that identified the '60s. Or should we re-agonize over the Vietnam War, or racial upheaval? How about the genesis of the drug culture?* I was privy to the candidate's background and found the furor of support and the political overtures excessive, so I stayed out of the kitchen, no longer caring to socialize. I saved the notes I scribbled during night runs and plopped back on the rack. In the morning I grabbed a cup of coffee and retreated to the quiet office to write my reports.

One of those mornings I found a note from an administrative chief whose department car was in our quarters. Her note admonished us bosses for notes to each other advising caution at a halfway house known to house AIDS patients. We did the same for other hazards, such as missing floors or faulty fire escapes. I told her she had no business rummaging through our memos. I couldn't take seriously her charge that we were discriminating. The times, they were a changin.'

I'm sure I presented as a character to some. It mattered little. I was never out to win a popularity contest. In fact, I said I was like scotch: you liked me or you didn't; there was no in between. Nor did I need a cheering section. I was content knowing that I held the trust and confidence of those around me. Working with skilled, competent people, even the simplistic tangibility of working with equipment, gave me satisfaction. I did not take lightly the fact that coworkers sometimes confided in me about personal matters, often eliciting my thoughts. I told Deb there were times I felt as though I were wearing a collar. I found people's perception of me interesting. I thought those who saw only aggressiveness missed the mark, because there was a flip side to that. In this line of work, aggression is a prime asset. It worked well for me in tough situations, on the job as well as in wartime, but it had to be reigned in, and that was no easy task. It would have been easier to say, "That's how I'm wired."

I harbored the feeling that there was always something more, something better that could be done. To quote Robert F. Kennedy: "Some people see things the way they are and say *why?* I dream things that never were and say *why not?*" It has always been about doing what's right and honorable, keeping values intact. I wasn't always successful, but as the saying goes: success is not a destination, it is a journey. I may never have hovered scalpel in hand over a patient in an operating room, scored a winning home run, or occupied the CEO's chair in a corporate setting, but I led firefighters in harm's way and brought them out, and that, to me, is special.

Often I indulged my sense of adventure. That fire has diminished over time but there remains a flame within. There must be a part of my brain that teeters between total self control and unbridled craziness. On the edge, I was keenly aware of how close disaster was. That in itself was fascinating. I felt confident, even comfortable, being on that edge. On that pinnacle is crystal clarity when all that matters is simply your next breath, your next move. For some it is filling a void or making a connection. It defines life. So high and spiritual were some of my adventures that I never really believed that I had nearly died. Death seemed an illusion with a guarantee that the dark, heavy curtain would not come down.

I joined the department knowing that death and injury were very real possibilities. I learned how frail life can be, how easily and quickly it can end. At Engine 31, like other places through which I had passed, I would see various ways the reaper tallied victories on his scoreboard.

The middle-age guy was having an MI, our term for myocardial infarction — more simply put, a full-blown heart attack. He sat on the edge of his couch, anxious, clearly in distress, scared of suddenly leaving his family. The paramedics knew. We knew. A slight gasp. His face turned ashen, and he closed his eyes and dipped his head, dying in front of us. The meds and my crew worked long and hard on him. I made it my job to stay with the family, to separate them from the flinching trauma of the flailing from the defibrillator's jolt, the needles, the throat tube, hearing ribs crack during chest compressions. I kept them apprised of what was happening. I sat down with them at the kitchen table, talking over the drama being played out in the nearby living room, making small talk, but not pulling punches either. "Your husband, your dad, is in good hands. They're the best and they're doing all they can for him right now." Recognizable background noise told me when all life-saving measures had run their course. I arose, went to the doorway, and made eye contact with the med officer, who shook her head. I would give them a minute to gather their equipment and straighten the scene, make the man as presentable as possible. Then I took his wife's hand and led her to the body. The son followed.

As her son and I each held one of her arms, she stood over him, hands folded in front of her. She tipped her head sideways, her eyes wet. Her trembling lips tightened into resolve and she whispered something, and then she smiled at him adoringly, replaying their life together, mournful eyes telling him how much she loved him. She and her son embraced tearfully. Then as if suddenly remembering something, she broke away and retrieved from a nearby table covered white with linen a small bottle. Stretching her hand toward us, she said quietly, "It's holy water. Would you give him last rites?" Unsure what that entailed, no one moved. I had never heard the request, but I was moved.

"Certainly," I said, squatting down on one knee. Uncapping the tiny bottle, feeling under my thumb an embossed cross, I let its contents dribble across his forehead and there traced with my finger a cross. "In the name of the Father, and of the Son, and of the Holy Spirit, may you rest in peace," followed by a collective murmur of "Amen." I wasn't sure my words constituted last rites, but the act was key.

"Thank you," she smiled. And I smiled.

Sometimes the last face a person leaving this world sees is yours; the last voice they hear is yours. Nothing in this world evokes such humility. I first realized that at 19 years old. Since time is a great illusion that can be compressed to make a moment years ago feel like yesterday, I'm a wet-behind-the-ears kid in a helicopter staring down at some goddamn kid younger than me who had tripped a booby trap. He wouldn't stop staring at me. I tried to keep the poncho over his face, more intent on covering those staring eyes than on the chunk of metal lodged in his forehead. But the violent rotorwash was too strong, and he stared at me as his young life drained away.

So you learn to smile. You smile at the dying. You smile because there is nothing else you can do. And maybe you say some kind words because we're told that hearing is the last thing to go. You chose to try to make a difference in the world, but you can't change this. So you smile for the dying, and maybe someone will smile for you. I wish I had smiled at that kid in the chopper, but I learned. Oh, how I learned.

I and my crew of Engine 31 saw how utterly simple it was for someone to end their life, and in the process shatter the lives of others. At 2 A.M. we were returning from a run when we were sent to a run-down apartment unit just a few blocks away. The dispatcher said it was for someone "unresponsive."

The victim's wife was outside when we pulled up. She was hysterical. I asked only, "Where?" and she bolted up the stairs, knocking aside kids and toys. She stopped abruptly short of a bedroom door and pointed to it, screaming hysterically. Wedged at the top of the door was a piece of plastic from a kid's toy.

Something on the other side of the door prevented us from opening it, so we heaved into it, shoving a body inward. John quickly produced a knife to cut away a cheap nylon cord that ran from the man's neck to the plastic block. Since we had been nearby, CPR was a viable action, but our efforts and those of paramedics didn't save him. He was only in his twenties. Two young cops that responded were curious about the method the young man had used to check out. Being too new to the streets to have yet seen a doorknob hanging, they were surprised when I told them it was a common and extremely simple method. I explained that usually the person merely puts a cord over the door to the opposite knob and hangs free. I was more bothered by what might have driven the young man to the brink, since he had a spouse and kids. It wasn't our job to figure out why, so I tried to shake off the insanity of it all.

My last run at Engine 31, which was the last run of my fire service career, involved the death of an elderly man. Although his end was hideous, his family's had the consolation that he hadn't been murdered, nor did he take his own life. The call was for a vehicle accident at the busy intersection of 13th Street and Lincoln Avenue, six blocks from our firehouse. Near the curb in front of a dime store was a car upside down. Surveying the scene, I didn't spot any other vehicles or bodies, but there were an inordinate number of onlookers. Walking to the inverted car it struck me that the large crowd was relatively silent, always a bad sign. I knelt and peered into the car. "Ah, shit," I muttered. Hanging upside down, still strapped into the seat, was a large body. Hanging where its head should have been was a large fleshy flap. Being inverted, the body had emptied much of its contents. When John dutifully ran up with the medical kit, I sighed deeply, "Won't need that, John."

It hit me that about 100 people crowded the intersection, gawking. I stood up, turning to sweep the shocked hordes with my angry eyes. I was filled with disgust. "What's wrong with you?" I barked. "Get out of here. And get those kids out of here!" Their morbid curiosity sickened me more than the gory scene. I hoped that they regretted rushing to the scene, many with kids, who shouldn't have seen that.

It wasn't until police arrived and immediately began scattering gawkers that I noticed the dimestore windows spattered with blood and gore.

Since the car was somewhat compressed, I had called for a truck company to help free and remove the body. Ladder 11 arrived, its crew led by a good truck boss.

"Take a look, Bob," I said as we knelt side by side.

He blew out hard. "Damn! Messy. It'll be tricky but we'll get him out."

"Got any cubs?" I asked.

"Yeah," he answered, turning his head to call someone over.

A young woman, no older than 20, wearing the clean turnout gear of a cub, walked to us. I saw her nervous gaze drop to the piles of bloody gore, which she gingerly stepped around. Still kneeling, Bob looked up at her. "Okay," he said with authority, "take a look, then we're going to brace this car and get him out." Bending over, she gasped, stood up, gulped and said, "Okay."

Bob rose, put a hand heavily on her shoulder and grinned. "Good. Let's do it." She looked past Bob at me. I nodded, smiled and said reassuringly, "This is the job you wanted. You'll be all right." And Bob's crew and mine got in there and did what few people can bring themselves to do.

Police Officer Pat Higgins, whom Deb and I knew, looked over the scene and surmised that the 81-year-old man had lost control when he hit a pothole and flipped the car. Although strapped in, the big man had come partially out of the car, which spun on top of him before coming to a stop. We ended up laying out a hose line to flush the street and the store windows. County EMS protocol required that I call an ambulance to remove the body from public view, but nowhere did it explain what to do with the hefty bag full of human remains my company had gathered. I was surprised that the medical examiner's office refused to accept it for disposal. We kept the final resting place of the man's partial remains under our hat. I didn't feel good about the indignity of our decision, but we were left with no choice. Thankfully, trash pickup at our firehouse was due the next day.

Such runs left me with little sense of accomplishment, but I wondered if there was a lesson in it for the cub. Knowing that being so close to a traumatic event can impact someone's career choice, I wondered if the young woman stayed on the job.

The fire we faced also held an important lesson — fear. And by fearing fire, you learned to respect it.

Fires were less frequent than during my previous years at Engine 6, but they were telling me something. Their ill effects were longer lasting and for the first time, my sense of immortality waned; my ship the USS *Infallible* was taking on water and listing. The combination of my youth — no longer sheathed in invincibility — slipping away, and the years of hard work, of "stick-toitiveness," was taking a toll. Cardiac problems too had surfaced, which only compounded my medical profile, which recorded back and hip trouble as well as shoulder surgery. Orthopedic surgeon Dr. McCabe said that I had the skeletal system of someone who had lived three lifetimes. Oddly, I found meaning and contentment in his words.

Doc Adlam was sterner this time. He told me mostly what I had been ignoring, and added that I had developed asthma and that my immune system was deteriorating. It was clear that I wouldn't see a normal retirement. A regimen of medication and treatment helped, but Adlam warned there would be little improvement if I continued going into fires. But he allowed me to return to work. He knew I'd be back.

My last fire was a garage fire, arson, a nothing fire, really. But it was enough to trigger breathing problems from which I had difficulty recovering. Reluctantly, back to Dr. Adlam I went, unwilling to hear what he had to say. After more tests, he concluded that I had Reactive Airway Dysfunction Syndrome, or RADS. Basically, it left me wide open to most any lung irritant or lung problem.

He was to the point: "Wayne, I'm sorry to tell you this, but you're done being a fireman. I'm putting you in for duty disability. You won't have to apply because I'll handle all the paperwork."

When I protested, he was adamant: "Let me put it another way. You're a company officer. If you take your crew into a fire and you go down, you've put all of them in a dangerous spot."

"Got it, Doc."

Doc Adlam's magnificent blend of gentleness and professionalism easily cracked my hard shell. He saw my eyes water, and he suffered my disappointment, my silence, with kind words about my dedicated service and accomplishments. "You certainly left your mark, Wayne," he said, breaking into a pleasant smile.

Regardless of the handwriting on the wall about my health, I abided by Doc Adlam's decision, but I wasn't ready to throw in the towel. In a letter to the chief I explained that I was qualified as an arson investigator, an instructor, and a public relations speaker. I didn't have to leave the department; there were other things I could do. In his response he cited the city ruling that to be a member of the fire department, one had to be fully capable of functioning as a firefighter. My pulmonary doctor found the ruling so absurd that every time he submitted his report to the city following an exam, he doggedly urged that I be used in other capacities.

The shortening of my fire service career was a change I hadn't programmed in to the master plan; nor had Deb when she suffered her disability. Getting a "duty" wasn't the pot o' gold at the end of the rainbow, as many professed and even strived for. Sure, I felt blessed to have a pension, but health was more important, and gone was the opportunity for promotion and overtime pay. A different lesson was driven home months later, when I felt sure that I was having a heart attack. A doctor in a follow-up session wisely deduced that this heart event had been derived from stress. I explained that

I didn't understand because I was off the job, and even while on the job I handled stress well. He explained that this was a deeper stress than I could imagine, repressed until it rose to the surface and hit me on the head. After he dug into my past and heard about the ending of my fire service career, he understood even better. "That wasn't a job," he said, "it was an identity, and when you lost it, it became deeply stressful." His analysis was so sensible that I no longer had such overwhelming feelings of impending doom, which is tied closely with heart attacks. Feeling foolish quickly gave way to gratefulness for the new perspective.

The transition had taken time. No longer would I look closely at the city and see things others didn't. *Will someone in this crowd turn violent and chaos erupt? Will ugly smoke one day pump from the upper floors of that old warehouse? Will the worn tire on that semi blow, sending the huge rig careening into a car full of people? Will the brothers and sisters one day have to scoop up a bloated body that washes up against this seawall?*

Nearly two years later, my lung condition had improved more than originally expected, so I again took up the chase. A former union official who had become an administrative chief was uneasy about my quest, implying that duty disabilities were sacred and I would be setting an unpopular precedent by returning to work. "Besides," he added, "the union isn't going to like it." A case worker with the city followed closely my pursuit, but in rethinking it, Deb's caution to be careful of what I wished for seemed logical. Friend and long time police officer Jim Oliva suggested I switch over to his department, a tempting prospect I would at times regret not pursuing. I was inspired by Deb and discovered that there was, indeed, life beyond the fire department.

In view of my medical problems — which, incidentally, I find insignificant in comparison to others, not to mention the alternative — people have asked if I have regrets. Of course not. How can anyone have regrets if people are alive today because they performed their job? Would I do it again? Silly question.

Epilogue

Discovering that there was life beyond the fire service, I re-invented myself and pursued other passions: that seemingly unobtainable college degree, and with honors, to boot, teaching, art, building projects, and writing. The idea of shaping my fire service stories into a book held promise. Long after my firefighting days had ended, I would add another story: a reminder that my life had purpose, and a clear sign that angels still huddled upon my shoulders.

It happened on April 26, 2002. I was driving my youngest son, Jason, to Milwaukee. Possessed by a sense of urgency, I pulled hard on the wheel to turn onto a road that veered from my usual route. Surprised, Jason asked, "What are you doing?" As though possessed, I stared straight ahead. "I don't know." I knew only that something down this road beckoned.

My foot was heavy on the gas pedal. Coming around a curve, clouds of light brown smoke carried by high winds grabbed our attention. My temples tingled. A familiar, eerie combination of dread and excitement washed over me. I answered Jason's "Wow" with "This isn't good." Assuming that firefighters were dealing with the source of the towering mass, I added, "Someone's got their hands full." The boiling columns darkened, telling me the fire was worsening. As we neared, the scene laid out before us was horrifying. From the top of a sprawling three-story apartment complex, dark brown smoke rolled skyward; bright orange flames danced among the billowing folds. My senses were electrified. Details jumped into view: wind direction, the building's size and layout, clusters of elderly people scurrying away from it, and, most horrifying, not one emergency vehicle in sight.

"Shit!" I floored the gas pedal, careening into a parking lot. Jason recalls that after slamming to a halt, I said calmly, "Time to go to work." I don't remember saying it. Before flinging open my door, my eyes bored into Jason's as I told him not to follow me, to stay away from the building, to tell people to call 911.

Running to the building, I brushed past elderly residents, some in night

Our "Brady Bunch" in 2002. From left to right are Jeff, Chris, Andy, Jason, Joanna, and Joe.

clothes. Grabbing my arm, slowing my momentum, a woman pleaded, "My husband, my husband's up there."

"What number?" I demanded. "What's the apartment number?"

"318," she sobbed, "top floor." Of course. They're always on the top floor.

Jerking on the door handle, I was surprised to find the large glass doors locked. It made sense. For security reasons, they locked when swung shut. Through the glass I saw an elderly man gingerly sidestepping down the stairs, his eyes wide with fear. *I hope that's her husband.* Slamming my palm against the glass, I yelled at him to hurry and open the door. Finally he leaned heavily against the lock bar. "What's your apartment number?" I knew from the terror in his face that I wouldn't get an answer. Pulling him roughly through the doorway, I felt a twinge of regret. *I'll apologize later ... if later comes.*

Leaning backward and looking up the building's slab side for a final quick size-up, the red flames jetting beyond the roof's edge humbled me, dared me. *You bastard. I was done with you. How many people are you holding up there?* I felt alone, overwhelmed, not believing I was doing this again. I felt small, naked. *God help me. This is too big. I need help.*

"Dad!" I spun to face Jason, his face flushed with anxiety. A new fear hit me. I couldn't let him meet my enemy. "Get away from here, now!" I barked, "See who needs help." Our eyes locked and he reluctantly ran. I turned and standing next to me was a young man in his early twenties, wearing a dark blue T-shirt with the familiar fire service Maltese emblem. Precious seconds were ticking away. *I don't have time for this.* He responded to my glare with, "What do you want me to do?"

"Are you a firefighter?"

"Yeah, a department up north."

"Can you do this?"

"Yes!"

"You gotta stick with me, man!"

"Got it."

His face never changed. His calmness for his age and what we were about to do seemed unnatural. *He can't possibly know.* Seeing that determination had replaced the fear in his eyes, I snapped, "Let's do it." A worn switch was thrown. A spark. Ignition. Fear and a millisecond of hesitation burst in a blinding flash, then vaporized. Power surged. Senses peaked. *I shall pass through this world but once ... Go-go-go! Get them!*

We flew up the stairs, gliding around people scurrying down. On the third floor landing, we were met by a wall of putrid, brown smoke — Lucifer's welcome mat, his dare. It became personal. *I'm back, motherfucker. Let's get it on.* Realizing that I still wore my glasses, I whipped them off, tossing them into a corner, knowing I'd never see them again. Turning to the young man crouching next to me, I asked, "What's your name?"

"Eric."

"Ready, Eric?"

"Ready."

"Then let's go."

Crouching, we ran into the acrid mass, the familiar pungent odor and sting attacking my eyes and throat. A pink nightgown appeared, floating in the smoke, a voice above it crying and choking. "Take her, Eric." I saw only his arm reach out into the swirling cloud, grabbing hers, and they disappeared. More pale colors drifted aimlessly in the smoke; coughing, wailing, lost. Reach out, grab, reassure, get them to the stairs. Eric was again beside me. "Good, good. Keep moving," I urged. The toxic concoction being pressed into my body challenged every vein and muscle. My tight lungs begged for air, every short, wheezing breath a grueling effort. *My God, I go off the job with a lung disability and look at what I'm doing. Let me do this last one.*

I heard the fire's roar overhead, as its huge, mighty red arms tore apart the building. "Gotta check apartments." My shadow answered, "I'll go left." Oddly, his voice didn't sound strained from the punishing smoke and deadly gasses. I felt better about him being there.

Apartments where doors were left open required a quick run-through, in a crouch, shouting, "Anyone here?" A locked door. *Damn!* I banged with a fist. "Anyone in there?" The door opened and there, in the haze, stood an old woman, terror stricken. Her deep-set slate eyes looked through me. "There's a fi…" Slam! *Jesus H. Christ! I don't believe she just slammed the door in my face!* "Lady — Open — Now — Fire — You have to get out!" *One second, two seconds....* "Get away from the door!" I spun around and mule-kicked the door, which nearly flew off the hinges. There she stood, motionless, thankfully a few feet away, clear of the door's arc. I grabbed her around the waist, bent her over and shoved her toward the stairs at the end of the hall. At the end of the darkness crouched Eric, ready to lead her to safety.

Back into the smoke, much closer to the roaring blaze, another closed door. With my face inches from the door, a number was barely visible — 318. Eric again was at my side. "Guy's in here," I coughed, straining to breathe through my constricted and spasming throat. He kicked this one in, and we flattened when a massive, hot hand pushed us to the floor. The fire was extremely close, racing overhead and through walls, devouring the next door apartment, trying to claim this one. "You with me?" I yelled. "Let's go," he snapped back. Crawling into the super-heated black smoke, I felt Eric's hand gripping my heel. *Good man.* I felt naked wearing only a T-shirt and jeans. We parted slightly, shouting for the victim, knocking over unrecognizable objects. Red flames sliced through the blackness overhead, the fire's rage now deafening. *Please let me feel the softness, the give, of human flesh.* Nothing. We couldn't inch forward, having met an impenetrable wall of searing heat. The demolition noise around us worried me. I swung a backhand punch, connecting with Eric's shoulder. "Look up!" I yelled. His faint "Shit" confirmed that he too saw the yellow glow through the splitting ceiling. "We have to get out, now!"

Crawling backward, we got to the threshold and closed the door, our futile attempt to contain the beast. Staring at the door, then at Eric's faint outline, defiantly I wheezed, "I can't leave him in there."

"I'm with you."

He now had my undying respect. I had seen him in action. I didn't have to wonder if he would go through hell with me. We were already there.

Back into Satan's den we crawled, his hand again squeezing us, playfully tossing us about like pathetic rag dolls, threatening to drop the building on us as we pushed, cursing, groping, hoping, now clinging to our own lives. *That's it!* A deep rumbling sound and fire leaping gleefully through the blackness spelled the end of our efforts. Scrambling back into the hall, from the dark depths I heard excited, high-pitched voices muffled by breathing apparatus, coming from bodies stumbling down the hall. I hacked to a shape in the smoke, "There's someone in here. Work your line overhead. It broke through." The shape screamed, "Okay, but you gotta get outta here!" I grinned, wondering if the shapes were confused about who I was or what I was doing there.

Groping our way down the hall toward the stairs, I looked up to see bright yellow fingers of flame dancing merrily along the ceiling. *I hope those guys don't get fixated, and remember to look up.* Now that the fire was consuming the top floor of the building, we would not reach safety until we were outside, clear of the structure. I longed for fresh air, and now I worried about Jason, as we stumbled drunkenly down the stairs.

At the bottom, Eric, anxious to get outside, reached for the door. Knowing the volume of fire atop the building, I tried to grab him, but he was out the door. Flaming debris fell on him, and I bolted through the door, shoving him forward. Embers rained down. Clear of the building, he hastily brushed smoking material from his shoulders. "Turn around." Pulling his burned and soaked T-shirt away from his back, I exclaimed, "Oh, man. Your wings are burned. You have to go to the hospital."

Spanning Eric's back from shoulder to shoulder was tattooed a huge pair of wings, which now bore the red and blistered battle scars of his foray into hell. "It's okay," he said quietly.

"Hell of a job you did up there," I grinned.

"Mutza!" I turned to see Mequon fire chief and old friend Curt Witzlib ambling toward me in the open grassy area where I stood. His curious stare reminded me that I must have looked dreadful. "What the hell did you do?" he asked. I avoided answering but reminded him that a guy might still be trapped in 318.

Curt broke his purposeful stride and turned, grinning and shaking his head in disbelief. "Just can't stay away from it, can you, Mutz?" Looking up at the top floor, now hidden by clouds of brown smoke, I didn't envy Curt having to tell the old woman that her husband would not be with her tonight.

I felt the all too familiar pangs of failure as I staggered away, when a paramedic I knew spotted me. "Wayne," Marian said quizzically, "what happened to you? You weren't in there?" Bending over to rest helped me avoid answering. She said something about my condition, but I waved an arm sideways, sputtered that I was okay but Eric here had gotten burned.

Bending over to look up at me, she asked, "Who?"

Standing upright, I scanned the open area. Eric was nowhere to be seen. "What th ... but, Marian, he's around here somewhere. His back is burned."

She grabbed my arm and ordered me into the rig. Jason, thankfully, appeared. "Jason," I wheezed, "Did you see the young guy with me?"

Puzzled, he answered, "I didn't see anyone with you."

In the gray fog, a nurse named Kathy floated at the foot of my hospital bed, shaking my foot, saying that I was a hero and that news stations were calling. I shook off her hero comment and asked that she please not say anything to the media.

"Okay," she said in a resigned whisper.

"A guy was missing. Did they find him?"

"I don't know."

Deb and our daughter Chris appeared. "Did everyone get out?" I had to know. As the fog cleared, I insisted on leaving the hospital that day, and they drove me home. Later that evening, they went to retrieve my truck. On the driver's seat were the glasses I had pitched onto the third floor landing and had given up for lost.

The media had a field day. Word got out and our phone was ringing. The next day Deb and I went to the site, where I stared in wonderment at what little remained of the upper floor, its charred, skeletal frame a bleak contrast to the bright blue sky. *Christ, I can't believe we survived up there.* I grinned at the reaper. *I spit in your eye one more time, didn't I?*

The husband in 318? It turned out that he had been sleeping, awoke to flames, and escaped the building ... ahead of his fretting wife.

Eric? I asked people who had been at the fire if they had seen him. No one had. I asked friends in the fire service to search for him. I called departments upstate. No one claimed a young firefighter named Eric. In a TV news clip I stated that he did an incredible job, and that I wished I could find him. Deb said that he was a young extension of my being. I have to believe that he was one of my guardian angels. After all, not only do I believe in angels, but I saw Eric's wings.

Me? I didn't remember my feet ever touching the many steps to the third floor. Everything clicked. It was as though I had never left the profession.

Holding back the years,
Thinking of the fear I've had for so long.
When somebody hears,
Listen to the fear that's gone...

I'll keep holding on,
I'll keep holding on
So tight.

— Simply Red

Index

Numbers in **_bold italics_** indicate pages with photographs.

acid tongues 123
acting positions 122–124
Adlam, Robert 153, 230
Adonnis, Maximillian 172–175
aides 39, **_43_**
AIDS scare 142–143, 171, 225
alarms, non-fire 38–39
alcohol abuse 124–125, 144, 175–176, 189
Allen, Glen 31, **_37_**, 39
Ambroch, Fritz 208
Ambrosia Chocolate accident 42
animal runs 152–153
apartment building fires 133–135, 180–181
Arlington Court 171
Army Airborne school instructors 25
arson 84, 136, **_139_**, 160–161, 206, 219, 221;
    investigation 200–201, 219
attic fires 186

baby deliveries 111–112
Balcerzak, Pat 67
Balistreri, Frank 47–48, 172
Ballering, Jerry 71
basement fires 73–74, 101, 105–107, **_154_**, 202
bats 152–153
battalions 31
Behling, Jack 133
Bett, Bob 81, 86, 114
BIT _see_ Bureau of Instruction and Training
"black cat" 123–124
boat fires 59–60, 78
boathouse fires 221
bonding 35
"Brady Bunch" 150, 185, **_233_**
Brady Street assignment: apartment

building fires 180–181; automobile accidents 168–170; ethnic makeup 172; first-in area 167; house life 179–180; ladder availability 167, 169; neighborhood personality 166, 170–171; night life 183–184; organized crime 172–174; personal conflict 166, 167; personnel problems 175–176; tar wagon fire 177–178
Brady Street characters: Burt 192; Colleen 190–191; Heather 212–214; Kelly 191–192; Marquette arsonist-murderer 194–195; mesc user 193; murderers 195–197; psycho woman 193–194
Brandt, Lenny 107–108
Brewer's Hill district 160
Brown Door fire 49
Bureau of Instruction and Training 61, 70, 72; _see also_ Fire Academy
burnout 144
burnt meat 131–132
bus fires 102
Busalacchi's 172
Butz, Dick 52

car 100, 171
car bombs 47
Ceretto, Larry 28
Chambers Street fire 136, **_139_**
chemical fires 200–201, 206–207
child fatalities 38, 145
child rescues 103
"child struck by auto" runs 58
Christmas tree fires 74–75
civil defense truck 75
Clay, Dennis 131, 132
Coast Guard station 182
Collova, Paul 46, 48
commendation letters 138

company policies 33
competitive spirit 131
confined fires 105–107
contract negotiation 96–97
CPR 199–200
crews 31, 33
crime-related runs 56–57
"crispy critters" 35
Critical Incident Stress Debriefing
    (CISD) 143–144
"cub" status 34–35, 85, 176

dangerous conditions 47, 100–101, 105–
    108, 132, 136–137, *139*, 206–207
dark humor 42, 48, 147, 211
Davis, Greg 89, 113
death calls 209
defibrillators 199–200
Deluge (fireboat) 28, 39
denial 99–100
Dirty Dozen 65
disability guidelines 171
dispatchers 48
dogs and cats 104–105, 134–135, 152
doorknob hanging 227–228
double houses 31
downtime 90–91, 110
downtowners 30
drug abuse 144, 162–163
drug-house fires 104
drunken firemen *see* alcohol abuse
Du De Voire, Pepie 45, 131
dumpster fires 94
duty disabilities 231

elder housing 171
elevator emergencies 51–52, 67
elimination events 25–27
Emergency! (TV series) 21–22, 23
emotional response 37–38, 51, 99–100
EMS/squad runs 95
Engine Company 5: beautiful moments
    90; crew *98*; downtime 90–91, 110;
    EMS/squad runs 95; false alarms 82–
    83; fatalities 85–86; fires 83–84; for-
    ward lay 84; horseplay 91–92; house
    layout 81; housekeeping and mainte-
    nance 90, 110; inner-city conditions
    83, 85, 88–90, 92–93; King Furniture
    fire 105–107; 1980 strike 96–97; post-
    fire booty 84–85; reputation for inno-
    vation 84; residential fire 86–88; run
    tally 81; shift work 81; suicides 85–86;
    typical day 108–111

Engine Company 6 166–167
Engine Company 10 123–124
Engine Company 13 107, *111*
Engine Company 20 31
Engine Company 28 74
Engine Company 29 124–125
Engine Company 30 38, 91–92
Engine Company 31 55, 56, 219, 222
Engine Company 32 141
Engine Company 33 119–123
equipment 34, 108, 132
equipment failure 87–88

false alarms 82–83, 95
farkels 90–91, 92
fatalities 36–37, *37*, 38, *43*, 51–52, 85,
    99, 133–134, 143; child 58, 60–61
Fazzari family 172
Fehr, Dick *37*
field assignments 28–30
Fightin' Engine 13 107
Fire Academy: first recruit class 65–69;
    library holdings 72; naming of 70;
    physical training (PT) routine 67; po-
    lice training 64–65; professional be-
    havior 68–69; public relations 71–72;
    smoke training 66; staff 63, 79; train-
    ing tower *64*; winter training *65*
fire behavior 105–106
fire inspections 72
fire-police arson unit 219
Fire Prevention Week 72, 73
firefighter-police relationship 95–96
firefighters, complex personality of 95
fireground conditions 136
fireground management 161
firehouse life *43*; *see also* housekeeping and
    maintenance; kitchen routine; pranks
first pipeman 31
flashover *221*
flat roofs 135–136, *139*
"floaters" 35
Forecki, Dick 165
forward lay 84
Frank, Jerry 126–127, 158
Frankowski, Gene 102

gallows humor 42, 48, 147, 211
gangs 93, 164
garage fires 104
gawkers 36–37, 86, 94, 228
Gernette, Howard 72–73
Gernette, Rosemary 72–73
Gimbel's Department Store fire 35

glass, vehicle and building 75–76
the Glass House 19, 30, 31
Glisch, Ken 202
Glorioso, Felix 172
Glorioso's 172
Glubka, Tom 143
Grabske, Ken 1, 35, *37*, 41, 50, 127
Greely, Jim "Griz" 102
Groth, Jim 136
ground ladders 28
Gumin, Stanley 119, 123

Hack's Furniture call 46
hand signals 33
Harambee Association 165
Harper, Leo 132, 160, 222
Harris, Pat 143
hazardous conditions 66
hazing 34–35
health problems 153–154
heavy equipment operators (HEO) 122
Heine, Tom 27, 88, 113
Heinowski, John "Heino" 176–177, 219
helicopters 70–71, 146–147
Heling, Arnie 103
Heller, Noble "Red" 200
Higgins, Pat 229
high-rise firefighting 35–36, 67, 70, 181
Holdmann, Mark 161
Holton, Doug 10
homosexuality 49
Hooks, Myron 85, 91, 98–99
hose maintenance 178–179; *see also*
  "spaghetti"
hotel fires 39
housekeeping and maintenance 90, 110
human frailty 86–88
human nature 114
Hurst power tool 103

independent action 97–98
Ingram, Bill 216
injuries 50, 101–102
inner-city conditions 83, 85, 88–90,
  92–93
innovation 69, 70–71
interdepartmental competition 131

Jaws 103
Jendrzejek, Bob 56, 58, 62
joker stand 34
Jones Island call 59–60
Journal Arms fire 40
judgment, reliance on 107–108

jumpers 42, 114–115
Juneau Village fire 47

Kaiser, Dick 136, 138, 151, 219
Kaminski, Bill 1, 35
Kardach, "Country Joe" 131
Kasierling, Fred 110
Kelscy, Jacque 216, 217
Kennedy, Robert F. 226
King Furniture fire 105–107
kitchen routine 34, 45–46, 108, 110, 120,
  179–180
Koleas, Gus "Casey" 44, 52, 60, 70, 72,
  204–206, *205*
Konetz, John "Radar" 117
Konicke, Tom 72
Kornburger, Ralph 177
Kovatch, Richard "Kogee" 13, *30*, 73–
  74, 81–82, 90, *98*, 99, 101, 160, 186
Kuehmichel, Clarence 13, 101, 143
Kuzminski, Cindy 130–131, 136

ladder availability 167, 169
Ladder Company 2 *32*, 33, 36
Ladder Company 9 128, *129*, 130–131
Ladder Company 10 221
Ladder Company 12 131
Ladder Company 17 123–124
Ladder Company 18 160–165
ladder company staffing 128
ladder rescues 134–135, 169–170
ladder training 26–27, 28
"The Last Alarm" *53*
laxity and unprofessionalism 119–121,
  122–123
leadership, failure of 107–108, 141, 162–
  163, 224
lessons learned 105–106
Lexan 76
Lincoln Avenue tavern fire 222–223
Lipski, Dan 69
Lipski Loop 91
Lisbon Avenue fire 100
living quarters 130; *see also* firehouse life;
  kitchen routine
loopers 30, 31

Mafia activities 172
maintenance routines 34
Manhattan Apartments fire *32*
manpower shortages 165
Marquette arsonist-murderer 194–195
marriage and family 110, 126, 139–140,
  150–152; *see also* Brady Bunch

Martins, Jim 160
mattress fires 131
McFarlane, Bonnie 142
McKinley Marina 180
Med 7 crash 216–217
media coverage 72–75, 201, 224
Megna, Mimma 172
mental observation (MO) 113–114
Michalowski, Dennis 74–75, 158
Midwest Express Airlines flight 105 144
Milwaukee Fire Bell Club 91
Milwaukee Fire Historical Society 72
minority hiring 24
Mitchell, Jeffrey T. 143–144
mob activity 47–48
Monaghan, King 4
Mother's Day emergencies 147
motor pump operators (MPO) 31, 33, 122
Mt. Sinai Hospital run 82
Mueller, Jim 161
"mushrooming" 25
Mutza, Dale (brother) 22–23
Mutza, Deb Dutkiewicz 139–140, *150*, 150–152, 164, 184–185, 215–218
Mutza, Wayne: basement fire *154*; "Brady Bunch" 150, 185, *233*; Brady Street assignment *178*; career approach 158; career end 230; early years 19–23; eligibility and hiring 23–24; emotional responses 37–38; Engine Company 5, *98*; enthusiasm for teaching 67; field assignment 28–30; firefighter training school 61–62; first transfer 54; "firsts" 35; health problems 153–154, 229–231; interest in photography *22*, 63–64, 69, 71; Ladder Company 9, *129*; last fire 232–237; leadership abilities 160, 162–163, 167; marriage and family 23, 24, 63, 71, 80, 110, 126, 139–140, *150*, 184–185; near-death experiences 137–138; officer ambition 155; personal danger 165, 174, 232–237; personal values 48–49, 63, 155; promotion to full status 53–54; promotion to lieutenant 155–157, *159*; recruit class 24; recruit training 24–30, *29*; self challenges 28; at training academy *68*; vehicle fire *37*; Vietnam experience 20–21, 61–62, 186–188, 211
"Mutz-ups" 27

Nell, Walter J. 53–54
Norquist, John O. 171, 197, 199

North Avenue Bridge fire 206
North Shore call 210
Norton, Bob 161
Nuge, Huge 48

officer safety training 198
"Oh, Darlin'!" exercise 67–68
old-timers 123–125
Oliva, Jim 170, 230
on-the-job training 33–34
organized crime 172–174

Pabst Brewery calls 46
Palmisano, August "Augie" 47
Papia, Sally 173
paramedic safety training 198–199
patches 152, 153
Paul, Bob 99
pay parity with police 96–97
Payne, Mike 131
people skills 50–51
personal danger 165, 174
personnel problems 162–164
physical fitness 27
pipe 41
Pitch's 172
Plankinton Avenue fire 103
police: chases 216; pay parity with 96–97; recruit training 64–65; undercover 95
police-firefighter relationship 95–96, 186–189, 192
population density 167
post-traumatic stress 145–147
pranks 43–44, 91–92
probationary status 33–34
professional behavior 69
Project FOCUS (Firefighters Out Creating Urban Safety) 145
Pross, Debra 77, 110
Public Relations Corps 72
puker runs 95
"pulling the hook" 82–83
pyromania 219, 222; *see also* arson

Raasch, Bunny 73–74
Radtke, James 174
Rajchel, Dick 31–33, 35–36
rappelling training 67
Reactive Airway Dysfunction Syndrome (RADS) 230
Rechlitz, Jim 143
recruit training 24–30
relinquished lines 186

rescue runs 69, 97–100, 103, 111–113, 115, 117–118
residential fires *61*, *111*
Rewolinski, Rich "Rev" 161
Ripple, Patrice 125–126
risk-taking 40, 100–101
roaches 115
Roman Coin bar 172
roof openings *79*, 128, 132, 135–136; *see also* skinning the roof
Rozek, Frank *43*, 44
Ruditys, Joe 77, 96
rules, use of 223–224

safety training 198–199
Sally's Steak House 173
Sauberan, Don 98, *98*
sauna fire 180–181
school fire 202–206
Sciortino's Bakery 172
Self-Contained Breathing Apparatus (SCBA) 27, *68*
self-doubt 99–100
Semenske, Roger 136, 138
sex discrimination 157, 163–164; *see also* women
sexual assault calls 164–165
Shea, Dan 39
shift work 31, 75, 81
ship fires 59–60, 78
shootings 95
"shouldn't have survived" episodes 50, 59–60
Singer, Paul 177, 202, 205
single houses 31
situational awareness 158
skinning the roof *79*, 128, 132; *see also* roof openings
"slow houses" 56
Slowey, Sean 132
Smith, Jon 144
smoke training 25–26, 66, 67
social events 126, 218
Soda Man 92
"spaghetti" *22*
Special Weapons and Tactics (SWAT) teams 75–76
Stamm, William 24, 70, 76, 77, 96
standard operating procedures 33; *see also* tactics
State Street fire 134
street violence 197–198; *see also* inner-city conditions
stress management 143–145, 151

strike 1980, 96–97
suicides 85–86, 121, 144, 147–148, 210–212, 227–228
summer fires 136, 165
summer rescues 149–150
Survive Alive House 145
Sweet, Mike 101
Sydney Hih fire 50

tactics 33, 84, 103, 107, 161
tar wagon fire 177–178
tavern incidents 222
technology failure 87–88
"textbook" fires 103
Thiel, Fred 179
third floor (Glass House) 31
Thomas, Dean 186, *187*
tiller position 148–149
Tischer, Harry 70
Tomasino, Dave 144
Tomasino, Tony 185
Tomasino, Wanda 185
tractor trailers 148–149
tragedy, emotional response to 37–38
"triple house" 30
truss roofs 135–136
turnout gear *29*

undercover cops 95
union activity 122, 128, 198
union dissatisfaction 109
University of Wisconsin Milwaukee (UWM) lab fire 206–207
unusual calls 42, 58–60, 168–170, 180–182, 206, 207–208
Up and Under Lounge 183
"Urinal Arms" fire 40

vacant burns 73–74, 78–79, *79*, 161
vehicle extrication 75–76, 94, 228–229
vehicle fires 36–37, *37*, 47, 94, 102
Venus, Jeff 140–141
Vietnam suicides 211
violence against firefighters 141, 197

Wachowiak, Brian 107, 200
Wagner, Tom 167
"waiting for water" 55
Walnut Street rescue 99
warming bus 116
Warzala, Don 38, 91, 103, 109–110
Warzala, Mike 38
Washcovick, Jim *98*, 101–102, 143
Washington Park pool rescues 149–150

water fights 44, 91–92
water rescues 58–59
weather conditions 38–39
Welk, Christine 77
Wells Street fire 133
Wichman, Norm 144
winter fires 132
winter training *65*
Witzlib, Curtis 66, 236

Wolf, Don 55
women: firefighters 76–78, 110, 126, 130–131, 157, 163–164, 229; paramedics 119–120, 121–122, 125–126, 139, 142, *150*; police 222; *see also* sex discrimination
"workers" 35

Zautke, Herb 33, 40–41